The Meaning of Life

A guide to finding your life's purpose

Nathanael Garrett Novosel

Written and Published in the United States of America

Published by Nathanael Garrett Novosel

Crownsville, Maryland

1st Edition, January 2020

Paperback ISBN: 978-1-948220-01-9

Library of Congress Control Number: 2019920080

Contents

Pre-Book Assessment   4

Introduction   7

Growth   13

Experience   31

Desire   47

Belief   73

Emotions   117

Ethics   161

Support   233

Choice   267

Conclusion   315

Post-Book Assessment   331

Glossary   333

Afterword   339

Bibliography   350

Pre-Book Assessment

Check your current ability to derive meaning in life

Rate the degree to which you agree or disagree with the following statements using this scale:

1	2	3	4	5	6	7
Strongly Disagree	Disagree	Somewhat Disagree	Neither / Uncertain	Somewhat Agree	Agree	Strongly Agree

Statement	Score
1. I understand the ways in which I can grow as a person.	_____
2. I understand how I define success in my life.	_____
3. I know what I can do to make progress in my life.	_____
4. I appreciate what I have in life.	_____
5. I desire activities, abilities, or things that I currently do not have.	_____
6. I believe that I can do, be, or have what I want in life.	_____
7. I understand what my emotions are communicating to me.	_____
8. I follow rules in life that protect and benefit myself and others.	_____
9. I know how to use the resources I have to support my goals in life.	_____
10. I feel like I have a choice in what I do or accomplish in life.	_____
11. I live my life with a sense of purpose.	_____
12. I am pleased with how my life is progressing.	_____
13. My life will be better in the future than it is today.	_____

Total: _____

Results

13-39: Struggling to find meaning in life; dedicate time to life exploration and analysis

40-65: Experiencing some issues or uncertainty in life direction; focus on clarifying specific areas

66-91: Living life with purpose; monitor for changes and opportunities for improvement

Save your total score so that you may see if your scores increase after reading the book and completing the post-book assessment. If you scored low in a particular statement and wish to focus on improving it, refer to the following mapping of the assessment's statements to the relevant parts of the book:

Section to Reference When Scoring Low in a Statement

Statements 1–2: Growth
Statement 3: Experience
Statements 4–5: Desire
Statement 6: Belief
Statement 7: Emotions
Statement 8: Ethics
Statement 9: Support
Statement 10: Choice
Statements 11–13: Each Chapter's Questions and Exercises

Introduction

How to think about life...not how to live it

"Life, under any circumstances, never ceases to have a meaning."

— Viktor E. Frankl[1]

"My life is my message."

— Mahatma Gandhi[2]

PRINCIPLES OF THE MEANING OF LIFE

- **Growth** – *The meaning of life is to grow*
- **Experience** – *You grow through experience*
- **Desire** – *Desires motivate you to have experiences*
- **Belief** – *Beliefs shape your perception and sustain your desires*
- **Emotions** – *Emotions indicate your life direction and progress*
- **Ethics** – *Ethics are principles for your growth within a society*
- **Support** – *Support enables you to realize your life's meaning*
- **Choice** – *Your choices create your destiny*

CONTEXT FOR THE MEANING OF LIFE

"What is the meaning of life?" is a complex question. People who ask it usually want to know four things:

- "How did life come to be?"
- "How does life work?"
- "How should I live my life?"
- "What should my goal in life be?"

The more important question, though, is why they are asking it. Ultimately, people want to know what to do with their lives and how to do it successfully. A rational person, then, is trying to use knowledge about where life came from and how it works to inform their goals and behaviors.

Unfortunately, life is so complex that no one set of instructions or rules could cover the infinite number of possible situations. Still, there are plenty of people looking for guidance and plenty of people willing to provide this guidance. As with any advice, the recipient has to decide whether any particular recommendation applies to his or her situation.

The problem with most life advice is that it combines the answers to these four questions and makes them interdependent. For example, one recommendation might be that life was created by God and follows the rules of God, so people should have an ultimate goal to worship Him and behave following His rules to live a pious life. These universal recommendations answer all four questions collectively, requiring anyone who only asks one of them to subscribe to the whole worldview.

By combining them, they often conflate them. Many religious and philosophical texts start with how life began, what the point is, and then recommend how to live based on that. There are two problems with this approach: subsequent scientific findings regarding how life works are filtered through the lens of that particular worldview, and life recommendations are based on who or what created the universe.

People should not be trying to use how and why life and the universe came into existence to determine what their goal should be and how to behave. An athlete does not need to learn who invented the sport and why to understand it, appreciate it, and excel at it. Instead, people should use their knowledge of how life works to define their own goals and behaviors.

Because how life works should be the basis of how to lead a meaningful, successful life, three of the four questions can be set aside for now. How life originated may have a scientific answer (i.e., a chemical reaction) or a religious one (i.e., God), but the former has no bearing on life's meaning while the latter can never be proven scientifically. Goals are subjective, so no one can say with universal applicability which goals everyone should have for their lives. Finally, you cannot understand how to approach life optimally until you understand how life works and what the goal is.

The reality is that no answer to the question of how to live life will satisfy everyone, and there is no single way to live life that is objectively best. There are plenty of successful approaches to follow when you have a specific goal, but people asking about the meaning of life are likely searching for what that goal should be.

Providing universal advice on how to identify the right goal and approach it in the best way possible is not easy. Philosophers have debated for thousands of years whether there are such things as objective, universal rules for living a successful life. Those conversations are often abstract, so most actionable guidance defines a set of common goals, such as health, wealth, status, and love, and explains to the listener what to think and do to succeed.

Unfortunately, telling people what to think instead of helping them think for themselves deprives them of the fundamental knowledge they need to find their own purpose. In addition, most life advice is heavily influenced by what the advisor believes is the right way to live. As a result, people receive guidance that may not apply to them with no way to determine whether it does.

To figure out the meaning of life, then, the only solution is to start by understanding how life works—how to think about life, not how to live it. How life works can be objectively answered, and those answers can be effectively used to inform what goals to have and how to behave in life.

Science, for example, is used to learn about and then explain how the universe works. There are "exact" physical sciences, such as physics and biology, and the "inexact" social sciences, such as psychology and sociology. Scientists have learned how life works from these sciences, yet most people separate science (the "how") and philosophy (the "why").

As a result, the most widely accepted life philosophies are based on pre-science theologies that start from how and why life came into existence and end with general rules for living. Science-based life philosophies, such as secular philosophy or atheism, have made significant progress but are frequently framed from the perspective of theology to help people live morally, happily, and purposefully without belief in a deity. In contrast, the most insightful, actionable philosophy would explain how life works and how you can systematically derive meaning from your existence.

Fortunately, philosophy and science have progressed to the point where there is now a logical explanation of how life works that can help you figure out the purpose of your existence for yourself. This book explains the eight most important life concepts that you need to understand to derive your own meaning:

The Eight Fundamental Concepts of the Meaning of Life
- **Growth** – Life's definition, purpose, and significance
- **Experience** – Life's medium for growth
- **Desire** – Life's driving force
- **Belief** – Life's sustaining force
- **Emotions** – Life's feedback mechanism
- **Ethics** – Life's rules for optimal growth
- **Support** – Life's protection and nurturing system

- **Choice** – Life's freedom to determine its own destiny

Understanding and mastering these eight concepts will help you live a life of purpose. Each chapter in this book explains one of the concepts in detail and contains supporting evidence from the fields of biology, psychology, sociology, philosophy, economics, and theology. The chapters are structured in the following way to explain the concept and apply it to your life:

Contents of Each Chapter
- The definition of the concept as it pertains to life's purpose
- The existence or evolution of the concept in living things
- The nature of the concept as it exists in humans
- The application of the concept in your search for meaning
- The difficulty in finding meaning without the concept
- Recommendations for how to proceed when you are unsure
- Questions for reflecting on how the concept applies to you
- Exercises to help you apply the concept to your life

You may wish to skip to the exercises to find your meaning as quickly as possible, but the most important part of searching for your meaning is knowing *why* these eight concepts are core to living a meaningful life. This book uses scientific, logical explanations of how each concept works to avoid the ambiguity of parables and the incredibility of spiritual explanations. Once you grasp the concepts, you can then use the practical guides at the end of each chapter to translate the insight into action.

In short, this book explains how life works conceptually and then provides an analytical process that you can use to find purpose in your existence. This approach can help you understand how to think about life so you can figure out your own direction without relying on an outside force to set it for you. There is no rigid belief system, no list of rules to follow without question, and no expectation to take anything on faith. Instead, this book contains the very core principles of life that serve as the basis for religions, philosophies, and personal success stories around the world.

If you are curious, lost, confused, depressed, searching for answers, or looking for more fulfillment, this book is made specifically for you. You want to find your purpose. You want someone to help you figure it out, not to tell you what it is or what it should be. After reading this book, you will understand how people find meaning in their lives and use that approach to live a life full of purpose. Your self-determined destiny begins here.

Growth

The meaning of life is to grow

"Life is a journey, not a destination."

— Proverb[3]

"Life is growth. If we stop growing, technically and spiritually, we are as good as dead."

— Morihei Ueshiba[4]

PRINCIPLES OF GROWTH

- Growth is the key difference between life and non-life
- Unlike early life forms, humans can grow in many ways
- To succeed in life, grow in the areas that are important to you
- Without personal growth, life seems pointless
- If your purpose is unclear, seek growth opportunities

GROWTH AND THE MEANING OF LIFE

The meaning of life is growth. Within the context of life, growth refers to the process through which a life form transitions from its current state to a greater future state. Growth is a vital part of the definition of what makes living things different than non-living things. It is what gives life its significance, and it is the intent or purpose of all life on Earth.

In short, growth is why life exists. More importantly, growth is why you exist. Growth is the foundation of all living things, and it is the most important concept to internalize as you aim to find your own life's direction and purpose.

Growth is the key difference between life and non-life

From a scientific perspective, life on Earth began with the replication of microscopic organisms. Scientists theorize that specific conditions (i.e., a mixture of chemicals and a catalyst such as lightning,[5] ultraviolet light,[6] or hydrothermal vent activity on the ocean floor[7]) triggered chemical reactions that eventually led to self-replicating groups of nucleic acids and proteins.

Most scientists define the origin of life as the point at which molecules begin to self-replicate. Andy Knoll, paleontologist and professor of biology at Harvard University, explains how self-replication is central to defining life and determining its origin:

> I think you can say that life is a system in which proteins and nucleic acids interact in ways that allow the structure to grow and reproduce. It's that growth and reproduction, the ability to make more of yourself, that's important.[8]

Growth is the key difference between life and non-life. Every living thing grows, including trees, animals, humans, bacteria, fungi, mold, weeds, and even cancer cells. Life is inherently defined by its ability to grow.

Growth is also life's purpose. Without growth, there is no

life. There is no point. Everything in the universe would exist aimlessly. Growth is the primary goal of all life on Earth.

Finally, growth gives life value and significance. All life can self-replicate, and this ability is unique in the universe. Advanced life has grown to the point where it can understand itself and the world around it. Given its unlimited potential, growth might be the most significant capability that has ever existed.

Growth defines life, is life's purpose, and gives life significance. Growth is the meaning of life. It is the core idea around which anyone can define a purpose for his or her existence.

However, this straightforward definition is not enough of an answer for many people. They continue to look for a grand insight into what gives their lives meaning and significance. In this search, people often erroneously conclude that they can find greater meaning if they can find a creator. They figure that if humans could identify the entity that created life, they could then determine the purpose of its creation.

The question of whether life is the result of divine intervention or a random chemical reaction is a fascinating mystery. It is one that will never be solved, however, because most theologies place the creator outside the physical universe where humans could observe it and receive direct answers about its intent. If the creation of the universe was a "big bang" without a divine cause, then no creator exists to answer the question. In that scenario, any and all effort to search for a divine purpose is a waste of time.

Fortunately, knowing whether a deity created life is irrelevant and unnecessary to understanding the meaning of life. Human beings are not tools; humans have their own intent. To understand the purpose of a tool, you can find who made it and ask the creator what his or her intention was for it. To understand the purpose of a person, you have to ask the person and not the creator because people have their own intentions.

Assuming for a moment that there was a creator, that creator's intent would not matter. If a person were to ask her biological mother and father—her direct creators—what the meaning of her life is, they would likely say that they did not have a specific intent for her or that they wanted her to go into an admirable profession (e.g., a doctor, lawyer, professional athlete). In cases where they had specific intent, the creators' intentions often differ significantly from the creation's intentions.

Of course, many people would reason that the best parents want to help their children figure things out for themselves. That reasoning is precisely why a life creator does not need to mandate meaning. When creating a being with intent, the intention of the creator is no longer relevant unless the creation considers it to be.

This same logic applies when someone finds a new use for an inventor's non-living creation. The inventors of fire, rubber, plastic, and the internet could never have foreseen all of the various purposes that humans have found for them. Purpose is ever-changing and not based on the creator's original intent. As such, knowing a divine creator's intent is not necessary to find purpose in life. While the scientific inquiry into the origin of life is a noble pursuit, the discovery would not bring any more insight into the meaning of existence.

Stephen Hawking says in his documentary, *Stephen Hawking's Grand Design*, "Meaning can only ever exist within the confines of the human mind, and in this way the meaning of life is not somewhere out there but right between our ears."[9] A purpose is something that a living thing gives itself. The meaning of **your** life is yours to determine, regardless of what a divine source may or may not have intended. The purpose of life is not the same thing as the intent of the creator of that existence, and knowing why it created life would not give you any better direction than what you could find from within yourself.

Any theist expecting a higher purpose to be bestowed upon them should consider the joke that Christians tell to explain how they believe God's divine assistance works:

A man is in the middle of a major flood and needs to evacuate the area to survive. He declines an offer from neighbors to leave in their car. "God will save me," he says. The water level rises, and a man in a small boat offers the man transport to safety. Again, the man declines. "God will save me." The flood worsens, and he becomes stranded on the roof of his house. A helicopter comes looking for survivors and offers an airlift to safety. "God will save me," he says yet again. The storm forces the helicopter to fly away. Eventually, the man drowns. He goes to heaven and rushes to meet God. He says, "What happened, God? I thought you would save me…" God says, "I sent you a car, a boat, and a helicopter. What more did you want?"

Monotheists looking for God to give them a higher purpose would benefit from the moral of this story. As per their belief, God gave them the capacity to think, feel, see, believe, intend, communicate, and cooperate. These abilities give them the potential to grow and achieve more than any other living creature on this planet. Everything that living creatures do today is because of the billions of years that life has pushed further and further to be more the next day than it was the previous day. They have an unprecedented set of tools at their disposal. If they squander their abilities, they could imagine God saying to them, "I gave you the means to find your own meaning. What more did you want?"

The purpose of life is built into every living thing, and humans have the highest growth potential of any organism that has ever existed. Growth is the common denominator that ties together all humans and all life forms. Because life forms have their own intentions, they determine their own life path and do not need another entity to assign them a purpose. Ultimately, humans find their own meaning in how they grow throughout their lifetimes.

Unlike early life forms, humans can grow in many ways

At a fundamental level, life forms have two general states based on environmental conditions: growth and protection.[10,11] In this simplified view, organisms are either growing and reproducing or protecting themselves from harm to their growth and reproduction. Sigmund Freud described the underlying psychological motivations in his Pleasure Principle, which states that humans have core instincts to seek pleasure and avoid pain.[12] In this context, pleasure is a neurochemical reward for behaviors that contribute to growth, and pain is a neurochemical signal denoting harm.

Reproduction is life's fundamental form of growth where an organism creates a copy or new version of itself to continue its existence. While the earliest forms of life were single-celled organisms replicating through basic cell division, life evolved to form complex organisms with tissue, organs, and organ systems. This cooperation allows organisms to survive the death of individual cells and acquire the resources they need to continue growing.

This complexity has opened up a multitude of different types of physical growth, such as sexual reproduction and regeneration. It has also enabled life to grow in adverse conditions. Some species are able to change reproductive functions to procreate, while others can regenerate limbs to recover from a predator's attack. Life has evolved over time to be incredibly capable when it comes to growing and reproducing.

Humans have evolved so much that they can grow and protect themselves in sophisticated ways. They have advanced brains, social abilities, and physical skills that no other creature can match. As a result, they can create structures to protect them from harsh environmental conditions, and they can work with other humans to make it easier to obtain nourishment and survive against competing life forms. They can learn how to develop sustainable food sources and manufacture weapons to ward off threats more effectively. These advanced capabilities allow them to survive, adapt, and grow better than any organism before it.

Humans still have the same basic forms of growth that other life forms have: physical growth and reproduction. They share intellectual growth with all other organisms capable of learning. They share social growth with all other social animals. However, their advanced capabilities grant them unique ways of growing and a greater capacity for growth.

As a group, humans can grow their intellectual capabilities more quickly and at scale through teaching, showing, and testing. They are so advanced that they no longer need first-hand experience to learn. For example, a mother can teach her son not to eat a poisonous plant without the son having to eat it and get sick first.

Additionally, humans can grow their social network to have better physical, psychological, and emotional support. They can accumulate resources so they do not have to gather food every day. They can combine their intellectual, social, and asset growth to create a system of exchanging goods and services so they do not have to do everything themselves. People can specialize in one area where they excel and achieve more as a group than they would individually. With these expanded forms of growth, human potential is exponentially higher than any other life form.

Below is a list of many ways that humans can grow, develop, and improve. With so many possibilities, no two individuals will have the exact same purpose. While the meaning of life is simple to understand, your meaning will evolve indefinitely.

Types of Growth

- **Physical Growth** – Growth of the body, including healing and reproduction
- **Intellectual Growth** – Growth of one's knowledge
- **Social/Interpersonal Growth** – Growth of one's friendships, social network, or social skills
- **Emotional Growth** – Maturation of one's ability to understand and manage their feelings
- **Familial Growth** – Growth of the family unit and its members
- **Financial Growth** – Increase in wealth, income, or financial well-being
- **Professional Growth** – Development in one's vocation, occupation, career, or field of study
- **Spiritual Growth** – Development of one's connection to the

universe, all living things, another plane, or a higher power

- **Relationship Growth** – Growth of one's relationship with a significant other (e.g., a spouse)

- **Asset Growth** – Accumulation of items of value, such as stamps, real estate, or books

- **Capability Growth** – Development or mastery of a skill, task, or ability

- **Technological Growth** – Advancement of technology to increase one's abilities and productivity

- **Artistic Growth** – Development of creative expression through music, art, poetry, literature, dance, video, or other art forms

- **Organizational Growth** – Growth of a group of individuals (e.g., a company or institution) with a singular goal or mission

- **Martial Growth** – Growth of a group's ability to defend against hostile forces

- **Political Growth** – Evolution of a society's effectiveness at governing and serving its citizens

- **Communal Growth** – Improvement of the safety, health, and well-being of a community

- **Cultivation** – The enablement of others' growth through teaching, feeding, protecting, financing, or other means of support

There are so many ways to grow, which may be both a blessing and a curse for people figuring out their meaning. From one point of view, it provides so many different options. You can contribute to society and earn a living in your strongest area, such as developing new technology to make people's lives easier or teaching the next generation how to read and write. Then, you can improve in secondary growth areas for personal fulfillment. You have the ability to make your life path unique.

From another point of view, the number of options can be

overwhelming if you want to do many things and only have so much time. Individuals who have reached the pinnacle of their fields—sports superstars, presidents, and Nobel prize winners, for example—may have had to sacrifice being involved parents or attentive spouses to achieve such success. While humans have the freedom to pursue one or several goals, they also have to make tough choices along the way.

Although everyone has their own choices to make, certain types of growth tend to have priority over others. Abraham Maslow's hierarchy of needs demonstrates how people typically prioritize their needs for personal growth. The hierarchy places biological needs at the bottom, as they are required for all life to maintain physical growth. Above that need is safety, which is necessary to avoid harm. The next priority is belonging, or social growth. Then, there is esteem, where self-respect and competence are necessary to feel good about oneself. Finally, self-actualization is at the top of the pyramid, and people who have addressed their other needs in the hierarchy can now focus on being the best version of themselves.[13]

Through this lens, a person may focus on the fundamental forms of growth (e.g., physical) to ensure survival and then make progress in more advanced forms of growth (e.g., social, familial, communal, intellectual, spiritual) to feel fulfilled. You will have to make these difficult selection, prioritization, and tradeoff decisions, so start getting a sense of which areas are important to you.

Understanding the practically unlimited human potential for growth is critical to finding a unique, tailored meaning in life. From endless possibilities, you can begin to dream and explore which specific purpose you wish to define for yourself.

To succeed in life, grow in the areas that are important to you

Since the purpose of life is growth, you are succeeding in life when you are growing. In this context, success can be defined as progress toward a desired outcome. Many people restrict the definition of success to the attainment of an outcome. They forget that most people describe someone as "successful" when they are in the process of building a great life for themselves. People wish each other "continued success" because success is progress and performance over time, not just a static result.

Success is also subjective and different for each individual. While you cannot control whether someone else views your life as successful or not, you have complete control over how you define and evaluate your success. Your growth and meaning are unique to you, so success is also unique to you.

Society tends to influence people's definitions of success based on what it glorifies at any given time, such as money, fame, status, or winning. While it is true that people who value financial growth and subsequently earn that money are indeed successful, that may not be how you define success in your own life. If the growth areas prioritized by society are not important to you, then you do not need to focus on them just to receive others' approval. Breaking through this incomplete list is critical to finding your purpose and identifying your own success criteria. If you do not define success for yourself, you will always be living your life on someone else's terms.

Teenage coming-of-age stories provide many examples of people trying to force their own perception of success onto the protagonist. In one story, a child will be told by her mother that she is worthless and will not amount to anything. In another story, a father will force his son to participate in an activity—a sport, for example—to fulfill the dreams that he was unable to realize in his childhood. In either of these situations, the conflict arises from the difference of opinion between the protagonist and his or her parents over what that child can or should achieve and how he or she should develop and grow.

Fortunately, many of these stories also demonstrate how to succeed and follow your dreams through adversity. Coming-of-age stories are often formulaic because they include the same eight key components of personal growth:

1. The protagonist has an **experience** that gets him or her interested in an activity.

2. The protagonist sees someone perform that activity well and watches with a sense of awe and the **desire** to do it.

3. They hold the **belief** that their life would be better if they had the ability to perform that activity.

4. Their first attempt at the activity makes them feel strong **emotions** of being happy, alive, or like their true selves.

5. They receive encouragement and **support** from a friend or family member to gain more experience with that activity.

6. They follow a code of **ethics** to perform the activity in the right way despite the temptation to cheat or take short-cuts.

7. They make a deliberate **choice** to continue working in the face of adversity and people questioning their decisions.

8. After enough practice, failure, and persistence, they **grow**, succeed, and attain their desired outcome.

The reason that this narrative is popular is not a mystery. These coming-of-age stories focus on the growth and development of a character as they come to find their purpose. These eight elements are essential to anyone finding success and meaning in life, so any good story involving personal growth will include them. Notably, the conflicts in these narratives almost always surface from differences in the characters' desires, beliefs, ethics, choices, or definitions of success.

Understanding that growth is the meaning of life and that you have practically unlimited options to grow should be a relief if you have felt powerless in your life. It is entirely up to you to identify which types of growth make you feel fulfilled. If you let others define which types of growth lead to success, you may be preventing yourself from finding your true purpose. Do not be misguided into thinking that becoming famous or getting rich is the sole indication that your life is successful.

You can define success for yourself and see an immediate change in your whole outlook. You can begin to make progress toward those goals and start to live a successful life. While there are eight concepts that you can master to live a meaningful life, growth is the most important to understand. To get started finding meaning in your life, find the right types of growth to pursue and define the right desired outcomes in those areas.

Without personal growth, life seems pointless

Imagine meeting someone who has been wandering through life without a purpose or a set of goals. Think about how you would describe that person. You may imagine that he or she is despondent, lost, in need of guidance, stuck in a rut, or in a bad place. Without growth, these people do not see the point of continuing and may experience depression, sadness, fear, frustration, confusion, or anger.

You have probably heard many ways to describe these people, and they are all metaphors for not growing. Their lives are going nowhere. They have no prospects. They are on the wrong path. They are going in the wrong direction. They are shooting themselves in the foot. They are not keeping up with everyone else. Success is measured by the direction and pace of growth.

Just as growth defines life, your personal growth defines your purpose in life. Without growth, life has no point. Without personal growth, your life has no point. If you want to feel satisfied, accomplished, successful, and fulfilled, you have to keep growing in the areas that matter to you. No purpose handed to you by someone else, a book, or a deity will ever truly be accepted unless you agree that it is right for you. When you identify an area of growth and a specific goal, you can better yourself every day so that you may realize that purpose.

If your purpose is to become a more spiritual person, you will try to do more and more things every day that will help you grow spiritually. If your purpose is to serve others, you will measure your success by how much you have improved their lives and helped them grow. Any purpose involves growth, and it will either expand or change every time you achieve a goal or milestone. Purpose and growth are intertwined, so finding the ways in which you want to grow is the most important action you can take to determine your purpose. No growth, no life, no purpose.

If your purpose is unclear, seek growth opportunities

Figuring out what you want to do with your life can feel like one of the most challenging tasks in the world. However, it is an important, constant pursuit that you must undertake. After all, you are looking for the meaning of life because you want to understand the meaning of **your** life.

To begin this journey, identify the growth areas that are important to you. You may find meaning in being a phenomenal athlete or raising a happy, healthy family. All forms of growth are valid if they are important to you, and no one can make you believe that your growth areas are wrong unless you let them.

If you have had a caring adult in your life, you probably have heard the phrase, "You can be anything you want to be in life." That person was trying to encourage you to follow your dreams. He or she is trying to tell you that you can grow in any way you want and that you can succeed in any area with enough effort.

While it can be liberating to hear this sentence, it can also be overwhelming because "anything" is so broad. To avoid being overwhelmed, start with core growth areas, such as physical, intellectual, and social, and then expand on them. It can also be unhelpful if you do not know what is possible or have a narrow view of the possibilities. You might also feel limited if your family, peer group, or community values some types of success above others. To avoid being limited by these factors, take time to learn about new fields and consider unconventional forms of growth and success.

Finding your growth areas can take time. Coming-of-age tales can be misleading in this regard because most of them have the protagonist stumble upon what he or she wants in a brief piece of exposition or a sudden moment of clarity. This part takes minutes in the story instead of the years it could take in reality. The story then focuses on how the protagonist overcomes adversity. The actual process of growing is usually glossed over using techniques such as time-lapse effects or montages. These methods are effective in moving a story along, but they are ineffective in teaching you how much time you need to figure out what you want in life and how much effort is required to succeed.

Fortunately, you do not have to have a sudden flash of insight to get started. The first step to finding your purpose in life is to look at the many ways in which you can grow and identify the ones that matter to you. Then, think about how you would like to improve in those areas and where you might want to be in the future. If you have trouble prioritizing, go through every growth area one by one and think about which changes would make you more satisfied with your life. Through this process, you will begin to determine which areas are most important to you.

If you are still unsure, experiment with a variety of growth opportunities. At worst, you will be better off in areas that you no longer wish to develop. At best, you will find your calling in life. If you continue to strive for growth, it is only a matter of time before growth opportunities become meaningful growth opportunities.

Seek growth, and you shall find meaning in your existence.

QUESTIONS

Questions That Help You Find Your Meaning

This section contains questions to help you think through which types of growth are important to you. Your answers to these questions will help you understand your life's purpose. This chapter's content will provide guidance on how to think about these questions, but only you can supply the definitive answers for your life.

1. What are examples of how you have grown over time?

- How have you grown in the past?
- How are you currently growing?
- How would you like to be growing now or in the future?

2. Which areas of growth are most important to you?

3. Why are these growth areas of importance to you?

4. Which areas are least important to you? Why?

5. What factors may be influencing your growth or your prioritized growth areas?

   - Do you have any personal limitations that hinder growth in an area? How does that affect your interest in it? How can you still grow in that area despite those constraints?
   - Do you experience peer or familial pressure toward or away from a specific type of growth? Do you want to focus on that type of growth, or do you feel forced into someone else's definition of success?
   - How would being free from these pressures or limitations change your priorities?
   - Does your belief in a higher power influence how you wish to grow? If so, how?

6. What does success look like for you? How is that different from how others define it?

7. What specific outcomes do you see yourself wanting in each growth area?

8. Where are you today in your growth areas? How does that compare to where you would like to be?

9. What can you do to focus more of your attention on growing in the areas that are most important to you?

EXERCISES

Activities That Help You Find Your Meaning

This section contains exercises to help you plan your approach to living with purpose. Completing these exercises will result in tangible prog-

ress toward living a meaningful life.

Thought Exercise: Imagine you are on your deathbed reflecting on your life. What should you have accomplished? What would you regret not having done? Returning to the present, what do you need to do to achieve those goals and avoid those regrets?

This exercise simulates hindsight as a means to identify what you want to do, be, or have in life. Like solving a maze more quickly by starting at the end, you may be able to find the shortest path to your goals by working back from the desired future state.

Brainstorming Exercise: If you are not sure of how you can grow or what success is for you, start listing out how you have grown in the past. Once you have an understanding of how you have grown personally, brainstorm ways you can grow going forward. Assume that anything is possible, and use examples from this chapter and your own research. Finally, brainstorm what you could achieve or accomplish in those areas if you grow enough.

The goal is to remove all restrictions and think of anything you can do with your life. What will you set out to achieve? What will you need to do, be, or have to succeed? How can you learn about what is possible? Use the ideas that you come up with in the following creative and writing exercises.

Examples:

Physical growth: I have grown from the fertilized egg in my mother's womb to the complex organism that I am today. I exercise three days per week to build muscle and increase my stamina and strength. Success for me is being one of the best athletes on my softball team and living long enough to see my grandchildren graduate from high school.

Artistic growth: I want to develop my painting ability so that I may create canvases worthy of art galleries.

Creative Exercise: Gather pictures of role models in fields that interest you. Examples include politicians, athletes, actors, entrepreneurs, business executives, and scientists. You may substitute people with outcomes, such as high test scores, a new home, or a healthy family. Paste or tape them to a piece of paper or poster. Below each person, list what attributes, skills, and abilities make them successful. If you use outcomes, list the attributes, skills, and abilities that you need to achieve that outcome.

You will quickly find that each attribute or quality you list—e.g., money, fame, athleticism, skill, philanthropy, leadership—requires you to improve upon it over time to succeed. Your role models or outcomes may indicate where you want to grow or which skills you wish to develop. Add any newly identified growth areas to your list from the previous exercises.

Writing Exercise: In the first column of a table, list the growth areas that you identified in the brainstorming and creative exercises. For each growth area, define success in the second column. In the third column, rate every type of growth you have listed on a scale of 1 to 10 (1 being unimportant; 10 being the most important) based on how important it is to your overall definition of growth and success.

This exercise helps you define and prioritize your growth areas and success criteria. Your highest score is your top priority because it contributes the most to your sense of meaning and fulfillment in life.

Example:

Growth Area	Success Criteria	Importance
Physical Growth	Bench press 215 pounds three times	7
Social Growth	Have three close friends Join the chess club and kickball team	9

Note: Keep this information for the next chapter's writing exercise.

OUTCOME

After reading this chapter, you should have a clear understanding of the meaning of life. More importantly, you should understand how you define growth and success to begin to find the meaning of **your** life. To that end, you should have a list of ways that you can grow in this lifetime and an initial idea of what the future state of your life will look like if you succeed.

The most important takeaway from this chapter is that these are areas of growth that **you** identified as being important or interesting. You did not need another person or entity to coax or coerce you into caring about them. Whether you find your purpose or define your purpose, it is up to you to carve out your own path in life that is full of meaning and fulfillment.

After this chapter, you may have found where your areas of interest differ from where people have told you to focus your entire life, and this may be the first time you prioritize your own opinion. Your self-determined destiny begins here.

When you have your list, you are ready to proceed to the next chapter.

Experience

You grow through experience

"People grow through experiences if they meet life honestly and courageously. This is how character is built."

— Eleanor Roosevelt[14]

"That all our knowledge begins with experience there can be no doubt."

— Immanuel Kant[15]

"All knowledge of reality starts from experience and ends in it."

— Albert Einstein[16]

PRINCIPLES OF EXPERIENCE
- Experience is how life grows toward an improved state
- Humans must have relevant experience to grow in an area
- To grow meaningfully, gain experience in an area of interest
- Without new experiences, life is boring, and growth stagnates
- If the right experience is unclear, analyze your options

EXPERIENCE AND THE MEANING OF LIFE

Life is a collection of experiences. While there are many different types of growth, experience is the sole medium through which you can achieve growth. Experience in this context refers to your observations and activities over time.

Fortunately, you have the power to focus your thoughts, observations, and actions. If you know how you wish to grow, then you can focus your attention on the experiences that will help you develop in that area. If you do not know which growth areas are most important to you, then you can choose experiences that help you reach a greater understanding of your interests.

As you grow, you will need more, new, or different experiences to progress further in those areas. If you continue to direct your attention toward relevant, appropriate experiences, you will continue to grow toward your life goals.

Experience is how life grows toward an improved state

For growth to occur, life must satisfy three criteria:

- It must exist in a current state
- It must have the potential to exist in a greater future state
- It must have the means through which it transitions between the current state and future state

The medium through which life transitions from one state to another is experience.

In early life, growth began with basic cell division. To grow, those life forms had to consume resources for energy, convert those resources into a usable form, and then expel the waste. For early single-celled organisms, that process involved the consumption of protein and sugars, the breakdown of these molecules with enzymes into individual molecules for use, and then the evacuation of any waste through the cell membrane. The digested food was then in a state that the living organism could use to grow and reproduce.

In this example, the beginning state is a single-celled organism. The future state is two single-celled organisms. The digestive process and cell division experiences enable the single-celled organism's growth. Without those experiences, the organism cannot grow.

Humans and other animals grow physically in a similar manner. They eat food, digest it, use the energy to grow the body, and defecate the waste. There are plenty of nutritional options for consumption, such as meat, vegetables, fruit, and grains. To optimize physical growth, humans need to consume the right amount of food and water with the right combination of nutrients. As a child grows into an adult, it needs more food to increase and then sustain its size. Eventually, it uses that fuel to engage in sexual activity and reproduce. After birth, the offspring repeat the physical growth process of their parents.

In physical growth, experience is the process through which life multiplies its cells. It is also the means through which life forms can learn which foods are best for them, where they can get them, and how much they need to consume. These experiences enable them to grow and also enable them to become more effective at growing in the future.

With advanced life forms and their numerous growth options, experiences to achieve growth are much more diverse and complex. When mastering a musical instrument, for example, a person may begin learning by observing how someone else holds the instrument, plays it, and creates a certain style of music. Then, she could build on that experience by holding the instrument and playing a few notes. She may mix practice and various forms of observation, such as working with teachers to play basic pieces and listening to the best musicians in the field play advanced compositions.

With more practice, she becomes better, and she then has to play more difficult music to advance her skill. Eventually, she will develop the ability to play those complex pieces. Throughout the experience, she is gauging whether she wants to continue developing her musical ability. At any point, she can decide to have the frequency and types of experiences that will improve the skill further, maintain it, or let it fade.

Positive psychology has conducted many studies over decades to find out what brings happiness, meaning, and satisfaction in life. One of those researchers, Mihaly Csikszentmihalyi, found that the "optimal experience" people could have was one where the challenge level of the activity was appropriate for their skill level. In this situation, people reach a state in which they describe being completely focused on what they are doing, being caught up in the moment, and feeling great joy and fulfillment in the activity. Mihaly called this state "flow" to reflect how engrossed people are in the activity.[17]

This "optimal experience" is essentially a set of conditions for optimal growth, as the research shows that the experiences that trigger flow are interesting to the individual and conducive to his improvement. If his skill outweighs the challenge, the person becomes bored with the activity. If the challenge outweighs his skill, the person experiences frustration and anxiety. This research uncovered that humans are genetically predisposed to seek experiences that help them grow toward an improved future state. If an experience is not enabling a person to grow at a satisfactory rate, he will be motivated to adjust his behavior accordingly.[18]

Because an individual organism has a limited lifespan, the only way for life to maximize growth is to make the most of its experience. As such, it can focus on experiences that optimize its health and nutrition, keep itself safe from harmful environmental factors, and nurture its family to pass its genes on to future generations. Because humans can grow in a multitude of ways, they must identify and select the right experiences to increase and maintain many areas, such as their finances, social lives, and knowledge. To reach their desired future state and get the most out of their lives, they have to select their experiences carefully.

Humans must have relevant experience to grow in an area

To grow in a specific area, humans must find and have experiences that are most appropriate given their current state and their desired future state. To grow physically, they have to eat, drink, exercise, and rest. For intellectual growth, they have to read books, listen to lectures, or perform scientific tests. For skill growth, they have to repeat an activity, increase its difficulty, or vary the experience to improve over time. With more time, effort, and attention, humans maximize their abilities.

Additionally, accelerated development comes from better experience. For example, a study conducted at the University of Texas investigated how learning ability was affected by the nature of the experience. The study found that people remember:[19]

- 10 percent of what they read
- 20 percent of what they hear
- 30 percent of what they see
- 50 percent of what they see and hear
- 70 percent of what they say
- 90 percent of what they do and say

The results demonstrate that people develop more quickly depending on how engaged or immersed they are in an experience.

The effect of effort and engagement on development may seem obvious, but plenty of people will give up on a goal before giving it the time and attention required to improve. For example, many who attempt to play a game will struggle and lose interest when they do not show instantaneous proficiency. Alternatively, they may be waiting to be proficient before pursuing the experience, such as when people want to lose weight *before* they join a gym. Worse, they may wait for years looking for the perfect opportunity. Humans cannot become good at something if they do not make an effort or quit after making one mistake.

One of the most influential factors that determine human effort is the belief that individuals have insurmountable, inherent limits from birth. This mentality, called the "Fixed Mindset" in

Mindset by Carol Dweck, prevents many people from pursuing areas of interest because they believe that their innate potential is low. Even if they try, people with a Fixed Mindset may quit in the face of their first failure or hurdle because they think that they have reached their limit.[20]

Fear of failure is one of the most daunting mental hurdles to overcome. Unfortunately, people often conflate failing at a task and being a failure. Failure is a temporary state of not succeeding at an activity and is an inevitable part of the growth process: a person attempts a task, succeeds or fails, learns from the experience, and improves. Describing someone as "a failure" is a derogatory assessment that a person applies to another based on arbitrary success criteria such as education, income, relationships, or social life. The only objective way to "fail at life" would be to die, and everyone dies. All failure is temporary, and there is no need for one person to meet someone else's life standards.

Additionally, there is a high degree of subjectivity in how someone perceives success or failure at a task. While a person can objectively define and measure success and failure, he can also change how he views an experience by looking at it in a different way. Based on that perspective, completing a task can either be the successful achievement of an objective or the failure to do it perfectly. The implications of this are that anyone can change the success criteria to make something seem better or worse than it is.

The reality is that failure is a behavior that does not achieve the desired outcome. Failure provides valuable feedback on what someone can do differently to succeed. A person who did not know what it would take to succeed may finally understand only after failing. She may then try a new approach or change her objective on the next attempt.

Once people identify where they want to improve and what outcome they want to achieve, their next step to finding meaning is to identify the experiences required to make progress. Then, they may gain that experience, learn from their mistakes, and improve until they achieve their goals.

To grow meaningfully, gain experience in an area of interest

Your personal development requires a clear understanding of where you currently are, where you want to be, and what you would need to do to get there. For example, if you would like to play soccer, you would look at your current proficiency and desired proficiency to determine the first steps and the estimated amount of effort required to reach that skill level.

Your current proficiency may determine whether you begin with an introductory class or an intramural league. You could ask other people who play soccer to teach you, or you could watch games to learn the rules and strategies. You could buy a ball and practice in your backyard. There are many options to get started growing in any area, so you need to identify those activities and select the best one for you.

Your desired future proficiency will determine what effort is required. If you wish to play recreationally, then once you learn the rules and join a league, you just need to attend the games. If you wish to play professionally, you will need to practice frequently and intensely, compete against experts, and develop the athleticism and knowledge to be an exceptional player.

Once you understand the journey, you will notice that past experiences and current restrictions will significantly influence your approach. You may have limited resources, knowledge, or time. You must consider these factors, but they do not close off all options. You just need to adapt to the situation and grow in the best way that you can.

For example, you may want to learn more about science but have no money, limited time, poor access to information, and a subpar school. Based on this restrictive situation, you can read books at a local library instead of purchasing a copy from a bookstore. You can use the library or ask a friend with internet access to do research online. If you do not have a library, there are book donations from charitable organizations. There are teachers who are willing to help students get more information. It may require effort to identify the opportunities at your disposal, but it is possible to find creative solutions to restrictions and barriers.

Extreme situations, such as being imprisoned, can inhibit many opportunities to grow. However, growth is still possible in the most restrictive of circumstances by focusing on experiences that are still available. In these cases, you are still able to grow psychologically or spiritually through activities such as reading or meditation. You can still exercise and practice certain skills under those constraints. Limitations in one growth area give you more time to focus on another. Despite life's obstacles, you can make the most of the experiences you have.

Even if creative approaches fail to help you improve in an area, giving up is not your only option. Instead, you can focus on another area for now while waiting for the right opportunity. If it is raining outside, you can reschedule your outdoor practice and use the time indoors to study the playbook. If you wish to grow intellectually and financially, you can choose between earning money now to attend college in the future and taking out a loan for college now to repay later. To stay on track toward your overall growth goals, you can adjust your planned experiences based on current circumstances and information.

No matter your circumstances, do not dismiss experiences or opportunities before you fully consider them. The mind can limit development much more than physical restrictions. Judgment from others, assumptions, self-doubt, and fear all contribute to people discounting potential opportunities for growth. To counteract this, you should identify and consider the merits of potential experiences before imposing any restrictions. If you dismiss your options to grow in areas of interest, you are relegating yourself to a boring, stagnant existence.

Without new experiences, life is boring, and growth stagnates

Imagine the fate of Sisyphus, a king in Greek mythology. Zeus punished him with the never-ending task of pushing a boulder up a steep hill. When the boulder reached the top, it would roll down the hill again, forcing him to repeat the task. An eternity of one repetitive, pointless experience would be intolerable.

Similarly, life without new experiences would be incredibly tedious. Monotony breeds restlessness, causing people to seek change. Boredom is genetically advantageous because humans that have more experience are better able to survive and thrive in their environment. For example, structured play (e.g., humans playing team sports) keeps their bodies prepared for potential future situations involving physical skills. Trying new food gives them another option if other food sources are exhausted. In survival of the fittest, experience makes life more fit to handle threats and succeed in future tasks.

New experiences are important to achieving life satisfaction. Research has found that experiential purchases tend to provide more excitement and anticipation beforehand and enduring happiness afterward than material purchases.[21] People are predisposed to finding value in experiences because of how critical they are to human growth and survival.

New experiences build and expand on past experiences. For example, originality is one of the criteria that critics use to judge movies. If a movie does not bring any new ideas, concepts, visuals, or plot points, a critic may dismiss it as stale or boring. However, people who have not seen this type of movie before may think that it is amazing because it is a new experience for them. Other people may love the genre and enjoy the new take on a classic formula. People are drawn to the new and the novel, and what is new is relative to that person's experience so far.

This instinct to seek the new and the novel pushes humans to continue to grow throughout their entire lives. Sometimes, it is seeking a new version of a familiar experience, such as reading a new book. Other times, it is an entirely new experience, such as creating an ice sculpture for the first time.

Even when repeating the same experience or activity, people can continue to develop by catching things they did not notice the first time. When watching the same movie for the 20th time, for example, they may see an actor in the background who became a star or catch an inside joke referencing the director's previous films. They get better at reciting the lines. When repeating a song or dance, they master the notes or the choreography. Repetition improves the efficiency and precision of the skill so they can focus on the next step in their growth trajectory.

If your life feels stagnant, you need to reevaluate your growth areas and experiences to look for adjustments that will get you back on the path toward growth. It is no coincidence that people cite travel, volunteer work, college, and child-rearing as events or activities that have opened their eyes to the world and their purpose in life. These experiences expose people to different perspectives and require new ways of thinking, acting, and relating to others. These people often mention that they were stagnant or unsure before, and these events forced them to get out of their comfort zones and figure out what truly mattered to them.

Because these events can put you into a completely new environment, they can change your worldview and life drastically in a very short period of time. While it is not necessary to overhaul your life completely at the first sign of stagnation, experiences that get you out of your daily routine will either help you to identify new areas to pursue or give you a greater appreciation for your current situation. If you are bored, the cure is to open yourself up to something new, different, or more challenging than what you are currently doing.

If the right experience is unclear, analyze your options

Experiences and growth areas act as a continuous loop: you identify a field or discipline to pursue, you gain experience, you grow in that area, and then you decide whether to continue or move on to something else. Alternatively, you find a new experience that may be of interest, you try it, and then you decide whether you are interested in additional or related experiences.

While many people can keep that cycle going for a while,

some cannot get started because they do not know which experiences will help in the area of interest. It could be because limitations eliminate the preferred options. It could also be that they just do not know how to get into a field, so the leap seems to be too great from where they are.

If you are facing one of these situations, do not give up before you research options. Take the area where you want to improve and find out how to get started. Read a book, browse the internet, ask an expert, or talk to people you know. Identifying the possibilities will help you understand how you can proceed.

It may be difficult to find a way into some pursuits. A child striving to become a world-renowned surgeon, for example, will need decades of education, training, and experience. Others might be easy; playing football requires having a football, space, people, and time. Whatever the goal and the situation, there is always a first step. Just learning about a subject gives you more information on whether it interests you and where to start.

If you are still struggling to figure out where you would like to improve, focus on having new experiences. Variety increases the probability that a person will find what is interesting, important, engaging, and satisfying to him or her. With a practically unlimited amount of information at an internet user's fingertips, finding the next journey to pursue just takes research, experimentation, and time.

When you begin that "purpose of finding a purpose" approach, the effort in and of itself becomes meaningful. It is why many say, "Life is what you make of it." You can shift from aimless meandering to a definite direction by having a goal—even if that goal is to find out what your goal is or should be. Be deliberate about your growth if you can; if you cannot, at least be deliberate about your experiences so that you may learn from them.

Ultimately, you can use experience in three ways: to determine which growth areas interest you, to explore opportunities to grow in those areas, and to perform the observations and activities that lead to growth. Make the most of your experiences to maximize what you can accomplish in your lifetime.

QUESTIONS

Questions That Help You Identify the Right Life Experiences

Your answers to these questions will help you identify life experiences that will allow you to grow in the areas you identified in the Growth chapter. This chapter's content provides guidance on how to think about these questions, but only you can supply the definitive answers for your life.

1. What life experiences can help you grow or develop in your growth areas?

    Examples: exercise for physical growth, quality time with family for familial growth, dating for relationship growth

2. What can you do to learn more about experiences you can have to grow in those areas?

    Examples: research the topic, interview/ask people with knowledge or experience, take classes

3. What do you need to do to have those experiences?

    Examples: take classes, apply for a job in the field, make time for family events, save money, volunteer

4. What do you need to refrain from doing or stop doing to have those experiences?

    Examples: stop making excuses, stop procrastinating, reduce time spent on other activities, eliminate bad habits

5. What can you do to learn more about new growth areas and experiences that you may not have considered?

    Examples: go to a different country, join a new club, volunteer in the community

EXERCISES

Activities That Help You Identify the Right Life Experiences

Completing these exercises will result in tangible progress toward having meaningful experiences.

Thought Exercise: To broaden your thinking of possible experiences that may be relevant to your identified growth areas, remove the following limitations and see if new opportunities present themselves:

- *Time* – If you did not have to work or had an extra day every week, what would you do with your time?

- *Money/Resources* – If you had endless funds, what would you do? Where would you go? What would you have?

- *Professional Connections* – If you knew the right people, what industry or field would you try to enter?

- *Knowledge or Skills* – If you already had great skill in a field, what would you do?

- *Looks or Personality* – If it did not matter what you looked like or who you were, would that change what you did?

- *Social Acceptability* – If an activity or field were more socially acceptable, would you show more interest in it?

- *Age* – If you were older or younger, would you be more likely to want to pursue an area of interest?

- *Location* – If you lived in a different location, would you want to pursue a different career or hobby?

- *Responsibility/Commitment* – If you did not have your current responsibilities, what else would you be doing?

Consider removing any other limitations that may be on your mind as you complete the above list.

Reapply the limitations one at a time. With each restriction, think about what you are still able to do to have those experiences.

Example: If you want to travel but lack money, can you save up for the trip? If you want to have a relationship with someone who does not know you, can you become friends with him or her first? If you would go to school if you did not have to support your family, can you set a time in the future where you will be able to share responsibilities so you can fit school into your schedule?

Brainstorming Exercise: If you do not know which experiences will help you grow, investigate classes, training, support groups, and other means of development to come up with possibilities. Continue brainstorming and researching until you have what you believe to be an exhaustive list of opportunities. Next, identify the potential barriers to having those experiences. Finally, think of creative ways in which you can overcome those hurdles.

This exercise can help you increase the probability of making progress in your growth areas by finding new options and troubleshooting hurdles before they stop you from proceeding.

Creative Exercise: Using the role models that you identified in the previous chapter's creative exercise, review the relevant experiences that they had in your identified growth areas. Specifically, evaluate these successful individuals' résumés, biographies, or backgrounds for which experiences were crucial to their achievements.

Then, create your desired future "Life Résumé" that forecasts the path you will need to take to succeed in your life. To create this document, put your name and objective at the top of a sheet of paper. Below your objective, list the experiences you want or need to have in reverse-chronological order. Use role models' experiences for guidance, and include your real-life past experiences. Finally, verify your list by envisioning yourself in the future looking back on your accomplishments.

This exercise should bring greater clarity to your ultimate goal and the numerous experiences you will need to have along the way. It will also show the continuous nature of growth; once you make that Life Résumé your reality, you can update it or create a new one.

Repeat for your other growth areas to explore and visualize your potential journey toward all of your life goals.

Writing Exercise: Take your list of prioritized growth areas from the Growth chapter's writing exercise. For each of the items on the list, write down the experiences you can have or need to have to grow in that area. If those experiences have a particular order (e.g., go to college and then go to graduate school), note which ones are prerequisites for other experiences. Then, write down the actions you could take to have those experiences or prepare to have those them in the future.

For this exercise, ignore whether you want to have these experiences or whether you think you can do them. All experiences should be under consideration at this point. At the end of this exercise, you should now have a full list of actions that you can take to pursue your priority growth areas.

Example:

Growth Area	Experiences	Actions
Physical Growth	Personal training Exercise three times per week	Schedule a session Sign up to a gym
Social Growth	Attend club social events Practice social skills	Mark meetings on calendar Join a communications class

Note: The above example does not show all of the information you will bring from the previous writing exercise; it is possible that this chapter's teachings may cause you to refine that information.

OUTCOME

After reading this chapter, you should have a clear understanding of how you have the ability to instill meaning in your life by pursuing experiences that enable you to grow and succeed. Experience is the medium through which all growth occurs, and you have a high degree of influence over your life experience. To exert that control, you should have a clear list of actions you can take to gain the experience you need to grow toward your desired future state.

When you have your list, you are ready to proceed to the next chapter.

Desire

Desires motivate you to have experiences

"The significance of man is not in what he attains, but rather in what he longs to attain. . . . We are all climbing toward the summit of our hearts' desire."

— Kahlil Gibran[22]

"Just don't give up trying to do what you really want to do. Where there is love and inspiration, I don't think you can go wrong."

— Ella Fitzgerald[23]

PRINCIPLES OF DESIRE

- Desire is life's driving force to seek growth and avoid harm
- Desire drives humans toward experiences that lead to growth
- To grow, find and build desire for relevant experiences
- Without desire, you feel unmotivated and lose your direction
- If your desire is unclear, then you desire to have a clear desire

DESIRE AND THE MEANING OF LIFE

Always be content; never be satisfied. Desire within the context of the meaning of life refers to the inner motivation or core drive of all living things to do, be, or have something. Live a life full of desire for what you have (i.e., appreciation) and desire for what you do not have yet but are working toward (i.e., drive, ambition, determination), and you will find meaning and purpose. Desire points you toward your life goals and instills in you the will to achieve them.

Desire is life's driving force to seek growth and avoid harm

Desire. Motivation. Intention. People describe it as the fire in the belly, the hunger, or the passion for something. All life forms, including humans, animals, plants, and even microscopic organisms, perform actions that help them to stay alive and to grow. For any life form to take deliberate action, they must first have a motivation or intention to do so.

Advanced cognitive ability is not required to have intent, as the primary directives to grow and avoid harm are even built into cells. Early forms of desire are observable in organisms that have the ability to move. Life that was able to control itself to move toward energy sources or away from sources of harm would be more likely to survive. Therefore, life that was able to sense an absence of resources and trigger the behavior to move toward the energy was more likely to survive than organisms that moved randomly.[24] Eventually, the organisms that survived contained an innate instinct or drive to act in ways that enabled their growth.

This instinct is desire. At its core, it is the ability of an organism to sense when something is required for growth and prompt itself to act in response. When it takes the action and attains the desired outcome, the drive subsides. This fundamental force underlies the behaviors and activities of living things.

Conscious, intelligent organisms differ from earlier organisms in their ability to understand and control their desires. For example, humans can use their advanced cognition to reason through what they want and how they should act. Impulse control is an advanced function of the prefrontal cortex that allows people to override primal instincts in favor of conscious intentions. As a result, they have the ability to think, act, and live deliberately.

In a civilized society, humans' desire to live in harmony supersedes their primal desires for food, water, shelter, and sex. People can also delay gratification in the short term for a larger payoff in the future. Most importantly, they can process multiple competing desires and determine the best path forward. This control over their drives and motivations allows them to focus their energy most constructively on their desired outcomes.

While desire originally motivated organisms to survive and grow physically, it can now drive humans to achieve growth and success in any part of their lives. People have a visceral understanding that overwhelming desire fuels the greatest achievements. Optimists will say, "Where there's a will, there's a way." Sports announcers will dramatize the end of a contest by saying, "The score is tied. There are five seconds left on the clock. Everything is on the line. It all comes down to who wants it more."

Desire can allow people to overcome many obstacles. Parents can lift cars off their children with desire and adrenaline. Olympic gold medalists can overcome severe financial and familial difficulties to achieve victory with desire and practice. When you see something you want, desire causes you to act.

While desire is striving toward outcomes you do not have yet, appreciation is acknowledging the desire for something you already have. Gratitude is important in social animals because they need to communicate to each other when a behavior was beneficial. This practice encourages prosocial behavior in the future.[25] Humans also have rewards systems in their brains that activate for both the deliberate helper and the grateful beneficiary.[26]

As for its role in growth, gratitude reminds you how much something or someone means to you, thus reigniting or sustaining that meaning you found when initially driving toward that goal. Desire for what you have as well as for what you do not have is critical to continue to grow while not losing or neglecting the progress that you have made to date.

Life has an inner mechanism that senses the lack of resources necessary for growth and drives it to take action. Humans must understand their drives to determine what they want to do, be, and have in life and what their motivation is for pursuing the requisite experiences. Because growth continues throughout life, human desire is inexhaustible.

Desire drives humans toward experiences that lead to growth

Human desire requires the perception of lack and the identification of a benefit that can address the lack. Masters of persuasion know this, as their goal is to get people to want to do something and not just to get them to do it. Advertisements and salespeople strive to make customers feel a need for their product or service so they are driven to satisfy that need with a purchase. People can build incredible motivation for anything by maximizing the contrast between life with and without it.

This motivation can drive a person to do anything. *The Adventures of Tom Sawyer* includes a story where Tom gets other children to paint a fence for him. In fact, *they* pay *him* for the opportunity. To pique their interest, he convinced them that he liked to paint and then expressed reluctance to let them try it when they asked. This approach fueled their desire to paint, changing their perception of the activity from a chore to a privilege.[27]

In this example, the other children sought amusement, and Tom convinced them that painting the fence would provide that benefit. As a result, they wanted to paint the fence. Most people are surprised by this story, as they consider painting a fence to be work and not play. In response, Mark Twain wisely narrates, "Work consists of whatever a body is OBLIGED to do, and . . . Play consists of whatever a body is not obliged to do."[28]

In his succinct narration, Twain describes both the difference and relationship between extrinsic and intrinsic motivation. Extrinsic motivation comes from external factors, while intrinsic motivation comes from a person's inner desire to do something. Pure desire is intrinsic motivation, and it drives people to succeed. Obligation is extrinsic motivation, and it can often diminish intrinsic motivation.

In this sense, obligation affects intrinsic desire like steroids affects natural testosterone production: the more a person receives externally, the less he or she produces internally. *Drive* by Daniel Pink provides several examples of scientific studies where extrinsic rewards, such as compensation, negatively impacted participants' intrinsic interest in the activity they were performing.[29]

External factors can also influence human desire toward behaviors that are better for society. In a capitalist system, money provides an incentive for people to have experiences that they may not want intrinsically. This motivation works well when an undesirable job needs to be done, such as paying someone to handle waste materials. Society benefits from the job, and the worker benefits from the financial compensation. Social norms also influence desires, as people adjust their behavior due to peer pressure so that they may achieve acceptance or status.

However, these same factors can lead people astray from their intrinsic motivation. For example, some people might have a desire to perform interpretive dance but lose it when they fear being judged or being financially insecure in that profession. They may also face familial obligations to spend time and money elsewhere. In these cases, external factors influence what people think they should want or cause them to dismiss their inner desires.

To avoid confusion, people should differentiate between the two types when evaluating what they want. The motivation that brings the most meaning to life is always intrinsic, so they have to find and build the desire within for the experiences and growth areas they wish to pursue. *Drive* provides examples of maximizing intrinsic motivation by seeking autonomy (i.e., self-direction), purpose (i.e., a greater goal), and mastery (i.e., continuous growth and improvement).[30] The monetary incentive can align to the internal desire to contribute to society, but no amount of money can keep people happy if they neither enjoy nor find meaning in an occupation that they spend the majority of their lives doing. Humans have to tie their experiences in life to an inner desire so that they build and sustain their drive to continue forward.

The strongest intrinsic desire that humans have is to live, and it requires extraordinary circumstances to extinguish. This instinctual desire for life drives people to seek basic needs for survival and growth, such as food, water, sex, and shelter. After meeting those needs, they have the opportunity for more advanced desires to accomplish greater achievements.

This desire for greater accomplishment is where greater meaning in life is found. Growth is the means to that achievement, and experience is the medium for growth. The instigator of that experience is desire. When people want something, they will take action to get it.

The difficulty, however, comes when people do not know what they want in life. Many people searching for answers will ponder and research what they *should* want in life. They will look to the origins of life for the intent of a higher power. They will look for guidance from others to tell them what they want.

However, each living organism is born with its own desires and intentions. Therefore, others' desires and intentions provide helpful guidance for what someone *might* want or *could* want, but they are mostly irrelevant to what that person *does* want unless he or she accepts their influence. A person's own intent to grow and thrive is the fire that drives the overwhelming majority of his or her actions. To find their true meaning, people must use their own analysis and experience to understand their intentions and use others for support, not dictation.

While desire comes from within, it is triggered by experience. You do not know what is out there until you explore. Since everyone wants to be, do, or have different things, exposure to a multitude of different places, things, events, vocations, and activities will give you a higher likelihood of finding something that piques your interest. The variety found in the world is of great value to life, as life would be boring otherwise.

For growth and meaning to exist, variety must exist. Many people ask, "Why can't everything be like (insert desired thing here) all of the time? Why is there (insert undesired thing here) in the world?" Alternatively, they might put it in more religious terms: "Why would God allow such bad things to exist?" The answer to that question is that growth requires contrast.

If you live in a world where you can make tomorrow better, then that world cannot be perfect today. There will always be a natural contrast between what is and what could be. As you grow, you will find more to do or something else to do because nothing is ever final. Variety provides contrast. Contrast triggers desire. Desire drives action to have an experience, and that experience leads to growth. Therefore, things you do not like must exist for you to have the desire for things you do like.

The Tom Sawyer example demonstrates the conclusion here: human perception and preferences determine whether something is "good" or "bad" in life. As William Shakespeare famously wrote in *Hamlet*, "For nothing is either good or bad, but thinking makes it so."[31] Sigmund Freud boiled down life into two basic drives: seeking pleasure (i.e., growth) and avoiding pain (i.e., harm). In the most basic sense, then, humans classify anything that supports growth and pleasure as good and anything that harms or detracts from pleasure as bad. Human perception of things being good or bad is seen as "positive" or "negative" in nature, and focusing on the good or bad is commonly referred to as having a positive or negative attitude.

Positive psychologists and New Age thinkers have expanded on this idea by saying that positive thinking is important for happiness and prosperity. This idea is true in its core point: focusing on wanting and attaining good things and not trying to obsess over bad things is a much more fulfilling approach to life. However, many have taken this to the extreme of always thinking positive thoughts, which can lead people to become complacent, avoid problems, and overlook risks.

With regards to growth and the meaning of life, something is positive or negative is based on how it affects progress toward desired outcomes. "Positive" is anything that contributes to desired outcomes. "Negative" is anything that detracts from desired outcomes or causes undesired outcomes.

In this context, you want to focus on desired outcomes and not on undesired outcomes. The former encourages you to keep moving forward, while the other tends to demotivate you. Positive thinking can be useful, then, because it fuels your motivation toward your desired outcome.

Critics of positive thinking are making a different point: you need to identify those detractors or hurdles to the desired outcome so that you may either avoid them or find solutions to overcome them. You may even find an alternative desired outcome. However, any additional focus on the undesired outcome is only going to decrease desire and inhibit growth. For example, once you know that you can fall off a ladder if you are not careful, you need to focus on securing yourself and climbing safely instead of thinking about falling.

Many people wonder what motivates others to do "bad" things that lead to negative outcomes for others. Most desires for bad things originated as desires for good things. People want beneficial outcomes, such as growth and safety, and so they want beneficial experiences, such as securing food, clothing, and shelter. What makes these desires lead to "bad" behaviors is when people believe that they can, should, or must commit harmful acts to achieve the desired outcome.

For example, people who steal not only want the stolen item but also believe that theft is the best or only way to obtain it. If they believed that a willful exchange was a better alternative and believed that they could secure the funds, their act would be to purchase the item. Their main desire is to possess the item, and their beliefs determine whether they desire to buy it or steal it to achieve that goal.

Ethics are a specific subset of beliefs that people use to judge a desire or action as good or bad. For example, a person may believe that harming others without provocation is wrong, but then they may also feel provoked and want to retaliate in self-defense. An observer may not believe that the harmful act is warranted, so he or she judges the behavior as immoral. This combination of desires, beliefs, and ethics determine whether someone's motivation for a beneficial outcome will lead to them being motivated to perform a harmful act to attain it.

If people believe that an act is harmful and that harming someone is wrong, they usually change their desire from a "bad" behavior to one that achieves the outcome without causing harm. If someone still desires to commit a harmful act, then, he usually is not aware of its harm, has convinced himself that it is not harmful, or believes that the other person is not worthy of his consideration. Through those beliefs, he transitions from desiring an outcome to wanting to perform the "bad" behavior to obtain it.

In almost all circumstances, "bad" desires come from faulty beliefs. A vandal may want to feel powerful, make his mark on the world, express his creativity, and prove his worthiness to his peers. Those desires are reasonable until combined with his belief that vandalism will achieve those goals and his ethics that justify the act in retaliation against oppression. A killer may believe that he is protecting himself from a threat and that it is a "kill or be killed" situation despite understanding that killing is wrong. These kinds of beliefs cause people to desire an action with negative consequences.

In those situations, people need to remember their true desired outcomes: growth, justice, or protection from harm. Any focus on a "bad" outcome is really a distraction from the desired "good" outcome that a person had before the slight, wrongdoing, or other factor triggered a desire for justice or retribution. If people are cut in line, they want to regain their position. If they are harmed, they want to recover. By focusing on those positive desired outcomes and constructive ways to attain them, people will minimize their desire for harmful actions.

Lastly, many people may question the merits of desire if they see addiction destroy someone's life. To them, addiction may seem like just a strong, uncontrollable desire. However, this powerful craving is not the healthy desire for growth that the human body normally has. Instead, a person is consuming chemicals or engaging in behaviors that temporarily boost certain neurotransmitter levels in the brain, causing him or her to feel pleasure. The subsequent absence of that neurotransmitter causes withdrawal and eventual dependency. Therefore, addiction is not a normal, natural desire but rather humans manipulating their brains' motivation and reward systems.

Healthy, natural desire is an instinct for life to sustain itself and thrive. All humans have an innate desire for growth in life, and it is up to each person to determine which experiences will accomplish that goal. Desire is the driving force for humans to live life with purpose, and it is the driving force for you to attain growth, meaning, and success.

To grow, find and build desire for relevant experiences

There are already things in life that you want. At the very least, a strong desire builds in you to eat, drink, and sleep every day. You most likely also have identified long-term growth areas that will require much experience, many resources, and a considerable amount of personal effort to attain.

Whether you continue to focus on those goals through adversity is significantly determined by your desire. As many people will ask about your intentions, "How much do you want it?" You can ask yourself what you are willing to do to get what you want. The time you are willing to put into a goal and obstacles you are willing to overcome to get there are indicative of your level of desire.

In addition to how much you want something, it is essential to understand why you want something. You may want something because it is socially acceptable, because others are doing it, because it is what other people tell you to want, or because you think you should want it. These external motivations will not sustain you through adversity because they will crumble under pressure. Find that internal motivation—the desire to do something because *you* want to improve your life, help others, achieve an outcome, or contribute to society—for the most sustainable drive toward your goal.

After identifying the motivation for growth, you can then evaluate the relevant experiences and determine which ones are of most interest. The intrinsic motivation you develop for these experiences will lead you to take action, and having the desire for both the outcome and the requisite experiences will maximize your determination. While a strong drive for the outcome can get you through the most unpleasant situations to reach your goal, it is easier to stay motivated when you also enjoy the experiences.

Given that you only have a set amount of time in a day, trade-offs often occur between competing desires. In those cases, prioritizing the most desired areas can help you progress more quickly. You may also switch between areas on different days or different weeks to make progress in multiple areas. However, neglecting one area too much will inhibit your long-term growth, so make sure that you identify how much you can sacrifice in other areas before it hurts your overall growth.

For example, you may work extra hours for many weeks because you want to complete a major project or make additional money to support your family. In the short term, anyone can make that decision with minimal impact on health, relationships, and well-being. Over an extended period of time, however, sleep deprivation, poor diet, infrequent exercise, minimal leisure time, and lack of social interaction will accumulate and inhibit your growth in all areas. While priority areas deserve more time, you should not make it the sole focus unless you are willing to make the appropriate sacrifices elsewhere.

In addition to prioritization, you can align your level of desire to how much you have to grow in that area. Some areas of growth only need to reach a certain point to satisfy that desire. For example, you eat enough food until you feel satiated, and then your desire diminishes so that you may focus on other areas of growth. Other outcomes require an almost obsessive desire and focus, such as being the world champion in a competitive game or sport. The drive that you have to sustain through the wins and losses, the failures and successes, and the injuries is immense. The best competitors in any area are select groups of people who are willing to do what is required to be as good as they are.

While you are analyzing your motivation, you have to check for deep-rooted issues that may negatively affect your behaviors and decisions in your life. Many dysfunctions occur when people find difficulty developing in one area of life and so overcompensate in others. If you have difficulties in one growth area, such as when developing social bonds, you may add focus to eating, exercise, or sex to an unhealthy point that is detrimental and destructive to your overall life goals.

For example, you may overwork to avoid difficulties in your relationship at home. You may overeat because you are being bullied in school. You may obsess over the news and current events as a result of being unemployed. In these cases, you may need to address that issue to adjust your desires and rebalance your priorities. Periodically checking your behaviors to make sure they match your priorities can make sure that you are moving in the right direction at the right pace.

Just as you must find, build, and maintain the desire for growth in life, you should continue to appreciate the growth you have made to date and the resources supporting your success. Appreciation prevents you from losing the desire for what that you already have and neglecting it. You can appreciate your friends, family, achievements, and possessions, or you can risk losing the support, lessons, and value you receive from them.

If you begin to take something in your life for granted, remember to show gratitude. Appreciate your car, and you will take better care of it. Appreciate your job, and you will work harder. Just as you will strive toward a goal if you desire it, you will maintain what you already have if you appreciate it. Desire and appreciation motivate you to put in the effort for continued success.

The proverb, "Life is a journey, not a destination," implies that you will find true meaning and happiness in the activities you perform to achieve long-term goals. Science supports this assertion. Research shows that any single event—no matter how large—affects overall happiness levels and life satisfaction for no more than a year before it returns to a baseline average.[32] Therefore, the idea that you only need to strive for a single desired outcome to be happy forever is flawed. You need to desire and appreciate everyday activities as well as major life objectives to raise your overall meaning and satisfaction with life.[33,34]

It is possible to be driven by the singular, unwavering focus on an outcome despite being miserable the entire time. However, it requires much less willpower to stay the course if you can find enjoyment in the journey. Build desire for the experiences and activities that help you achieve your objective. Show gratitude for what you do, who you are, and what you have that helps you get there. With strong desire and appreciation, you are more likely to succeed, and you will have a strong sense of meaning along the way.

Without desire, you feel unmotivated and lose your direction

The state of a human being with no desire or appreciation is depression. Individuals in this state may not even have the desire to get up in the morning. The typical cause of a depressed state for individuals with healthy brain function is that there is nothing to look forward to in their lives.

These people may have experienced a traumatic event or had their hopes for the future dashed. As a result, there is no desired outcome to strive for, and there is no motivation to grow, learn, improve, achieve, or develop. Desire motivates us to act; without intention, there is no action. Growth cannot occur. Life cannot move forward. It results in stagnation, depression, and listlessness.

Many people associate wanting with either greed or disappointment. They believe that if you want too much, you will take from others or take too much. Alternatively, if you "get your hopes up" and fail, you will be disappointed. Some philosophies even encourage you to suppress desire because wanting something you do not have leads to disappointment, pain, and suffering. While you can balance your desires to want well-being, happiness, and success for yourself and others, people cannot suppress all desires for anything more or new in life without also losing the will to live.

Everyone wants something, from basic needs like food and shelter to greater aspirations like a bright future for a son or daughter. It is not the wanting itself that causes problems; even philosophies that caution against strong desire still promote appreciation, which is just desire for what you already have. Instead, problems arise when desires conflict with beliefs and ethics. The goal, then, is to keep them in harmony.

For example, if you fall in love with someone who does not feel the same way, the cause of your pain is accentuated when you believe that you will be alone and miserable forever without the person. The appropriate response is not to lose your desire to find love. Instead, it is to believe that the heartbreak will help you find the right person for you. Alternatively, if you want money and believe that stealing is an appropriate option, the solution is neither to steal nor to suppress your desire for money. Instead, you should want to find ethical ways to earn it. Seeking love or money is not inherently bad, but you may need to redirect your desire toward better options through different beliefs.

If you try to suppress all of your desires, you are almost guaranteed to feel unfulfilled with your life. Instead, refocus your desire on finding a person who returns your affections or a way to earn money that benefits both parties in the transaction. These kinds of adjustments allow you to drive toward your outcomes without harming yourself or others.

While medical conditions or psychological disorders can cause unhealthy desires, most desires for negative outcomes occur in response to the loss of an appreciated asset or the inability to achieve a positive desired outcome. If a person's negligence causes harm to someone in your family, you may have the desire to retaliate. If someone without a mental disorder wants to commit suicide, the beliefs that life is too hard, the pain is unbearable, or there is no reason to live are likely involved. When otherwise ordinary people commit atrocities, it is very likely that they are struggling with their inability to get what they want in life and are trying to bring others down with them.

Fortunately, most people who do things for their own benefit at the expense of others would desire another approach if they were aware of the harm and could get the same benefit without it. Therefore, if you have a desire for a harmful outcome, you have the power to change it to a desire for a beneficial outcome.

Desire is a powerful force that you should properly develop, temper, and direct. Suppressing desire will demotivate you. To develop it, find an outcome, thing, or activity that brings you great anticipation and focus on why it triggers a strong drive within you. To temper it, focus the desire on goals that are tangible and achievable. To direct it, ensure that the desire is beneficial to yourself and others.

To track your progress, monitor how much you anticipate your desired outcomes. Not only does this emotion indicate how much desire you have for an outcome, but it also contributes to the amount of happiness and satisfaction you get from your experiences. A study conducted by George Loewenstein and published in *The Economic Journal* found that just the anticipation of positive future events had utility for the anticipator.[35] Use anticipation to confirm your interest and improve your life satisfaction.

If you feel unmotivated, you can jumpstart motivation with either temporary pleasures, such as food or sex, or long-term goals, such as graduating from business school. Temporary pleasures can quickly change your mood to get you back on track, but you should not to confuse it with a long-term solution. If you do, you are at risk of self-destructive behavior.

Imagine eating ice cream or drinking alcohol when you have a terrible day. As a one-time mechanism, it can be a temporary stress relief to help to keep you on track. As a repeated habit, it sends you off track and inhibits your growth. The growth-enabling enjoyment is what you are looking for, so you should only use these pleasures for temporary relief and rejuvenation.

The long-term solution is to start with areas of your life that you can improve, identify opportunities to have those experiences, and build your intrinsic motivation to have them. There is nothing else that can give you a stronger will to live. Successful people do not point to sex, drugs, fried food, or gambling as key to having meaning and success in life. They find their true purpose in high-effort endeavors such as family, financial success, scientific discoveries, record-breaking achievements, personal growth, or spiritual enlightenment.

In addition to fueling the desire for what you wish to attain, you have to strengthen your appreciation for what you have in life. Without an appreciation for your relationship, you may no longer treat your partner with love and respect. Without an appreciation for your health, you may make poor food choices and live a sedentary lifestyle. Just as you will work hard toward a goal if you desire it, you will spend the time maintaining what you already have if you appreciate it. Strive to have what you want and want what you have.

Ungrateful behaviors have consequences. Your friendships will weaken without at least an occasional phone call or conversation. Your health will decline without proper nutrition and physical activity. Your drive and passion for a career can quickly diminish if you forget to appreciate all that you have achieved to this point. Appreciation is just as important as desire in keeping you motivated so that you continue to put in the necessary effort.

If you have tried to keep motivated and yet still cannot find the desire and passion for something, it could be that you no longer want it. There is nothing wrong with losing interest, as you can and will always desire something else. The point of life is not to pick something and stick with it no matter how miserable you become. It is not to keep going because others think that it is best for you or because it is socially acceptable. It is to find things you want and to make progress toward those outcomes. When you achieve those outcomes, you can seek new growth areas.

You may learn through the course of pursuing one growth area that another area is what really matters to you. You could find through your efforts that you do not want what you thought you wanted or that you want something else. Your desired outcome can change over time. Life is continuously changing, so your desires will change as well.

Before you change direction, though, make sure that it is your desire that has changed and that it is not because the journey is too difficult or you are being discouraged by others. The result of giving up on something you really wanted is usually feeling regret. You should neither abandon a strong desire before you try to overcome the adversity nor give up on something before you can confidently tell whether it piques your interest.

No matter the situation, you have two options when you have lost your desire for the outcome or the growth area: rediscover your passion or find a new one. Losing desire because of your beliefs or circumstances likely requires you to see if you can adjust them and stay motivated. Losing desire because you have changed likely requires you to shift your focus. In either case, you need to reignite your motivation. Both options can get you back on track toward growth.

If your desire is unclear, then you desire to have a clear desire

While rekindling desire can be difficult, you might consider your biggest challenge to be figuring out what you want. Usually, you have this problem if you do not have enough information about you could want or you have to choose between multiple options that each have pros and cons. In either case, do not fret because you already have identified a desire: **you want to know what you want!** This desire can motivate you to investigate possible experiences and decide which ones you wish to pursue.

Before you assume that you are indecisive, though, check to see that you are not just ignoring or dismissing what you want because you have been discouraged from wanting it. This problem is not one of figuring out what you want. Rather, the problem is figuring out what to do when you believe that you should not want or cannot have something you desire. In that case, you are better served by shifting your beliefs, adjusting the desired outcome to be more believable, or finding alternative means to making progress.

For example, you may want money but believe that people have to exploit others to become wealthy. You then convince yourself that you do not want money but feel miserable that you cannot acquire the goods you wish to own. Instead of pretending that you do not desire money, you can change your beliefs about how you can make money, identify an actionable monetary goal, and find ethical ways to make money. In this case, you knew your desire but kept it suppressed because of your beliefs.

In another example, you may want to play a sport but have a physical or psychological limitation. Rather than looking into a less desirable field, you could rethink how you can be involved in the game, organize a group with the same limitation, or think of a way to work past your constraints. If you already know what you want most in life, it is much easier to find a different way to pursue that path than to deny it and look for something else that ignites a similar passion inside of you.

Assuming that you genuinely do not know what you want, you can use many methods to understand your desires. One approach is to note when you enjoy an experience or like something so that you may come back to your list later and look for patterns. Consciously assert that you want to know what you want, and your brain will be more likely to notice your likes and dislikes. As a result, you will more effective at identifying desirable experiences in the future.

This method is known as priming, an effect where the exposure to one stimulus influences your response to future stimuli. A common example of priming is when you purchase a car and begin to notice the same model more frequently while driving. Because the model is fresh in your mind from the purchase, it is more noticeable when you see it on the road. By bringing your likes and dislikes to your attention, you will begin to notice other things in life that you may want to have or experience.

A similar method is the "you might also like" approach used by online retailers to maximize their sales. These businesses identify products that people frequently purchase before/while/after purchasing other items. They then place ones that you might also like next to the product you were originally seeking. As a result, you are more likely to spend more money. Use this method to see if you can identify related causes, occupations, places, events, products, or people associated with your areas of interest that you might also desire.

Once you have surfaced new interests, you may want to gauge your desire for one or multiple options. With one option, you can visualize having obtained the item or attained the goal and use your reaction to assess how much you want it. With multiple (un)desirable options, you can use the "assume you've already picked" method. Pretend to make a choice and see how you feel about the decision. Your emotional reaction may give you insight into your preference.

In either example, uncertainty and hesitation signals that you need more information, research, or experience before making a firm commitment. Instead of using the indecision as an excuse to procrastinate, identify what you need to make a more confident decision and what you can do to get it.

If you are still having trouble identifying what you want, start with what you do not want. Anyone who has tried to help another person decide knows that *everyone* seems to know what they do not want. Knowing what you do not want is a great asset. If you understand what you do not want, then what you do want will contrast with that dislike for the unwanted thing.

For example, if you do not want to get sick, you want to be healthy. If you do not want a job where you sit in a cubicle for eight continuous hours, you do want a career where you set your own hours and get to travel or work outside. You can use what you do not want to eliminate options and get closer to figuring out what you do want.

Many people of differing philosophies debate the merits of thinking about the undesired outcome. Some advocate for thinking as many positive thoughts as possible, while others say that negative thoughts help you avoid problems. They are both right. While *focusing* on what you do not want is unproductive in the long-term, *identifying* what you do not want is the easiest way to begin to uncover what you do want if you are uncertain. Undesired outcomes are often more obvious, so use them to find your desired outcomes more quickly.

Your aversion to the undesired outcome is also an effective means to build desire for the desired outcome and its requisite experiences. People who have or witness heart attacks become motivated to eat healthy foods and exercise. People who are failing a class, losing the love of their spouse, falling behind in a game, or underperforming in their job redouble their efforts. The fear of the undesired outcome can motivate people to do whatever they can to avoid it.

If you use the undesired outcome for motivation, though, remember to follow the "don't look down" principle: focus on the goal in front of you to avoid the fear and decreased performance that occurs from focusing on the undesired outcome. If you look down for too long, you are actually more likely to fall.

When trying to figure out what you want, be wary of others' influence. You will often need help to find what you want, and others are often willing to provide that help. However, they may want to help you for your benefit, for theirs, or both. As a result, they will make their case for what you should do and why their recommendation—an experience, product, or way of life—is right for you. Persuasion is the act of getting a person to want to do something, so people with an agenda, product, or worldview to sell will use many different approaches to convince you that whatever they are selling is what you want or what you need.

If you are looking to understand what you should want and why you should want it, then you hope that people provide you with this information. However, you probably also seek financial security, freedom, truth, fairness, and safety. The people trying to persuade you may be doing so for validation, income, or control. You have to determine for yourself whether their desire conflicts with your desires because they will have different priorities— even if they have your best interest in mind.

If you are feeling extra pressure to decide what you want, remember that you can always take time to consider competing wants and needs. Protect yourself by giving yourself time to think in a pressure-free environment before acting on your desire. This way, others' attempt to recruit you or sell you a product does not overwhelm your own sense of what you want.

Given all of these internal and external considerations, you may tend to procrastinate out of fear of an undesired outcome. If you know what you want but cannot decide between a couple of options, then you have to build the desire to make a decision. When the urge to move forward outweighs the fear of being wrong, you will act. If you are wrong, remember that a mistake will trigger a new desire, and you will adjust over time toward the new desired outcome. Your intentions evolve as you grow.

Desire is a powerful tool that drives you to have the experiences you need to grow. It also enables you to appreciate what you have so that you maintain it. Practically, it is the difference between taking deliberate action and wandering around aimlessly.

Growth requires motivation, and your next step after identifying your growth areas and experiences is to find the motivation to pursue those goals. When you find the desire—the intent, the drive, the hunger—in your life, you will have a purpose.

QUESTIONS

Questions That Help You Find Your Motivation and Drive

Your answers to these questions will help you understand what you want in life: the types of growth you want and the experiences you want. They also help you to understand your intrinsic motivation and help you think through your options when you do not know what you want. Your answers to the questions in the Growth and Experience chapters will be useful for this section. This chapter's content provides guidance on how to think about these questions, but only you can supply the definitive answers for your life.

1. What do you want out of life? What do you want to do, have, or be in your lifetime?

2. Does what you want align with what you have already identified as growth areas and experiences in the previous chapters?

3. Which of your desired outcomes do you want the most?
    *   How much hunger, passion, desire, or motivation do you feel when you think about those things?
    *   Does any area get more desirable as you think about doing, being, or having those things?

4. Why do you want what you want? Is there a common theme connecting the things that you want?

5. Does knowing why you want something change what you

want?

6. Are other people trying to discourage you from pursuing the things that you want? Should you listen to them?

   Example: If people tell you that dancing is silly, you can ignore them or free yourself from their influence to continue without detractors.

7. Are there things that other people say you should want or have to do that you do not want to do?

   - Do you have to comply? Why?
   - Can you make your mandatory activities more desirable?

     Examples: If you have to do chores, you can listen to music to enhance the experience. If you have to exercise, you can remind yourself of the "endorphin high" your body provides after physical activity. You can find pleasure in helping others, developing skills, and making money while working an after-school job.

8. How can you strengthen your current desire for what is important to you in life? What will keep you moving toward your desired growth opportunities or life experiences?

9. What do you appreciate in life? Why?

10. What can you do to increase your appreciation and maintain your passion and joy for that person, thing, or activity?

11. Are you uncertain in your desire for a particular life path?

    - What can you do to gain the information you need to be sure about whether you want to pursue it or not?
    - Are there alternatives to that path that are more desirable?

EXERCISES

Activities That Help You Find Your Motivation and Drive

Completing these exercises will result in a stronger drive to pursue your life goals.

Thought Exercise: To find your current motivations, take a mental inventory of what you appreciate doing/being/having now, look forward to being/doing/having in the future, and what drives you personally to get up each day and to get through tough times. Then, ask yourself why you have these motivations.

Next, think about your growth areas and experiences from the previous two chapters. Consider what drove you to choose those items. Identify what about those areas makes you want to pursue them.

The goal of this exercise is to understand your motivations so that you may leverage them when you get discouraged to help you stay on your life path.

Brainstorming Exercise: If you are not sure of what you want, then you want to know what you want. Research things you can do, be, or have and create a list of experiences, achievements, or possessions that might interest you. Then, next to each item on the list, think of three reasons why you think you want it.

The goal is to uncover motivations that will help you understand what you want, how much you want it, and whether there is something deeper or broader that you want by looking for commonalities across your list.

Example: If you want to buy new clothes, join a club, and to win a dance competition, then you may have underlying interests in fashion, relationships, and physical fitness. With this understanding of your desires, you can look for a club that focuses on these areas.

Creative Exercise: Make a collage of what you want out of life.

Start by creating two columns on a large sheet of construction paper. Label one column "Appreciation" and the other "Desire" at the top. The Appreciation side is focused on what you have that you (still) want, like, and appreciate. The Desire side is focused on the things you do not have (yet) that you want.

Next, take catalogs, magazines, internet photos, and other visual representations of things you appreciate or want and create your collage. If the things you want are intangible, find pictures to symbolize them (e.g., a photo of a family gathering if you want more time with family).

The goal is to have a vision of your desired future state. Getting your mind focused on what you want is the easiest step toward building desire for it. This activity also primes your brain to notice when you can make decisions or take actions that will get you closer to what you want in life. It also ensures that you never take the things you have for granted.

When your life gets difficult, the output of this exercise provides a motivational reminder of what you are striving for in life. If your life ends up resembling the Desire side of the collage, you can move everything under the Appreciation column and add new experiences and things to the Desire column.

Note: You may wish to leave space on, next to, and below your collage for future chapters' creative exercises.

Writing Exercise: Take your list of growth areas and your list of possible experiences from the previous chapters' writing exercises. Rate your desire to have those experiences on a scale of 1 to 10 (10 being the highest).

Next, list the desired outcomes for each growth area and describe what makes the experiences and their outcomes desirable. You may also note past experiences or current assets that you appreciate having that will help you attain your future desires. Then, rate your level of desire again and see if your scores change or you identify more preferable experiences.

This exercise will help you clarify your desired outcomes and build your desire for them.

Example:

Experiences	Desire	Desired Outcomes	Reasoning	Appreciation
Personal training	8 9	Attractive physique to attract a mate	Looking good feels great	I played sports in high school
Attend club social events	5 6	Make close friends while having fun	I love relating to people	I had friends before I moved

Note: The above example does not show all of the information you will bring from the previous writing exercises; it is possible that this chapter's teachings may cause you to refine that information.

OUTCOME

After reading this chapter, you should have a clear understanding of how your desires motivate you to have experiences that allow you to grow toward a future state. Your identified growth areas and experiences should now have scores for how much you want them as well as information that will help you build and sustain your desire and appreciation for them. You may have added items to the list or reprioritized them if your desire (or lack thereof) has guided you toward or away from certain areas.

When you have your updated list, you are ready to proceed to the next chapter.

Belief

Beliefs shape your perception and sustain your desires

"Whether you believe you can do a thing or not, you are right."

— Henry Ford[36]

"The mind is the limit. As long as the mind can envision the fact that you can do something, you can do it, as long as you really believe 100 percent."

— Arnold Schwarzenegger[37]

"Believe that life is worth living and your belief will help create the fact."

— William James[38]

PRINCIPLES OF BELIEF

- Belief is life's sustaining force to grow through adversity
- Belief allows humans to overcome fear, doubt, and setbacks
- To sustain growth, align your beliefs with your desires
- Without belief, you will abandon your efforts
- If an outcome is unbelievable, start with a believable step

BELIEF AND THE MEANING OF LIFE

Perception is reality. A belief is an idea or thing that you accept as true or existing. A subset of belief is knowledge, which in this context is an idea that you accept as true because you have verifiable proof. The remainder of your beliefs, then, are based on partial or no evidence. To form a belief, you take what you know to be true from past experience and fill in the knowledge gaps with assumptions and conjectures about what is likely to be true.

Beliefs are necessary because you must make decisions and take actions in life with incomplete information. Over time, both knowledge and belief shape how you take in and process new information. Collectively, they determine how you perceive the world and interpret life experiences.

Because beliefs alter your perception of reality, they shape what you determine your purpose to be. You can have an experience that triggers a desire or intent, but your beliefs about whether that desire is good/bad, right/wrong, possible/impossible, safe/dangerous, or praiseworthy/shameful influence whether you decide to pursue that course of action.

Therefore, belief's relationship to purpose is that of confirming and sustaining that purpose (or denying it and terminating it). Your desires light a fire inside you, and belief can either fan the flames or extinguish them. Your life's meaning is what you want it to be if you believe it is; it is not what you want it to be if you do not believe it is.

Belief is life's sustaining force to grow through adversity

Living things must have beliefs because not everything is knowable. Because of how time and the universe work, life cannot perceive anything that its senses are not observing at its current point on the space-time continuum. For life to know that something exists, it must be observable (i.e., physical) at the time in which it is being observed (i.e., in the present moment). While things can exist in reality regardless of whether someone is observing them or not, you cannot be absolutely certain that anything exists unless it is physical and presently observable.

Your assumption that something is true outside of those exact conditions is a belief. You believe that the sun will rise in the east tomorrow because you understand the physics behind the solar system and because it has every other day in your existence. You believe in ancient civilizations because the remains of their architecture, artifacts, and documents still exist today. You believe that the door in your house is locked because you remember locking it.

None of those beliefs have to be true. An asteroid could hit the Earth and knock it out of its orbit before the next sunrise. Documents studied by historians could have been forged or could contain inaccuracies, bringing a false understanding of past societies. Someone may have unlocked the door that you locked earlier in the day. The information you have, though, caused you to conclude—to believe—that these things did/do/will exist.

The world changes, so a belief or assumption that was true yesterday may not hold today. For example, a belief that Pluto was a planet was accurate until astronomers found other bodies in space and reassessed their definition of a planet. Scientists believed that diamond was the hardest material on Earth until they discovered wurtzite boron nitride and lonsdaleite. You may hold accurate beliefs that become erroneous when conditions change, and then you might learn about these changes and update them.

Because no one can know everything at all times, living things are able to decide and act as if something is true without having direct observation of it being true. If this were not possible, life would not be able to avoid harm in the world without having to observe or experience it directly. You believe that jumping in front of a fast-moving vehicle would hurt, so you behave in a way to avoid that experience based on that belief. You could test that belief, but it is safer to act as if it is true without having to try it first. In this regard, beliefs are critical to life's survival.

The earliest forms of belief appear in the physical response of organisms to stimuli in their environment. Early responses included cells moving away from harmful stimuli such as intense heat and moving toward beneficial stimuli such as food. Eventually, organisms began to respond to stimuli in ways that equipped them to be more effective at dealing with them in the future. An example of this adaptation at the cellular level is when human skin cells produce additional melanin in response to ultraviolet light. Not only do the skin cells repair the damage from the sun's ultraviolet rays, but they also prepare themselves for future sun exposure.

These automatic responses get more complex in more complex systems. An animal grows or shrinks its muscles based on physical exertion and nutrient intake. An animal's heart rate increases when a predator attacks. While these actions at the cellular level may be automatic responses due to natural selection, they occur because the cell or organism has certain expectations for the future based on their recent experience. For example, the body increases or decreases its muscle mass because it expects that it will need more or less to survive given the physical requirements and nutrients available. The animal expects that it will need to exert physical effort to respond to a threat, so the body immediately prepares for action.

Advanced life forms such as animals and humans have a greater degree of control over their responses to stimuli and have to choose how to act in response to complicated, ambiguous situations. In these cases, they use their beliefs, assumptions, and expectations to fill in their knowledge gaps and make the best decision possible. For example, predators hunt for prey in certain locations at certain times of day because they expect them to be there. Like automatic responses, these organisms' unconscious and conscious beliefs significantly affect their survivability.

Because there is so much that an organism can possibly know and so little that it actually knows, beliefs form the majority of its interpretation of reality. That interpretation includes what a person, thing, or event means to them, so belief is the mechanism through which a person assigns meaning. In essence, your life has importance and significance because you believe that it does.

While all life exists to grow, the full meaning of your life is highly subjective. Life could be a great journey to find happiness or just a bunch of creatures fighting over resources so they can reproduce. The objective facts are the same, but the perception of those facts' meaning is open to interpretation.

As a result, key parts of life are up to belief, not knowledge, to determine. Your unique purpose in life is a belief. Greater meaning cannot objectively exist; it requires a person to believe in it subjectively. The existence of an ethereal entity is also a belief because science—the study of the physical world—cannot prove something that humans cannot observe in their physical reality.

Despite the fact that your meaning in life is subjectively defined, the system through which you derive that meaning can be objectively defined. Life's central purpose is to grow, it grows through experience, and it is motivated by desire to interact with the physical world to carry out its purpose. Belief allows life to combine its knowledge and assumptions to determine how it should pursue its desires most effectively.

For example, if an organism believes that changing its location will lead to death and that hiding in its current position will reduce its chances of being harmed, it will do the latter to realize its innate desire of staying alive. It has no way of absolutely knowing which action will result in the desired outcome, so it can only act based on what it believes is best for itself.

Beliefs can have a wide range of impact. Their impact ranges from altering a specific behavior to significantly influencing how life perceives and understands its reality. Because beliefs are an imperfect substitute for knowledge, that perception of reality is not always accurate. In any given situation, there are four possible relationships between an organism's belief and its reality:

- A living thing believes something that is true.

- It does not believe something that is not true.
- It believes something that is not true.
- It does not believe something that is true.

The closer that an organism's beliefs are to reality, the more likely it is to make the right decisions to continue to survive.

Holding false beliefs in an environment full of danger can be deadly. An organism can believe that something is beneficial when it is harmful, or it can believe that something is harmful when it is beneficial. Because being wrong about how harmful a threat is can kill them, life forms tend to be risk-averse. Prioritizing loss aversion over reward seeking keeps them alive.

However, there will always be risks. The organisms that take risks, survive, and gain the reward will have the best outcome. Also, organisms that live in perpetual fear and take no action will suffer the same fate as the ones that take the risk and fail. Life has basic needs that it must obtain to survive, so it must be willing to take some risks to grow.

What results is a delicate balance of being risk-averse enough to avoid unnecessary harm but risk-tolerant enough to pursue valuable rewards. Because growth requires obtaining the necessary resources, organisms must believe that they can obtain them and that they will grow as a result. This growth bias leads to the assumption that the future will be better than the present. Since growth is life's purpose, there would be no motivation to continue living otherwise.

Psychologists refer to this default assumption of a better future as the optimism bias. The optimism bias is the tendency for humans to overestimate the likelihood of a positive outcome and underestimate the likelihood of a negative outcome.

Tali Sharot analyzed this effect in her book, *The Optimism Bias*. She explains that people are less likely to perform the activities that will protect them from negative outcomes because of this bias. For example, if people believe that they are healthy, they may not go to the doctor regularly and get cancer screenings.

Avoiding the screenings increases the risk of a late diagnosis.[39]

Despite the clear risks, Dr. Sharot emphasizes the many benefits of believing in better future outcomes:

- Anticipation makes you happier
- Belief in a positive outcome makes you work harder toward the goal
- Optimists are more likely to recover from challenging circumstances due to their ability to find meaning and takeaways from the experience

While she recommends that humans take more preventative measures despite being optimistic, having the instinct to believe in a better future is critical for humans to pursue growth.[40]

This research validates the role of belief in the meaning of life. Belief sustains an organism's pursuit of future outcomes, making it the difference between perseverance and surrender. Humans experience substantial inner conflict reconciling realistic beliefs that aim to minimize harm with optimistic beliefs that aim to maximize growth.

The future is unknowable, so beliefs are organisms' best guesses as to what it could be. To live with purpose, people have to believe that the future will be better than the present and that what they do now can influence the outcome. People who do not believe that they have control over their destiny are susceptible to resignation, depression, and even suicide. If they did not believe in their ability to attain their goals, they would cease to grow toward those desired outcomes.

Spaceflight, the four-minute mile, circumnavigation, and the microscope did not exist until someone had a desire for space travel, a world record, a single round-the-world trip, or a way to view microorganisms. To attempt to achieve those goals, that person also had to believe that they were possible. Growth requires belief because the desired outcome has not happened yet—and no one can be sure that it will happen.

Therefore, belief sustains the drive brought on by desire. Everyone wants to be, do, and have more. The only reason people bother to strive for more, though, is because they believe that they can be, do, or have it.

Despite this fact, many people restrict themselves to only believing in things that have already happened. This "I'll believe it when I see it" approach tempers their inherent optimism with critical thinking and skepticism, which protects them from dangerous false beliefs. However, it also limits their potential. Before a new feat is achieved, many people will say that it is impossible. Afterward, many people will say that it was inevitable. It only happened, however, because someone believed enough to try.

A famous example is Roger Bannister running a sub-four-minute mile, an event that has elevated the power of belief to mythical levels. The myth claims that everyone thought that it was impossible for humans to run a mile in under four minutes until he did with relatively little training by modern standards. It then claims that it was broken many times in succession because people suddenly believed. The myth exaggerates the power of belief to a supernatural level. *Not* everyone thought that it was impossible, and it was *not* broken multiple times in succession by other athletes shortly afterward.[41]

The truth, however, still suffices in showing the power of belief: no one who thought that breaking the four-minute mile record was impossible was training to break it. The people who believed that it was possible and wanted to break it—including but not limited to Roger Bannister—pursued the goal with the effort required to achieve their desired outcome. While there are other factors such as genetics that make this feat possible, the lack of belief will make it impossible.

Society celebrates broken barriers because of how difficult and unbelievable the achievement is to the average person given their current reality. The world revered the first people to land on the moon because it was such a physically improbable feat. Similarly, the first person of a certain age, race, gender, nationality, or creed to win an award, hold an elected office, or to join a professional sports team receives recognition as someone who overcame great adversity so that others could have a chance in the future.

However, the laws of physics do not render these outcomes physically impossible. They are just incredibly difficult due to limitations in technology, biology, or human rights, so most people do not believe that they are possible until they happen. That difficulty causes people to give up or not even try, which prevents them from ever achieving the goal. The end result, then, is the same as if it were actually impossible.

Belief does not by itself make everything magically happen, but you will not accomplish much without it. Belief can just as easily hold you back as it can sustain your drive. Letting others discourage you can bring down your belief in yourself and therefore stop you from growing in a certain area. Even people with an intense desire will not try if they believe that their peers will make fun of them or that their best effort will not be good enough.

Beliefs are more difficult to manage than desires because so many of them are unconscious, implicit, and assumed. Desires generate noticeable attraction toward desired outcomes and repulsion from undesired outcomes. Beliefs, however, are often underlying a person's decisions, actions, speech, and motivations.

For example, a person might say, "I want to lose weight and know that I should be able to if I eat well and exercise, but I just don't seem to do anything about it. The reality is that I can't lose weight. Why kid myself?" The "I can't lose weight" part is not reality—it is a belief. It is one of many unconscious beliefs and assumptions that are preventing the person from taking action.

For example, this individual might believe that exercise is painful or tedious. He might believe that he does not have the time to exercise. He might not want to go to a gym because he believes that people will judge him. He might believe that healthy food is expensive. He might believe that he will abandon his diet as soon as his life gets stressful. These are all beliefs that he may not realize are demotivating him and preventing him from accomplishing his goal.

If that person believes that losing weight is a gargantuan effort that is incredibly unpleasant, then that person may *say* that he wants to lose weight, but he surely does *not* want to experience the process of losing weight. The beliefs squelch the desire for the experience. Few people could overcome those beliefs with sheer willpower.

Meanwhile, the many small changes that he could make to achieve that outcome are now discounted. He could use the stairs instead of the elevator. He could park farther away from stores and walk. He could drink water instead of sugary beverages with his meals.

None of these actions require significant time, effort, cost, or sacrifice but could add up to noticeable weight loss. For one floor trips, elevators can take longer than the stairs. With a crowded parking lot, walking an extra fifty feet can save several minutes driving around to find a closer spot. Switching drinks can save hundreds of calories per meal (this equates to about 15 pounds per year for each daily 150-calorie drink avoided) without changing what he eats at all. Because he believes that weight loss is difficult, though, he will probably miss those options for immediate improvement.

Another example of how belief can inhibit growth is a person saying, "I want $1,000,000. I want it more than anything in the world. Why don't I magically get it?" It is likely that someone would use this as an example because he or she thinks that it is unbelievable. As a consequence, it is not going to spur that person to action to grow financially toward that goal.

People who genuinely believe they can attain financial wealth will create business plans and identify opportunities to earn more income. People who do not will play the lottery, implicitly showing that they believe the odds of winning (which can be 1 in 292.2 million[42]) is higher than their likelihood of being able to invest that dollar in themselves to earn that money. If they only believed in their financial potential enough, they could learn that putting the equivalent of three $2 lottery tickets in a retirement account per day (over a 40-year period at 10% interest) could lead to a million dollars. If they just believed, they might increase their chances from practically impossible to mathematically probable.

Instead, people with an intense desire for improved financial growth but a lack of belief in their current prospects are susceptible to false promises from sources such as gambling, salespeople, con artists, cults, and get-rich-quick schemes. They want money but do not see how to gain it doing something that they find meaningful. Con artists will exploit their victims' need to believe in a better future for themselves by promising incredible success with no risk and minimal effort. It is no coincidence that most victims of these predators have low self-confidence and are dissatisfied with their current situation. These people want to believe in something because they do not currently believe in themselves.

People who can honestly say that they want something but then do nothing to start their journey have a problem with their beliefs. As a result, they may look for a quick fix or give up before they start because they believe that the best solution is too hard or out of reach. Destructive beliefs inhibit even the strongest desires.

Desire and belief do not magically make everything happen instantly. However, they are the two forces driving people toward desired outcomes. Without them, growth ceases.

Belief is anything that an organism accepts as true. Life forms have to fill in knowledge gaps with assumptions that guide them toward the best decisions and actions. In practice, belief can enable people to continue through adversity or prevent them from pursuing their dreams. The most useful beliefs balance realism and optimism to sustain desire and help people succeed in life.

Belief allows humans to overcome fear, doubt, and setbacks

Beliefs squelch desire and prevent growth when they conflict with a person's goals. However, beliefs that are in alignment with a person's desired outcome can help him or her overcome almost any obstacle.

Carol Dweck discusses in her book, *Mindset*, the scientific evidence for the relationship between belief and growth. Dr. Dweck has conducted thorough research on people who have what she calls the "Fixed Mindset" and the "Growth Mindset" to see if their beliefs had an impact on their lives. The Fixed Mindset is the belief that intelligence, athleticism, and other abilities are innate, while the Growth Mindset is the belief that people can grow and improve.[43]

Her findings show time and again that the Growth Mindset makes people:

- more effective in handling life's challenges
- more likely to continue to try something instead of giving upmore likely to succeed and continue to improve
- less likely to stagnate and retreat at the first sign that they do not immediately succeed

The belief that it is possible to grow and improve over time is one of the most significant factors in determining whether humans succeed in life—more than a multitude of other variables tested.[44]

Countless inspirational stories from successful people tout the power of hope. Hope is the belief in an improved future state despite the current circumstances. It helps individuals survive wars, jail, famine, and other terrible situations where despair can result in failure or death. People who want something strongly enough and believe that they can get it are very powerful; they will not stop until they succeed.

Often, motivational speakers will contrast the power of hope with the debilitating nature of worry, which is a belief in a negative outcome given current circumstances. Worry provides obsessive focus that can protect people when they face real threats that they can influence or control. However, excessive worry—especially when factors are uncontrollable—can prevent them from living their lives and keep them in a constant state of protection instead of growth. A person who is overcome with worry cannot strive toward their goals because they are so focused on the undesired outcomes (e.g., pain, failure, loss) that they abandon the effort for the desired outcome altogether. In this state, the probability of achieving an aspirational goal is low.

The biggest hurdle to overcome in life is the current situation, which is the most cited reason for low expectations. Realists pride themselves on how aligned their expectations and beliefs are with reality. However, aligning belief with reality can be difficult and restrictive. Pure realists would limit themselves to accomplishments that had already been proven by others, meaning they could not invent anything new. While they protect themselves from harm and disappointment, they are more likely to refrain from pursuing ambitious goals because of the risk, sacrifice, and effort involved. What is possible is not as restricted by the current situation as people think, yet the current reality will dictate the majority of their beliefs and hinder their progress in life.

Ironically, beliefs about the current reality are often more important than the actual situation. Self-fulfilling prophecy, for example, is a psychological effect where a person's belief regarding the outcome makes the outcome more likely to occur.[45] In research on the effect, teachers who believed that certain students in their class had great intellectual potential will treat them differently, leading to greater development.[46] The reality could have been that every student had similar potential, but teachers' beliefs led to behaviors and results that validated them.

In this example, the students' beliefs affect their performance as well. If the teacher treats the students as if they can learn the material, the children may have more confidence and begin to behave in ways that match those expectations. They start to study harder and receive better grades. These students may have underperformed in the past, but their updated beliefs that they could learn changed reality by changing their behaviors.

Collectively, the teachers' beliefs affected their own effort, the students' beliefs affected their own effort, and the teachers' beliefs influenced the students' beliefs. Both sets of beliefs affected the students' potential, leading some to succeed through greater effort and others to fail through resignation.

There are many scientific examples of how beliefs influence reality. Scientists conduct double-blind studies (where neither the administrators nor the subjects know critical details of the experiment) because the expectations of either party can influence the results. Psychology, biology, and pharmaceutical studies also have to factor in the placebo effect, a phenomenon where study participants will see beneficial results by simply believing that they will improve. These beliefs have measurable, tangible effects. In their attempts to eliminate belief from scientific testing, scientists have demonstrated its role in attaining a desired outcome.

One of the most interesting, controversial scientific examples is the observer effect, which suggests that the mere act of observing an experiment affects its results. The double-slit experiment, a study of wave-particle duality, demonstrates this effect in quantum mechanics. In the experiment, an observer can influence how light behaves—either as a wave or a particle—merely based on the act of observing it.[47] The effect is so pronounced that quantum physicists have theorized that the idea of an "observer-independent state" may need to be replaced with a model that factors in the relationship between physical systems.[48]

The observer effect occurs when the measuring device is a machine, so it is not direct evidence of the power of belief. However, the observer effect, priming, and the placebo effect are all examples of how perception can have a tangible impact on reality. If merely observing reality influences it, consistent belief can have significant consequences for everyone involved.

People who believe can accomplish extraordinary feats. Humans can now fly, talk to people on the other side of the world in real time, live in space, and access the cumulative knowledge of humanity from a hand-held device. These achievements were deemed impossible until relatively recently. However, none of those things were possible until someone wanted them and believed in them strongly enough. The desire inspires action, and the belief enables them to continue to make progress through a multitude of setbacks until they succeed.

While people are much more likely to persevere with optimistic beliefs about the future, they can make more effective decisions toward that outcome with accurate beliefs about the current situation. The difficulty is in figuring out how beliefs differ from reality and whether that difference is beneficial, neutral, or harmful. Beliefs are intended to be beneficial; that is why people hold them. However, the same ones meant to be protective can be limiting, and the same ones meant to be helpful can be harmful.

While it may seem strange that false beliefs can be beneficial, they have contributed to the survival of the human race. For instance, if early humans who were seeking shelter associated a specific cave with a bear, the belief that they should avoid it protects them from harm. In this case, they are safer if they assume that the cave is occupied and stay away from it than if they assume that it is empty and then potentially die walking into it. Once the group sees evidence that the bear is gone and is not returning, it can update its outdated belief to align with reality.

Beliefs can also be neutral. Superstitions, such as believing that photographs steal your soul or that a black cat crossing your path is bad luck, have no scientific validity but are beliefs in some cultures. There is no harm in not having your photograph taken, nor is there harm in avoiding black cats. People can give up these superstitions because they are inaccurate and can lead to strange behavior, but they affect neither growth nor survivability.

Lastly, many inaccurate beliefs limit growth or cause harm. Ones that lead to harmful behaviors, such believing that guns are toys or that people can survive a ten-story fall, clearly add unnecessary risk. However, the ones that limit growth are less obvious because they are usually done in the name of protection.

For example, people may believe that they will never be able to play the piano, so they should not even bother trying despite being interested in the activity. They may believe that they have to be a doctor/lawyer/construction worker because that is what one of their parents did. They may believe that they cannot have something because other people will judge them. If they want to get out of their own way, they have to change those beliefs.

Despite everyone's best efforts, inaccurate beliefs are inevitable. One person cannot know everything, and the future is unknowable. To add to the difficulty, facts are continuously changing, and beliefs may be correct or incorrect depending on the situation. As a result, reconciling beliefs and reality is a constant, strenuous mental exercise.

Because being wrong is unavoidable, the goal should be to maximize knowledge (i.e., reducing both inaccuracies and the need for beliefs) while minimizing the potential harm of false beliefs. To achieve that goal, people need to understand how knowledge is acquired, where beliefs go wrong, and how to minimize the impact of being wrong.

Knowledge is acquired through an experiential process that starts and ends with beliefs. The scientific method, which is an effective approach to knowledge acquisition, begins with a question about how the world works and a hypothesis about why. It ends with a conclusion based on the results. Hypotheses and conclusions are beliefs supported by observation, and they become knowledge when repeated experiments fail to falsify them.

Inaccurate beliefs come from a misunderstanding of science or incorrect conclusions from their observations. Many people, for example, explain things they do not understand by invoking supernatural forces. As Sir Arthur Clarke once said, "Any sufficiently advanced technology is indistinguishable from magic."[49] In other examples, human brains are genetically predisposed to look for patterns and may erroneously assume causal relationships between coincidental events. Correlation, however, does not necessarily mean causation.

Lastly, any belief inherently has a probability of being wrong and an impact that it has if it is wrong. If a person believes that he or she cannot become physically fit, the probability and cost of being wrong are high (i.e., probability: likely; cost of not trying: poor health), and the probability and cost of being right are low (i.e., probability: unlikely; cost of trying: "wasted" effort). In another example, a person may believe that her business will succeed. That person may believe in it enough to put all of her money into her business, but she could also save some of it because of the probability that she may experience financial difficulties if she overcommits. The goal is for people to hold beliefs that get them the best outcome.

Unfortunately, optimally aligning a person's beliefs with both reality and their desired outcome is one of the hardest parts of life. Some people are *more likely* to succeed if they put their savings into their business. This approach forces them to believe in the outcome, erase doubt, and overcome adversity. Other people who completely disregard their current reality may behave irrationally and have to face the cost of their willful ignorance later.

Monotheists may use the probability and impact model to invoke Pascal's Wager, which argues that the infinite reward for belief in God—rendering probability irrelevant—justifies religious faith. Alternatively, skeptics may find the most success in never being certain and assuming that anything that can go wrong will go wrong. There is no perfect combination of realism and optimism that guarantees success. The only certainty is that some hope is required, and some grounding in reality is required.

This combination of knowledge and belief—of certainties and uncertainties, of facts and conclusions—leaves the world open to many different interpretations. For example, if someone wants to play a sport professionally, detractors will appeal to improbability by pointing to the small number of professional players. However, their perspective ignores the higher conditional probability of healthy, hardworking athletes succeeding. They also discount the value of playing the sport to stay fit and healthy, to earn a scholarship, and to develop social and leadership skills.

Detractors implicitly believe that the person does not have the potential to do it. The fact that professional sports positions are rare leads to the belief that the person will probably not succeed and the decision to tell the person to aim lower in life. They are trying to align that person's beliefs and desires with reality as they believe it to be.

The problem with facts is that they are often used selectively to support a certain belief and discounted or ignored when they do not support it. This issue is known as confirmation bias, which must be eliminated in scientific experiments for validity but could result in demoralizing fear, uncertainty, and doubt if removed while in pursuit of a desired outcome. Confirmation bias is helpful when people need to stay committed and motivated toward their goal, but it should be eliminated when they need to make an objective decision. Unfortunately, when people are trying to persuade someone and have limited time in which to do so, they will often select only examples that support their position.

In the sports example, the detractors are trying to use the fact that there are few positions in an elite professional sports league to support their belief that the aspiring athlete should find other interests. This fact ignores the millions of people who play sports recreationally and the millions of jobs in the industry, including players, coaches, staff, trainers, broadcasters, commentators, reporters, international leagues, gambling businesses, and sporting goods stores. Trying to discourage someone with one data point only serves to bring down the person's desires and beliefs to match the detractors'.

These same people could have reached alternative conclusions with the same fact and different beliefs. They could have encouraged the athlete to emphasize the teamwork and fitness aspects. They could have insisted that the sport is a privilege that only comes with a sufficient grade-point average. They could have ensured that the person understands finance so that he manages his money well regardless of whether he makes millions or thousands per year in the sport.

Instead, they decided to combine one fact with a string of assumptions to try to crush a person's dreams. With additional knowledge and a different perspective, they could have cited the multitude of sports-related opportunities and made a valid argument for pursuing a career in such a large field.

Given how many interpretations there are, the best approach to balancing beliefs and reality is to gather knowledge and establish beliefs that support the pursuit of the desired outcome. Additional knowledge and new beliefs may change someone's desired outcome or even his or her view of reality. Both possibilities demonstrate the power of belief.

To find fulfillment in life, people need to analyze their desires, maximize the believability of those desired outcomes, and then keep their faith through setbacks and detractors until they succeed. Desires and beliefs are constantly changing, however, so people should be monitoring how they affect each other.

There are often going to be setbacks to growth. Growth requires change, and change is difficult. Many people resist change and will resist other people's desire to change. As a result, some people will tell you to keep your deepest desires to yourself so that others will not try to crush them with their beliefs. Belief is sometimes the only thing that will get you through the toughest situations, so you have to align your beliefs with your desires and strengthen your conviction if you are to persevere.

To sustain growth, align your beliefs with your desires

To maximize your ability to persevere, you can change either your desired outcome or your belief. For example, if you think that your wish to become president is an unattainable outcome in the near future, you can set your immediate sights on a seat on the city council. That adjustment reduces your goal to something that you believe is attainable in a shorter time period. Alternatively, you could increase your belief by improving your qualifications, thereby making the path to the presidency more believable. In short, you can increase your belief by bringing the outcome closer to you or bringing yourself closer to the outcome.

A quick analysis of *why* you want what you want could help you adjust the goal to something that is more attainable or more appropriate for you. In the president example, you may want to be president for fame, power, status, or global impact. If you realize that your motivation is to make a positive change in the world, you can identify numerous alternative and intermediate options to achieve that goal, increasing the probability of success.

You now have options outside of politics, such as starting a charity or inventing a life-saving product. In the political sphere, you can lobby for the legislation you support or become a diplomat to negotiate the peace you wish to see. With these additional options, you have many potential paths toward your objective. Knowing how many ways that you can have your desired impact increases your confidence, which keeps you moving forward and gives you options if you experience setbacks.

In this process of aligning your beliefs and your desires, you do not have to give up on your aspirational goal. On the contrary, expanding your options or setting more believable intermediate goals reduces your likelihood of abandoning the effort altogether. Intermediate goals address lofty goals' imbalance of high desirability and low believability. Alternatives allow you to feel safe putting full effort into the original desired outcome because you know that you can change direction if you fail or lose interest.

Similarly, when trying to bring yourself closer to the goal, you do not have to make significant progress before you can feel more confident. While it may be easier to believe that you can win the championship when you are in the championship game, you can increase your confidence at the beginning of the season by acknowledging the attributes that make your team's success possible. Just looking at what you have, what is possible, and how you could succeed can boost your belief without your current situation changing in any way. This approach brings you closer to the goal mentally without necessarily making visible, tangible progress.

Before you put in the effort to build belief, you may be curious about its limits. After all, wanting something and believing it is possible do not guarantee that you will attain it—soon or ever. However, if you do not want it and you do not believe it, you will certainly not achieve it because you will not bother to try. No one ever won an Academy Award or even the lottery without wanting the outcome and believing that it was possible. Desire and belief drive behavior, and success is a result of a combination of controllable (e.g., effort) and uncontrollable (e.g., circumstance) factors. Maximizing your desire and belief maximizes your willingness to work on what is within your control.

For example, you have to put in years of effort to win an Academy Award. You have to study your craft, gain experience in many productions, get your work noticed in the industry, and possibly move to Hollywood or New York. You could win in your first role in an obscure indie film, but the likelihood and believability are much lower. While you have to face uncontrollable factors such as attractiveness, talent, and age, all you can do to increase your probability of success is build the desire and belief to make the right decisions and take the right actions.

In the lottery example, you may use the logic, "If you don't play, you can't win," to purchase a ticket. However, your goal is to win the prize money; you would probably not pay to participate in a random drawing just to hear someone call your name. Knowing that your goal is financial growth, you can find more believable means, such as labor, investing, saving, or starting a business.

Belief by itself does have short-term limitations. When temporal, genetic, and physical constraints are combined, certain outcomes are not possible. You cannot flap your arms and fly like a bird whether or not you believe it. You cannot become the CEO of one of the world's largest companies tomorrow with no experience, degree, connections, or knowledge of the industry. Your current reality is hard to overcome in one day.

However, that fact does not negate the power of belief. Growth takes time and effort, and belief does not magically eliminate these requirements. If you instantaneously transformed from your current to future state, the whole point of life would be removed. You would gain everything and earn nothing. Instead, belief opens up opportunities and puts you in a "solutions mindset" to focus on possibilities, not obstacles.

In the previous examples, you cannot become CEO of a large company tomorrow, but you could become a CEO of your own company or start working at a large company in an entry-level position. You cannot fly by flapping your arms, but you can accomplish your goal of getting from one point to another through a variety of physical means. When you believe, you find solutions.

In the long run, belief makes what is impossible today possible in the future. That desire to fly like a bird existed for a long time, and human flight via airplanes is now commonplace. However, it took millennia of studying physics and biology to understand how other creatures fly and how to design a craft that could fly while supporting the weight of a human. Society lauds Orville and Wilbur Wright for their audacity and dedication to their dreams. Anyone today who says that the controlled, sustained flight of a powered, heavier-than-air aircraft is impossible would be ridiculed, even though that statement was accurate until 1903.

You can now fly in an airplane, a space shuttle, or a variety of other aircraft. The desire for human flight and the belief that the laws of physics could support it were necessary for scientists to continue through failed experiments to achieve the outcome. When scientists see that birds can fly but they cannot, they try to understand why and then figure out how they can create the conditions that allow for human-controlled flight. They neither give up because they cannot flap their arms to achieve flight nor continue to flap their arms hoping to see different results.

That achievement, however, required constant change to

what scientists believed was possible. Humans have difficulty accepting changes to their beliefs. People will hold on to their core beliefs as much as anything they know for a fact. Holding beliefs was useful to protect early humans because it would prevent them from assuming too quickly that a threat had subsided. However, it could also hinder them when pursuing an objective.

Because growth is change, your experiences need to change, your desires need to change, and your beliefs need to change to continue your growth. You cannot achieve your desired outcome if you believe that you have only one desire, that there is only one way you can attain that desire, and that this option is impossible. Something has to change for you to find meaning and happiness in life. You can change your perspective on what you want, you can change your thinking on how to get there, or you can find a way to make the best course of action possible. Change your perspective or risk getting depressed, giving up, or trying a futile approach in vain.

If you have this narrow view of your life, open yourself up to any and all change that allows you to progress in life. There is no such thing as, "I only want this one thing, and there is no meaning in life if I can't get it." Meaning evolves as experiences, desires, and beliefs evolve. The meaning of life is growth, and meaning itself is capable of growing.

Because beliefs often need to change, you should frequently test your beliefs and assumptions. You might believe, for example, that you do not need to be good at math to be successful in studying the arts, your desired career path. Then, five years later, you decide that you want to open your own performing arts studio, which requires you to manage a business.

If you are starting the business with minimal operating costs, you may choose to do the accounting by yourself. You now need to be good at math so that you may keep yourself in business and avoid fines or jail time for (accidental) tax evasion. Your beliefs about math may have been true at one point, but this new situation requires that you adjust them to keep yourself on the path to success. At this point, you may improve your math skills or hire an accountant. It is up to you to determine which beliefs serve you and which you need to change to succeed.

Beliefs that you need to test include what your meaning is and what your desires and experiences are. You may believe that your life has a particular meaning but later discover that the path you are setting is pointing you in a different direction. You may believe that certain experiences will help you succeed but then determine that they are ineffective or harmful. You may believe that you want something but then realize after you attained it that you actually did not want it. All of these scenarios are possible, so you need to continuously monitor your beliefs and change them as you come across new information.

Because beliefs vary from person to person and are constantly changing, everyone will have different perspectives. Fortunately, they do not have to be the same. Diversity has always been life's strength. Just as genetic diversity increases the probability of survival, freedom to believe different things allows for new ideas and innovation. Diversity in desires and beliefs allow people to fill various jobs and pursue different life paths. Although differing beliefs do cause many conflicts, they are necessary for humans to accomplish more as a group.

The conflict over beliefs usually arises from people wanting you to believe what they (want you to) believe. Many people spend their entire lives trying to get others to adopt the same worldview. Assuming positive intent, they usually do this to validate their own beliefs and educate others about their values and ethics. However, you may need a different set of beliefs to achieve your life's purpose. If their ideas direct you away from healthy, beneficial desired outcomes, they can disrupt your path to meaning and fulfillment in life.

One of the most blatantly damaging examples is the parent who tries to set his or her children's expectations low for what they can achieve in life. That parent may tell the children that high expectations can lead to significant disappointment in life.

This limiting statement likely came from his or her own past experience of having a dream, striving for it, and failing. However, the variables in that equation were significantly different: a different person, time, situation, goal, support structure, degree of determination, and education level. These factors could change the outcome, but the parent may not be thinking about them.

While managing their expectations could make success easier to achieve, it could also be stopping them from finding what they want and realizing their potential. This act—despite being done in the children's best interest—may be very damaging to their ability to find life satisfaction.

If you are an influencer and your child, friend, relative, or colleague believes that she can do something beyond what you think is possible, it is more useful for you to help her find practical next steps on that path rather than more modest long-term goals that limit her potential. With this approach, you are supportive and pragmatic without crushing her dreams. If she wants to fix appliances or design interstellar spacecraft, she has to learn math, physics, and engineering first. There is no need to lower her expectations when the next step is the same.

On the receiving side of influence, make sure that you are ready to hear what others have to say if you ask for their opinion. Most people are willing to criticize and bring "a heavy dose of reality" to your ambitious goals. Go into any belief-testing session with a clear reminder of what you want and why so that belief-busting does not demotivate you.

It is tough to discover that the path to success is much more perilous than you imagined, but that does not mean that you should abandon it. Instead, you should take the opportunity to test how much you want that outcome and use the belief-testing process to figure out the right way to approach your journey.

When discussing your beliefs with others, you should be wary of how someone with negative intent might influence them. They might be trying to control you, sell you something that you do not need, or discourage you. Sleazy salespeople and con artists, for example, will use any information they have about you to manipulate your desires and beliefs so that you give them money.

It is difficult to detect these scams because they hide the harm they are doing behind irresistible benefits. Manipulators will make you believe that you want what they are selling and that they can give it to you, and they keep you convinced just long enough to get you to do what they want you to do. To protect yourself from manipulation, test new beliefs by viewing the potential risk and harm to you before you adopt them. If someone tries to convince you of the incredible, check to see if they have an incentive, if they are preying on your insecurities, and if you have alternatives to their "too good to be true" approach.

Beliefs are powerful, and you need to have them to push through adversity. However, they can also be detrimental and inhibit your growth. Keeping your beliefs constructive and focused on attaining the right outcome is a continuous process, so adjust them frequently. An effective approach is to align your beliefs with the current reality, expand your beliefs based on the best possible future state, and bring your current state closer to that future potential by adjusting the near-term goal or your ability to achieve it. Without a means to align your beliefs with your desires, your growth will be self-limited.

Without belief, you will abandon your efforts

Growth requires effort, and effort requires desire and belief. Desire drives you, and belief sustains you. If you do not *want* something, you will have no motivation. If you do not *believe* that you can have it, you will eliminate any motivation you had. Losing belief can extinguish passion as quickly as desire can ignite it.

You may know that you face even worse consequences for inaction, which is why you may act even if you neither want something nor believe that you can have it. You may also want it so much that you are willing to push through disbelief to attempt it. While they are both possible, those situations require much more willpower than if your desires and beliefs are aligned.

There is no such thing as having no beliefs at all, as assumptions underlie all decisions. In practice, however, having no belief in your ability to grow is the same as living a life with no hope. You cannot live life for long without any hope, as you will have no reason to continue on your path.

One of the highest risk factors for suicide is depression, which indicates a belief that a person's life is miserable and will never improve. Humans have a natural instinct to want to live, grow, and thrive, so it takes an overwhelming amount of belief in the impossibility of growth for them to develop a desire to end it. Belief is necessary for life to strive for a better future.

For you to grow, you must believe in a future state that does not reflect your current reality. You were not born a master chess player, an Olympic athlete, or a parent of a family of four with a house, a car, and a dog. You have to grow into being that person with those things. It also requires you to believe that any growth-limiting situation, such as being bullied, working at a job you hate, or living with someone who makes you miserable, has the possibility of being overcome.

Similarly, humans cannot grow as a species if they do not believe in things that do not exist today, have not happened yet, or have not yet been proven. It is commonly known as having faith, and although that word has a religious connotation as belief in the divine, everyone needs to have faith in themselves and their potential to grow. You never know what is possible until you try. If you do not believe in anything that you do not already know, you will never learn anything new. If you do not believe in the possibility of anything changing, you cannot invent anything, influence public policy, or make new discoveries in your field.

Because growth is the point, the two most useful beliefs you can have about life are that you can grow in areas that are important to you and that the process of growing is an enjoyable experience. Even if you believed that you had low potential and that the whole world was trying to stop you, you could still get to a meaningful life instantly by adopting those two beliefs. They are the foundational beliefs for success in life. Without them, life would be a miserable existence of doing things that you do not want to do and loathing the process.

The Tom Sawyer story is a perfect example of how painting a fence can be an enjoyable experience or work depending on your beliefs. Tom was able to get the other children to believe that it was a fun activity that *they* should compensate *him* for allowing them to perform. A simple shift in your beliefs can have the same effect. If you believe that an activity can be fun or that you can make it fun, you will put forth more effort, be more successful, and enjoy doing it. Your beliefs shape your experience, so you have control over whether your experiences are meaningful.

Unfortunately, there are many people who do not believe in anything that has not already happened or that does not already exist, and they are often the most vocal in giving you their opinion on how bad of an idea something is. They could be right; something may be extremely difficult. If you want to set a world record for holding your breath, then it is probably a good idea to learn about the risks before you try it. Take the information that they provide and use it to mitigate the risk of failure or harm.

However, many of the reasons they give will be biased based on *their* beliefs. For example, they may say that you cannot play on a professional sports team because no one of your height, weight, gender, or race has ever done it before. You can consider that information, but make sure that you test their beliefs. If you want something enough, believe that there is a way despite the obstacles. No great feat was achieved without doubt, mistakes, failure, and naysayers. No one has to believe but you.

If you are worried that other people will discourage you, you may want to keep your desires and beliefs to yourself. It is much easier to succeed when you do not have to continually reassure yourself against a slew of doubters giving you their thorough arguments for why your goals are unattainable. Alternatively, you can confide only in people who will listen and be supportive. These people are more likely to help you surface risks and find solutions without trying to deter you from your desired outcome.

The choice to share your goals is ultimately your own, and there are tradeoffs for either approach. For example, research shows that weight loss benefits from public declarations of intent because the social support (i.e., encouragement) and pressure (i.e., risk of embarrassment) hold you accountable.[50] However, sharing your identity goals (e.g., becoming a good parent) with other people can make you feel like you have already attained them and lull you into premature complacency.[51] Choose the option that maximizes the believability of the outcome for you.

There are benefits to looking externally for information. The experiences help you to figure out what you want in life, and the input helps you test your beliefs by opening you up to different perspectives. As you get new information, your beliefs—and, consequently, your purpose—will evolve. Those external sources should inform (but not dictate) your ultimate direction.

While belief is necessary for meaning, success does not require that you never have any doubts. On the contrary, arrogance inhibits growth because it contains an implicit belief that there is no way to learn or improve from another's input. In that respect, arrogance and humility are opposite perspectives that may lead to the same result. With arrogance, you may think that you are already good enough. With humility, you may think that you will never be good enough. In either case, you do not pursue growth. The right balance is to be confident enough in your ability to improve and humble enough in your willingness to improve.

Excessive belief is usually not an issue for people looking for meaning in their lives; arrogant people assume that they already have the answers. However, if you ever think that you know everything, consider opposing viewpoints and the reasoning behind them. You will often find that people who disagree with you are not ignorant, stupid, or evil; they just have different ethics, desires, and beliefs. You may not agree with their viewpoints, but you can still learn from them. If you believe that you can always learn and improve, you will find it difficult to be arrogant.

More frequently, people looking for meaning do not believe that they can get what they want. If they did, they would already have the purpose of attaining it. If you are in this situation, you need to find ways to overcome that disbelief so that you can proceed toward your goals.

If you find it difficult to increase your belief before you take action toward a goal, you can instead suspend disbelief long enough for your desire to drive you to act. The "fake it 'til you make it" approach is one method that you can use when you have the will but not the confidence to do something. In this approach, you pretend and, as a result, act as if you can do it. As you gain experience, you replace that pretend belief (i.e., "fake it") with real belief when you increase your proficiency enough to succeed (i.e., "make it"). This approach works when you cannot find easy tasks to build confidence and have to start with something difficult.

Another approach is the "admit reality, but do it anyway" approach. In this case, you acknowledge the low probability but make up for it with enough drive and belief to put forth your best effort. This technique was used before the USA men's hockey team won against the Soviet Union in the semi-finals in 1980, an event known as the "Miracle on Ice" in U.S. sports lore. Defenseman Jack O'Callahan recalled coach Herb Brooks saying in his pre-game speech, "If we played 'em ten times, they might win nine. But not this game. Not tonight. . . . Tonight, we are the greatest hockey team in the world."[52]

This game is often considered to be the greatest upset in U.S. sports history because it came shortly after a 10-3 loss to the Soviets in an exhibition game. In that speech, the coach openly admitted to the improbability of winning. He left just enough room for belief that they could win one game. Even with the tireless training and preparation, this group of amateur college hockey players needed to believe that they could overcome the incredible odds to defeat the best team in the world. They had an unparalleled desire and just enough belief necessary to score one more goal than their opponents and win the biggest game of their lives.

The latter approach is especially useful for overcoming external resistance, as you do not have to disprove the critique of the critic to move forward. A similar way to overcome resistance is the "objection noted" technique, which allows you to note opposition, factor the risks into your plan of action, and then move forward with the plan while taking the risks under advisement.

For example, if you want to be a professional athlete but face critics telling you that there are few openings for players, you can note their concerns by responding that you will also study hard in school. That way, you can prepare to play sports professionally and to contribute to society when your athletic career ends. This technique quiets objections because you show that you understand their concerns and have factored them into your plan.

While the "objection noted" technique mitigates risk, it might lower your chance of success if it causes you to turn to the alternative options too quickly. If you are prone to this behavior, you may prefer the "no other option" approach: eliminate alternatives, forcing you to commit completely to your desired goal. This high-risk, high-reward technique is the inverse of the previous one, replacing the risk of settling with the risk of failure. In theory, you exchange safety for increased motivation and immediate dismissal of all contrary beliefs out of necessity.

This technique uses fear as a motivator to drive you to succeed, but it is a drastic measure used by people who know that they will abandon their goal otherwise. It does involve some self-deception like the "fake it 'til you make it" approach because there are *always* other options. The deception makes you think that other options are not only undesirable but also unavailable.

These techniques allow you to overcome disbelief and drive you to action and success. They are temporary remedies, as you cannot suspend disbelief forever. You have to build belief in the outcome to replace your belief that it is not possible. While you may not be fully aware of the possibilities, you can at least get out of your own way long enough to learn what they are.

To stop being your own barrier to success, you need to test and address limiting beliefs wherever possible. If you do not, your confirmation bias will shape your interpretation of events to reinforce your beliefs. When you believe that something is impossible, you will find roadblocks and use them to justify quitting. Instead, you could adopt a mindset of proactively identifying hurdles so that you may find solutions before they stop you. Obsessing over your trials and failures will make you less likely to want to continue. Believing that you have the potential, support, and capabilities to succeed does the opposite. In these cases, use confirmation bias and priming to your advantage.

No matter which beliefs you hold, be careful. Perception heavily influences your interpretation of facts, so you can use facts to rationalize almost any belief you have. If you are looking for reasons to give up, you will find them:

- "The probability of success is low."
- "Many people have failed."
- "Salaries in the field are low."
- "I lack the necessary education."
- "I have poor genetics."

Those could be the facts, but you could just as easily build a rebuttal with competing reasons to continue pursuing your goals:

- "The industry employs millions of people."
- "People can make money doing what they love to do."
- "I can get a degree."

Since conflicting evidence exists in most ambiguous situations, you will likely acknowledge and emphasize the facts that support your beliefs and understate and ignore the ones that do not.

This effect is demonstrated in formal debates where opposing sides gather facts to confirm their pre-existing beliefs. Each side cites its evidence as incontrovertible proof and dismisses opposing data. The audience is left to filter through the evidence and come to their own conclusions. Similarly, you will have to form beliefs and make decisions in your life based on many conflicting facts and opinions, so you should do so in ways that maximize your potential while minimizing unnecessary risk.

With this understanding, you will quickly realize that it is a waste of time to find reasons that you cannot have what you want unless they inform changes you can make to be successful. You will also start to realize that people who cite lack of time, resources, or money as hurdles are often trying to rationalize their inaction. Excuses are an indication that they are in a situation where they either do not want something enough or do not believe in themselves enough to go after it. If they had enough desire and belief, they would have acted. Without belief, excuses will hold you back forever; with belief, you will eventually find ways to be, do, or have what you want in life.

Because desire and belief are both factors within your control, you have autonomy in your life. If you want something that is unattainable, you can begin by finding a prerequisite that is attainable. If you want something that you believe is impossible, you can change your beliefs. If you think you want something but keep making excuses, then you can build your desire and test your beliefs. When belief and desire are in alignment, decisions and actions that get you closer to your objective are inevitable.

Belief is key to finding and having meaning in your life. If you believe that you can find it, you will look for it. If you do not believe, you cannot have meaning. Anyone saying that there is no meaning in life is usually trying to tell you that purpose is a belief from within rather than a gift that an external party bestows upon you. Asking another person or entity for what your life's meaning is would be like asking someone to tell you what your opinion is. You look outside for ideas and experiences that will inform your beliefs, and then you derive meaning from within. Your purpose in life is whatever you believe it is.

If an outcome is unbelievable, start with a believable step

Strengthening your belief can be challenging for monumental tasks. For example, it may be difficult for an overweight individual who has never exercised to believe that he can run a marathon. However, it is believable for that person to walk a mile just by going outside and strolling around the block. To paraphrase the Chinese philosopher Laozi, "A journey of a thousand miles begins with a single step."[53]

After a couple of weeks, he could improve and walk two miles per day. With enough conditioning, he could begin to run for a portion of that distance. He could work up to five, ten, and fifteen miles of walking and running. Eventually, he could progress enough to run the 26.2 miles necessary to complete a marathon.

You may not think that you can complete a marathon, but you know that you could start training regularly and eventually be able to finish a 5K race. People do not usually overhaul their worldview with one insight; they reshape it slowly over time. Growth and change require time, so you can gradually strengthen your beliefs. You do not have to be sure of your long-term potential to get started. Your desire drives you, so you just need enough belief (or lack of disbelief) to prevent you from quitting.

As you improve, you can test your beliefs about your abilities. For example, if you want to dance but think that you are a terrible dancer, commit to attending every session of a beginner's class and assess your progress at the end. If you want to go into physics but believe that you cannot do the math, seek a tutor who can try a different approach to teaching you. By testing your beliefs, you check to see whether they are protections or constraints.

Stand-up comedians understand how to test boundaries, as comedy tests people's assumptions and beliefs and risks crossing the line from funny to offensive. When they write their routines, they have no idea which jokes are going to work with the audience. When a joke does not elicit laughs, they do not know whether it was the joke, the delivery, or the target audience that was wrong until they change one of the variables and repeat it. They believe that a certain style, set of topics, or delivery type will work in a particular situation, but they have to test those beliefs continually through experimentation to improve their effectiveness. Given the risk, they may spend months polishing a single joke before they use it in front of large audiences.

Consistently delivering a great set is extremely difficult because of the diversity of audiences they run into as they tour. As they continue to develop their craft, however, it becomes possible for them to succeed in a variety of different scenarios, and their accuracy of applying the right humor to the right situation improves. If they are too tame, their jokes are lame. If they are too bawdy or offensive, they may disgust the crowd. Many assumptions and beliefs have to be made for a set to be successful, so they have to test both the jokes and the audiences continuously.

Similarly, you have to continuously evaluate your situation as it changes and adjust your desires, beliefs, and approach accordingly. If you identify and define reasonable steps that you can take to move forward, you gain confidence that you can progress and are more likely to stay motivated. This process includes identifying why you can succeed, who can help, what your obstacles are, and how you can overcome them. Then, you learn through trial and error and adjust accordingly. Throughout the process, your belief sustains you until you achieve the desired outcome.

Arguably the most significant belief to check is your attitude toward failure. Two indicators of this belief are worry and resignation. Worry is the expectation of a negative outcome, and resignation is a defeatist response to failure.

Before a negative outcome occurs, you can manage worry by reducing the perceived risk or impact of not attaining your goal. You do not worry about being able to perform menial tasks, such as getting out of bed, because the risk of you not being able to do them is low. You also worry less about goals with contingency plans because they reduce the impact of failure. If failure is likely and disgraceful, you may not even try; if it is unlikely and surmountable, you may do it without giving it a second thought.

After a negative outcome occurs, you can reduce resignation if you change what failure means to you. If you fail and believe that you will continue to fail, you will not try again. If you believe that it is a setback with lessons learned, then you will probably persevere. Whether you see failure as a learning opportunity or see it as the end can make all the difference in how you respond.

The pain of failure is difficult to attenuate. That pain comes directly from the belief that failing makes you a failure who cannot achieve anything in life. As a result, you may do whatever you can to avoid it on your journey toward your goal. You may break down your long-term outcome into a series of incremental milestones that are easy to achieve. You may lower your expectations. You may study and practice for years before showcasing your skills in public. These techniques reduce the likelihood of failure and make you more confident in success.

However, no matter what you do in life, you will fail. Failure is a natural part of growth. Growing requires you to be able to do something later that you cannot do now. You will fail along the way, and you will likely still be alive afterward. Assuming you are, there will always be another attempt, another approach, or another goal. Thomas Edison failed thousands of times during his development of a light bulb and a storage battery, and Abraham Lincoln lost several elections before becoming president of the United States.

Fear of failure is unproductive once you already know the risks. It does not help you; it inhibits performance. Once you have done everything possible to prepare and mitigate the risk of failure, you must convince yourself that you are ready. Your previous incremental successes should have strengthened your confidence, but realizing your full potential requires you to tackle challenges with high risk and major consequences eventually.

When you reach that point, you must know how to manage worry as a list of controllable and uncontrollable risks that you choose to avoid, mitigate, or accept. You must know how to embrace failure as a learning experience. You can "trick" yourself into making it so far without belief if you want something badly enough, but you will eventually have to believe that success is possible and that failure is a natural step in that journey.

Finally, when you strive for that "unattainable" outcome, believe that no setback will deter you. If you do that, then failure will not be so discouraging. You will do what you can with things you can control and not worry about things you cannot control. You just need to learn the difference, as experience will teach you.

Belief is critical to finding meaning in life because it is both required to have meaning and necessary to persevere through adversity. Beliefs can be wrong, so you have to test them continually. However, you should always believe in your ability to grow and pursue your desires. This faith in yourself keeps you moving forward. If it seems too unbelievable, spend time increasing your belief by finding a believable first step. Align your desires with your beliefs to maximize your growth and improvement. Create a virtuous cycle of your progress, your desire for more, and your belief in your ability to pursue the next goal. Keep moving toward your goals, and you will succeed.

QUESTIONS

Questions That Help You Build Your Belief and Expectations

Your answers to these questions will help you understand your beliefs about your growth areas, experiences, desires. If you believe that you cannot get what you want, they help you to understand how to build greater expectations for life. Finally, they offer insight for when you do not know what to believe (without telling you what to believe). This chapter's content provides guidance on how to think about these questions, but only you can supply the definitive answers for your life.

1. What do you believe your meaning in life to be?

2. What keeps you going when you face adversity?

3. Do you believe you can be, do, or have what you want in life? Why or why not?

   - What assumptions underlie your answer?
   - What can you do to test your assumptions?

4. Do you have a person or people telling you that you cannot do something that you want to do? Why?

   - How can you address legitimate concerns?
   - How can you acknowledge concerns when you disagree?

5. What can you do now or in the near future to build your confidence in your ability to grow in life?

6. Are there intermediate or alternative goals that are more believable? What are they?

7. Does a belief system (e.g., a religion, a philosophy, a parent's belief system) you follow place certain types of success or forms of growth as more important than others?

   - If so, are these beliefs in conflict with your desires? How can you reconcile them?

8. What can you do before and during stressful situations to help you through them and reinforce your belief in the outcome?

9. How do you view failure?

   - Can you mitigate the risk and impact of failure without compromising your goals? If so, how?
   - How can you embrace failure as a growth opportunity?

10. If you are struggling to believe in your ability to achieve a goal, what can you do to suspend disbelief long enough to take the first step?

    - How can you maintain resolve through early setbacks?

11. Are you worried about pursuing certain goals in life?

    - What can you do to address your concerns?
    - What uncontrollable factors must you accept?

EXERCISES

Activities That Help You Build Your Belief and Expectations

Completing these exercises will result in beliefs that are more conducive to growth.

Thought Exercise: Take your list of growth areas and answer the following questions about each one:

- What do I believe is possible in this area? What is not possible?

- Why do I believe these things are possible or impossible?

- If I believe that something is not possible:
  - What would have to be true for it to be possible?
  - Can I influence the situation to make it possible?
  - If not, can I start with a more believable goal?

- If I believe that something is possible:
  - Can I change my beliefs to make my goal more desirable?
  - Can I adjust my goals or beliefs to increase my confidence?
  - What can I do to increase my probability of success?

- Which experiences can I have that will shift my perspective?

If your answers to these questions indicate that you do not believe you can grow how you want to grow in life, think about what you can do to change your beliefs a little every day or make your goals just a little more possible.

If your answers to these questions indicate that you do believe you can grow, continue to monitor your desire and belief for when progress and setbacks require you to reevaluate them.

Revisit your assumptions periodically to see if they have changed. If they have, determine whether you can make a decision or take an action that will increase your confidence in the future.

Brainstorming Exercise: If you are not sure about what you believe, then your goal is to surface and test your beliefs. Choose a goal, growth area, or experience and complete the following statement repeatedly to uncover your most influential beliefs:

I believe that _[goal/growth area/experience]_ is _____.

Examples:

- *easy/difficult*
- *worth pursuing/not worth pursuing*
- *what others want me to do/what others do not want me to do*
- *fun/boring*
- *great when you succeed but terrible when you fail*
- *too expensive*
- *heavily based on luck*
- *the reason that I get up each morning*
- *too hard to convince others that it is right for me*
- *a hobby but not a career*

Next, select the most limiting belief you wrote down and complete the following statement about it:

I hold this belief because _____.

Examples:

- *I have seen others do this*
- *I have had difficulty in the past*
- *my parents always said this to me*
- *my peers made fun of me when I told them*
- *I love every minute I spend doing this activity*
- *my father did this, as did his father*
- *no one like me has ever done this before*
- *I love the end but hate the beginning of the process*

Then, check how your belief influences your behavior by completing the following statement about it:

Because I hold this belief, I _____.

Examples:

- *procrastinate*
- *have not had a chance to get started*
- *work on other things for now*
- *set my sights lower for now*
- *spend all of my spare time working on it*
- *don't stress too much about it*
- *try to find balance with other demands*

Now, test your belief by completing the following statement with the most contrarian evidence you can cite:

The reason that this belief may not be entirely true is _____.

Examples:

- *I don't know that for a fact*
- *my friend could have been wrong*
- *I tend to overdramatize things*
- *other people like me have achieved that outcome*
- *I do have time that I currently spend or waste elsewhere*
- *I could find a club or group that could help me focus on my goal*
- *I could approach the situation differently and avoid the issue*

Finally, see how your behavior might change when you adjust your belief by completing the following statement:

If this belief were not true, I would _____.

Examples:

- *spend more time practicing*
- *sign up for a beginner's class*
- *go to college to study the field*
- *work harder toward my goal*
- *have more fun along the way*
- *stop procrastinating*
- *buy an instrument and start learning*
- *audition for a role in that play*

The goal is to identify your beliefs, understand their cause and effect, test them, and change them if they are holding you back. If you disprove a belief, state your new belief (i.e., "I now believe _____.") to acknowledge the change. Repeat this exercise for your other beliefs, goals, growth areas, or experiences.

Creative Exercise: Take the collage that you made in the Desire chapter. Below the Desire column, create a "Beliefs" section that includes the qualities you possess that make you capable of doing, being, or having the things you want in life. Write down what they are, paste words you cut out of magazines, or find pictures of people who have the qualities you possess (e.g., a person smiling, an athlete, a person who exudes ambition or confidence). Then, add anything that you know or believe to be true about your reality that makes your goals possible. For example, you could paste survey results of people who say they want to lose weight if you are writing a book on dieting. Finally, add anything that you *want* to believe to be true about yourself or your reality that would make your goals possible.

This exercise will add to your picture of your desires to include a picture of the beliefs that will help you attain them. Getting your mind focused on what you believe will allow you build the confidence you need to sustain your growth. It also enables you to overcome doubt and resist others' discouragement. Through this process, you may even think of new ways to get what you want.

Note: You may wish to leave space on, next to, and below your collage for future chapters' creative exercises.

Writing Exercise: Take your lists of growth areas, possible experiences, action items, and desirability scores from the writing exercises of the previous three chapters. For each experience or action item, rate the feasibility of you taking these actions or having these experiences on a scale of 1 to 10 (10 being the highest).

Next, list what makes these experiences possible ("Evidence") and what you could do to make sure that you have those experiences

("Reinforcers"). Also, list hurdles to taking action or achieving success and write down what you could do to overcome them.

For low-scoring items, think of similar, alternative, or prerequisite experiences that are more feasible and could boost their scores.

Finally, repeat the rating exercise to see if your level of belief has changed, and rate any new action items or experiences you have identified as being more believable initial steps.

This exercise will help you build upon your belief that you can grow in your areas of interest. It will also break down unbelievable outcomes into believable initial steps. If your feasibility score is still low or you are unsure of an experience's feasibility, you can do more research to find out what is possible for you to do.

Example:

Experiences	Action Items	Feasibility	Evidence/ Reinforcers	Hurdles	Alternatives
Exercise	Sign up to a gym	7 10	Gym is on my commute	Working late	Run at home
Club activities	Mark meetings on calendar	5 7	Set reminders	Work-related travel	Join once per month

Note: *The above example does not show all of the information you will bring from the previous writing exercises; it is possible that this chapter's teachings may cause you to refine that information.*

Outcome

After reading this chapter, you should have a clear understanding of how your beliefs can affect the strength of your desires and influence whether you continue to pursue the experiences required for you to grow. You should have assessed the feasibility of your goals and identified evidence that reinforces your belief. Finally, you should identify hurdles and intermediate or alternative goals to help you prepare for adversity. You may reprioritize items on your list if you have enough belief to move toward some goals while you take time to fortify your belief in others.

When you have your updated list, you are ready to proceed to the next chapter.

Emotions

Emotions indicate your life direction and progress

"Your intellect may be confused, but your emotions will never lie to you."

— Roger Ebert[54]

"Happiness is not a goal; it is a by-product."

— Eleanor Roosevelt[55]

"I say [happiness] is neither virtue nor pleasure nor this thing or that but simply growth. We are happy when we are growing."

— John Butler Yeats[56]

PRINCIPLES OF EMOTIONS

- Emotions are life's feedback mechanism
- Human emotions indicate the existence and degree of growth
- Your emotions reflect your experiences, desires, and beliefs
- Without emotions, you could not know what matters to you
- If you are not happy, find the root cause and address it

EMOTIONS AND THE MEANING OF LIFE

Find what makes you happy. Emotions are your personal indicators of whether your experiences are in line with your desires and beliefs. Your emotions can tell you whether you have found your meaning and purpose in life. They will provide you with positive feedback that your life's direction is correct if you want to achieve a goal, believe you can, and are having the right experiences.

Do not confuse your indicators, emotions, with your goal, growth. Many people will tell you that the meaning of life is to be happy, which is inaccurate. Happiness is not the end goal; it is feedback on your progress toward your goal, growth. Happiness is one of many emotions that provide real-time updates on your current state relative to your growth. Happiness is an indicator that you are growing and thriving.

Emotions are life's feedback mechanism

If life needs to seek growth and avoid harm to survive and thrive, it needs a mechanism to tell it whether something is beneficial or harmful so that it may change its behavior accordingly. Microorganisms' cell membranes are selectively permeable, meaning that they can let in and keep out different substances. This attribute is an inevitable result of natural selection, as organisms that let in harmful substances or kept out beneficial ones would die while the ones that let in nutrients and kept out toxins would survive. Most successful organisms would be able to identify these substances, receive feedback on their benefit or harm, and exhibit control over their interactions with them.

Complex organisms need sophisticated methods of detecting, signaling, and controlling the presence of beneficial or harmful stimuli. Their bodies evolved nerve endings and senses to detect stimuli and send signals to their central nervous systems so that they may respond appropriately. When those senses detect something beneficial or harmful, the pleasure or pain signal that they send triggers a physical response. The organism then acts to receive the benefit or avoid the harm. Since each cell of an organism cannot evade physical harm on its own, it has to rely on the brain to use those signals to behave in its best interest.

Humans have developed a sophisticated, multi-layered feedback system. When nerve endings detect external stimuli, their signals take time to travel to the brain and back. That time could be the difference between life and death, so the body evolved to respond to those signals from the spinal cord (via reflexes), the limbic system (via emotions), or the pre-frontal cortex (via reason).

Reflexes are rapid muscle movements triggered by the spinal cord in response to pain or other stimuli. It is the fastest response and does not even involve the brain. On the more thorough side, a reasoned, conscious response requires the signal to travel to the brain, be processed by the prefrontal cortex, and return to the muscles of the body. This process has the advantage of allowing the brain to interpret the data and formulate the most appropriate response based on knowledge and not just instinct.

In between those extremes, the limbic system provides a more advanced mechanism for responding to stimuli than reflexes and is faster—but less thought out—than reason. The limbic system developed in early animals as a means to provide neurochemical responses to internal and external stimuli. These responses, known as emotions, inform the rest of the body about how to react to those stimuli. An emotional response includes rapid bodily changes to prepare for action as well as activation of the brain's rewards system to drive and incentivize behaviors.[57]

Because the rewards ultimately drive the behavior, many people ignore the value and role of emotions as feedback. The feedback is meant to help them learn which behaviors, things, events, or people are contributing to or detracting from their growth. The rewards, which include chemicals such as dopamine, endorphins, serotonin, and oxytocin, are meant to encourage them to experience more of those behaviors, events, things, or people to continue growing. By focusing on the latter instead of the former, people are simply acting to experience pleasure rather than understanding why a situation causes them to feel a certain way.

Pleasure is such a powerful incentive that many seek to maximize it by any means necessary. These people will quickly conclude that the meaning of life is to be as happy or to experience as much pleasure as possible. This conclusion is the epitome of mistaking the signal (emotions) and reward (pleasure) for the goal of life (growth). While the signal-reward system works very well in earlier life because it was the best way to survive, humans' advanced physical and cognitive capabilities allow them to "game" or manipulate the system and miss the point.

Unfortunately, confusing the indicators with the goal can lead to catastrophic mistakes. For example, call center managers trying to create success measures for their staff will tell you that employees will focus more on making the metrics look as good as possible than achieving the intended goal. The managers may want the team to provide great service to customers, and so they think that the best indicators of service quality are when service interactions solve the problem in as little time as possible and do not require follow-up conversations. With the best intentions, they may then create monetary incentives to ensure that staff provide rapid service and solve the problem the first time.

Quickly, though, they could see their staff ignore the purpose of the measurements. Instead of providing exceptional service that solved problems quickly and effectively, employees try to get customers off the phone as quickly as possible and make sure that they do not call back. The same indicators that were supposed to provide helpful feedback on service effectiveness led to behaviors that elicit the reward without achieving the intended goal.

Similarly, many civilizations put a premium on learning (i.e., intellectual growth) in life, so they may establish grading and standardized scoring systems to measure and track progress. This approach is consistent with the maxim, "What you can measure, you can manage."

However, what you can measure **will be gamed**. Once administrators establish metrics and provide incentives, the students and teachers will find ways to work the system in their favor. The teachers may only cover material that will be on the test. Students may cheat. Entire classes will be dedicated to improving test-taking ability instead of accumulating knowledge. The goal, learning, becomes secondary to maximizing a grade or score.

Not surprisingly, people often manipulate their emotional indicators. Alcohol, tobacco, opioids, non-reproductive sexual activity, gambling, and other addictive substances and behaviors affect their emotions and trigger their brains' rewards systems in ways that are not conducive to growth. Unlike the manager or the school system, humans cannot change their indicators to prevent these manipulations. As a result, overindulging in these behaviors is possible and even rational if they genuinely believe that the point of life is to maximize happiness. These pleasurable activities can cause them to feel happy, so they may initially conclude that seeking pleasure leads to a happy life.

If that reasoning were accurate, psychology has already found the most direct way to game this system: stimulating the septal region of the brain. In 1954, James Olds and Peter Milner of Mc-Gill University were testing whether stimulating the limbic system would make rats uncomfortable. During their experiments, they found that electrical stimulation of the septal region produced feelings of pleasure. When they attached electrodes to this part of the brain and enabled the rat to stimulate itself by pressing a lever, it would repeatedly press that lever up to several hundred times per hour.[58] Subsequent studies found that rats preferred the stimulation to the consumption of food or water, and many of them died from exhaustion.[59]

Human experiments on this region of the brain had similar results. In a 1972 experiment, researchers attached electrodes to a man's pleasure centers as part of a study on human sexuality. During each three-hour session, the subject was given the opportunity to stimulate his septal region. He did so up to 1,500 times per session. Robert Heath wrote of the experiment, "During these sessions, B-19 stimulated himself to a point that, both behaviorally and introspectively, he was experiencing an almost overwhelming euphoria and elation and had to be disconnected despite his vigorous protests."[60]

These examples demonstrate that happiness is an indicator and not a goal. Like any indicator, emotions can be manipulated. If the point of life was to be happy as much as possible, everyone could just hook his or her septal regions up to electrodes and experience utter euphoria until dying like the rats in the experiment—this technology already exists.[61]

However, happiness is not the end goal of life, and people who attempt to game the system are missing the point. Instead of manipulating, suppressing, or ignoring their emotions, people should be learning to understand and manage them to achieve the real goal, growth. They can begin with the happiness emotion, as many are likely misunderstanding their most coveted emotional indicator.

Extensive research in psychology has found that happiness can be broken down into at least two types of emotional feedback: pleasure and fulfillment. While people need both for long-term happiness, the former is usually more temporary in its effects than the latter.[62]

Pleasure is short-term happiness triggered when the body satisfies its primal needs such as eating, drinking, defecating, urinating, sleeping, and procreating. Science has shown that happiness from these kinds of activities is short-lived, with people returning to their typical happiness levels quickly. For example, if someone eats a pizza, the enjoyment of the pizza will improve his or her mood, but the happiness boost will subside relatively quickly. Psychologists call this happiness set point that a person eventually returns to regardless of life events and circumstances the hedonic treadmill.[63] Because pleasure is fleeting, dedicating life to temporary highs is ultimately unrewarding.

Fulfillment, on the contrary, is long-lasting. If a person volunteers at a soup kitchen, masters a new song, or tutors a child, the impact of those kinds of growth activities on his or her happiness levels last for a much longer time. A series of studies have found that while the happiness set point and a person's circumstances have a significant impact on happiness, the rest is influenced by intentional activity.[64] Over time, a person's focus on intentional activities that lead to fulfillment may help him or her achieve sustainable gains that shift his or her happiness set point.[65]

These two types of happiness work together: fulfillment is the long-term indicator that people are successfully growing in life, while pleasure is a short-term incentive and indicator to perform the basic life duties that allow them to grow. People must balance the two types. Focusing too much on pleasure will lead to a hollow feeling as they continuously seek the next pleasurable experience; focusing too much on fulfillment may be exhausting if they have to sacrifice too much to achieve a long-term objective.

Without understanding the difference between these two forms of happiness, many people will look to maximize pleasure and then wonder why they are still not truly happy. In these situations, they may see labor, service, or learning as unpleasant experiences that they should avoid as much as possible. They will never be able to find true happiness if they actively avoid fulfilling activities while they pursue pleasurable ones.

An absence of fulfillment is an absence of purpose. Feeling fulfilled is the ultimate indication that you have meaning in life. If you do not continue to grow, however, that fulfillment will be temporary, and you will have to find new ways to develop. Fortunately, people are able to feel fulfilled as they are progressing toward their goal, so continuously achieving objectives is not as important as continuously pursuing those growth opportunities.

While you are developing, you must maintain a healthy body, strong relationships, and safety. Physical pleasures act as incentives to take care of yourself, such as the feeling of being with a loved one or the solace of drinking hot cocoa in front of a fire on a cold winter night. It is essential to get the nutrition, love, and protection you need, but overindulging will eventually detract from your long-term growth and happiness. Use life's pleasures as a reprieve to regain your strength and resolve for the setbacks in life; they can help you sustain your passion and commitment.

The writers of the Declaration of Independence knew about the importance of striving to achieve long-term fulfillment, as they stated that the three unalienable rights of all humans were life, liberty, and the *pursuit* of happiness. Pursuing the people, experiences, and things that make you happy and fulfilled is the point. True happiness (i.e., not gamed through neurochemical manipulation) provides feedback that you are on the right track.

With the core of life to pursue growth and avoid harm, humans would seemingly only need two emotions: one to indicate that things are going well (i.e., happiness), and another to indicate that something is wrong (i.e., sadness). However, emotions are very complex indicators that can tell a person what is wrong, how bad things are, what the cause might be, and what he or she can do about it. For emotions to perform all of those functions, they have to be more sophisticated than a simple dichotomy (i.e., "happy" or "sad"). Emotions provide nuanced feedback to help humans adjust their course and speed accordingly.

Human emotions indicate the existence and degree of growth

The purpose of human emotions is to provide insight into whether people are growing or being harmed and to what degree. Positive emotions, such as love, happiness, and excitement, provide feedback that their current experiences are contributing to their growth. Negative emotions, such as anger, fear, and depression, indicate that their experiences are threatening or causing harm. Neutral emotions, such as boredom or indifference, provide feedback that they are neither moving toward nor away from their goals and therefore need to find new experiences.

To understand and manage their emotional indicators, people first have to identify them and define what they are indicating.

Because emotions gauge the relationship between experience and growth, people can create a list of them in order from the strongest positive indicator of alignment to the strongest negative. They could then add descriptors of what these emotions are indicating to them so they can interpret these nuanced signals more accurately. Below is a sample continuum of emotional indicators:

Identifying and Defining Human Emotional Indicators[66]
Illustrative, Organized by Degree of Growth

- **Happiness** (i.e., fulfillment, joy) – Reaction to growing, living, and thriving to great satisfaction
- **Flow**[67] (i.e., complete immersion and focus, being "in the zone") – State associated with an immersive experience that is optimal for improving in a desired growth area
- **Excitement** (i.e., anticipation, optimism, hope) – Anticipation of future opportunities to experience new things and grow
- **Contentment** (i.e., satisfaction) – Satisfaction with the current state; usually a state of rest after growth or accomplishment
- **Boredom** (i.e., tedium) – A level of dissatisfaction with current stimulation and growth in an experience
- **Frustration** (i.e., annoyance) – Dissatisfaction with a hurdle that is slowing progression and preventing growth or attainment of the desired outcome
- **Anger** (i.e., rage, fury) – Strong dissatisfaction with and opposition to an obstacle that is thwarting growth or causing harm
- **Fear** (i.e., worry, uncertainty, doubt) – Expectation that desired outcomes may not occur or undesired outcomes may occur
- **Regret** (i.e., sorrow, grief) – Reaction to loss, mistakes, or missed opportunities, signaling attachment to what was lost or missed and a desire for a different outcome
- **Sadness** (i.e., disappointment, misery) – Reaction to an undesired outcome, signaling harm, loss, death, or decline

- **Depression** (i.e., hopelessness) – Expectation that an undesired outcome is inevitable; a sense of helplessness regarding the ability to pursue, influence, or attain desired outcomes

In this structure, emotions provide feedback as to where people *believe* they are with respect to their *desired* progress toward their objectives. For example, fear shows that they believe that there is a threat to their growth in their current experience that could cause them significant harm. Excitement shows that they are currently expecting a positive experience that could help them reach their next desired goal. The happiness associated with success is the feedback that they receive when they get where they want to be. Each emotion indicates where they believe they are and where they believe they are going.

Once people understand what each emotion is signaling to them, they can use this information to diagnose what might be wrong and what they can do to improve their state. For example, depression shows that they have almost completely lost touch with what brings them fulfillment and happiness in life. Anger shows an obstruction or conflict that they have an opportunity to resolve. Excitement shows that they have found the right thing to focus on and are looking forward to the desired outcome. They can now assess the range of nuanced emotions they feel, determine the root cause, and decide what action to take in response:

Using Emotions to Diagnose the Situation
Illustrative Self-Assessment, Organized by Degree of Growth

- **Fulfillment** – I am achieving my goals. I should continue to grow and improve.
- **Pleasure** – I am meeting an immediate need. I should continue until satiated, then return focus to toward long-term fulfillment.
- **Excitement** – I really want to have an experience. I should prepare to make the most of it.

- **Hope** – I believe that the future will bring me what I want. I should strive to achieve my goals.

- **Admiration** – I know someone who has grown in a way that I want to grow. I should learn from them, associate with them, or emulate them to follow their path of growth.

- **Contentment** – I am satisfied with my current state. I should appreciate the moment until my next growth opportunity.

- **Boredom** – My current experience is not engaging me. I should look for new experiences.

- **Frustration** – Something is impeding my progress. I should look for solutions or alternative approaches.

- **Jealousy** – Someone has something that I want, and I have negative beliefs about my ability to get the same thing. I should find ways to change my desired outcomes or change my beliefs about my ability to achieve them.

- **Anger** – Something or someone is in sharp conflict with my desires and beliefs. I should determine whether I can resolve this conflict or find a way around it.

- **Disgust** – Something or someone offers a threat to my health or well-being. I should not consume the food or participate in the activity.

- **Shame** – I have had an experience that is not socially acceptable. I should learn from the experience and adjust my behavior accordingly.

- **Fear** – I believe that an experience will be harmful. I should identify solutions to avoid that harm and move back toward safety so that I may continue growing.

- **Pain** – Something or someone has caused me harm. I should find a way to protect myself or avoid the experience in the future.

- **Regret** – I have missed an opportunity, made a mistake, or experienced a loss. I should find a way to properly mourn the loss, make up for the mistake, or identify alternative opportunities.

- **Depression** – I lack desire, have extremely negative beliefs, and am not growing in any meaningful way. I should find ways to reignite my desire and change my beliefs as quickly as possible. I should seek support, new experiences, or other means of reversing this trend.

Many psychologists recommend that people should "be in touch with their feelings" because their emotions are providing valuable feedback that they should be using to improve their lives. No mentally healthy person randomly experiences an intense positive or negative emotion for no reason at all. Their feelings are telling them something about their current experiences, desires, and beliefs. Listening to them and constructively responding to them can give people the ability to improve the situation instead of being at the mercy of random chance.

Unless a person has a mental illness or disorder, emotions are temporary indicators of a person's response to a situation. Therefore, happiness is not a state that someone needs to try to maintain at all times. This misconception is what causes so many people to focus on temporary pleasures or highs and to miss the opportunities that will lead to long-term happiness. People need to feel bored occasionally to realize that what they are doing no longer engages them. They need to feel bad when something is harmful so that they learn to protect themselves and find alternative paths to their goals. They only need to feel joy long enough to receive the feedback and reward from the experience. Each time, however, their bodies return to an emotional state that allows them to continue their growth journeys.

Once they receive that input and address that situation, the emotion is no longer needed. However, some people who feel strong negative emotions and cannot address the cause will hold on to them. Holding on to the negative emotions can trigger a stress response that suppresses the immune system or even prevents people from living their lives. Over time, that chronic stress can lead to poor mental and physical health.[68]

Many people recommend practicing a technique known as mindfulness for this reason. Mindfulness is a way for people to clear their mind of all thoughts and become detached from them so that they may view their emotions objectively, accept their feedback, and then release them when they understand them. This approach allows them to process their emotions and return to a positive, peaceful state.

Over time, people who practice this technique improve how they control their thoughts and process their emotions, increasing their overall life satisfaction. While any method that works for you to keep you in touch with your feelings is constructive, scientific studies support the emotional and psychological benefits of mindfulness meditation[69,70] and similar relaxation or deep focus activities such as yoga[71] on emotional stability.

Understanding what emotions are telling you and identifying opportunities to make constructive adjustments are your first steps toward using this feedback mechanism. Emotions are complex, however, so reading them will sometimes take time and effort. The direct cause of an emotional response may not be readily apparent; psychiatrists and psychologists have found that many behavioral disorders are due to childhood trauma.[72] These traumas can cause deep-rooted emotional problems that are difficult to unpack in adults years later.

For example, a person may have a phobia that prevents her from entering large bodies of water, and it could have stemmed from watching someone drown as a child. She may not even recall the event because she has forgotten or suppressed it, but the strength of the emotion had triggered an extreme behavioral reaction of never wanting to swim. While there are less severe adjustments she could make, such as always swimming with a friend, the harbored, unprocessed emotion of fear will cause physical and psychological paralysis near water.

Similarly, to handle an overwhelming emotional reaction that comes seemingly from nowhere, you may have to ask yourself whether your desires, beliefs, and past experiences are affecting your response to an external stimulus. For example, you may have a bad day at work, and later you may reply harshly when your spouse asks an innocent question about whether you were planning to wash the dishes. It could be that the reason for your anger is that you are being asked to do too much at work, and it never seems to be enough. When you get home, those beliefs and emotions regarding work creep into your personal relationships.

Your emotions can get very complex when childhood trauma, current stress, and an uncertain future combine. When an emotion builds without being addressed, a seemingly innocuous event can lead to a disproportionate response. The single, seemingly inappropriate reaction may require simple willpower to address in the immediate term, but it may also require in-depth analysis to address the root cause of that deeply held anger in the long term.

Analyzing emotions can be an arduous process for many who have been told their whole lives to ignore them or keep them suppressed. Additionally, it can be hard to unpack complex, conflicting emotions. However, knowledge of your desires, beliefs, and growth areas will give you the information you need to understand why you are reacting to an experience with a specific emotion or set of emotions.

Your emotions reflect your experiences, desires, and beliefs

With an understanding of how emotions work, you can use them to derive critical information about your current state so you can make better decisions and take better actions in response. However, you have to learn which situations trigger which emotions for you so that you can properly understand and manage them.

Grades are an appropriate analogy for understanding how you can read and diagnose your emotions. Your goal in school is to learn. Your grade (e.g., A, B, C, D, or F) is the primary indicator of how much you have learned in the class, and your grade-point average (e.g., 0.0-4.0 GPA) is the overall indicator of how much you have learned or your ability and willingness to learn. When someone who normally earns a high GPA receives a poor grade, people try to diagnose what might be wrong:

- Is it trouble at home?
- Is the material particularly difficult?
- Is the student's health failing?
- Is he or she not interested in the topic?

Family and teachers work together with the student to fix problems and return the grades to a level that their prior GPA suggests they can achieve.

If someone has a low GPA, people start to question whether the student has a learning disability, whether he or she lacks the discipline and drive to learn, or whether he or she has a low level of intelligence. Again, the goal is to identify ways to develop the student to his or her full potential given the current situation. A single low grade is an indicator of a specific issue; a low GPA signifies deep, long-term problems.

Similarly, emotions are your primary indicators of the current state of your growth and well-being. Your overall outlook on life is the aggregate indicator of how much you have been able to grow and how much you may be able to grow in the future. If you have a positive disposition overall but suddenly become depressed, people who care about you will try to diagnose the issue and find out what might be wrong:

- Did you just leave a relationship?
- Did you lose a loved one?
- Did you fail a test or lose a competition?

Family, friends, teachers, or colleagues want to help you return to a more positive emotional state.

If you have a negative outlook on life or have significant emotional problems, people will begin to question whether you have a mental illness, were abused as a child, or experienced severe emotional trauma. In this case, people want to identify the issue so that they can help you raise your typical emotional state and outlook on life so that you may live a healthy and fulfilling life.

In this analogy, grades are indicating alignment between the knowledge that the student should have gained through the course and the information that they actually learned and retained. Emotions are indicating whether the experience that is the focus of your attention is in alignment with your desires and beliefs. Falling grades signal that you need to change your approach. Your negative emotional reaction signals a need to change your desires, beliefs, or experiences because they are not contributing to your growth. In either of these cases, the signal tells you that something is wrong, and then you have to figure out what exactly is wrong so that you can correct it. As shown in both examples, issues can have direct causes or deep-seated influences.

To evaluate issues and find their source is called root-cause analysis. Just like a weed will keep growing if you cut it near the top instead of ripping it out from the root, eliminating the symptoms of a problem without addressing the source will not completely solve it. For example, if you feel bad because an injury dashed your dreams of playing a professional sport, drinking alcohol temporarily alleviates the pain but does not address the cause of the sadness, which will return at some point in the future. The only healthy way to recover emotionally is to address what is causing your emotional reaction.

Emotions primarily work in stimulus-response terms: something happens in your environment, and you react to it. However, that response is not just based on external stimuli but also your perception of it. Because your desires and beliefs influence your perception, they are involved in your emotional response.

Most people are familiar with experience, the "stimulus" in the "stimulus-response" example. The experience of touching a hot stove is harmful, so you will recoil in response. The pain will tell you to move your hand away and not touch the stove in that way again. Your experience is the primary cause of your emotion.

However, if the reason that you touched the hot stove was to protect a child from touching it, then your emotional response will change because of your desire to protect the child and the belief that blocking him can achieve that goal. Now, you may feel pain at the harm, relief at the child not being hurt, and anger if the child was being careless. The experience of touching the hot stove is the same, but your emotional reaction was different because of your desires and beliefs.

In a different situation, the cause may not be the experience itself but rather just your beliefs and desires about it. For example, you may hear that you will be having pizza for dinner and become happy or sad depending on whether you were in the mood for pizza. You may believe that the pizza you are going to have will be terrible and dread the thought of going home to eat it. The experience of hearing someone talk about dinner does not directly trigger an emotional response like touching a hot stove does. Instead, your emotional response came from your desire to have something else and the belief that the pizza will be unappetizing.

Together, these three factors determine your emotional response. If you hear that someone died, you may feel sorrow if you believed that he was a good person or relief if you believed that he was a bad person. You may have actually wanted him to die because he was at the end of his life and was suffering. You may also feel regret because you wanted to tell him how you really felt about him before he died. The death, your beliefs about its implications, and your desires related to the person who died all go into your reaction. Because these factors create complex combinations, your emotions are often nuanced and complicated.

If you want to understand your feelings in any situation, evaluate the relationship between the experience, your desires, and your beliefs. When you feel good, there is alignment between the three factors. When you feel bad, they are misaligned. If you are conflicted or unsure about how you feel, then you have complex, competing desires and beliefs that are creating confusion in your emotional response.

Use this analytical approach to trace any emotion back to its root causes. For example, you might get mad when someone asks you when you are going to get married. In this situation, you might be recalling past experiences where people were asking so that they could pressure you. You might not want to get married and believe that they will judge you for your response. The person may have just been making conversation, but your beliefs about their intentions and your desire to avoid being asked this question cause you to respond with irritation. By repeatedly asking yourself why you feel a certain way and why your experiences, desires, and beliefs are causing that feeling, you can always find the root cause of your emotional response.

Through this analysis, you can now understand why you reacted in a certain way in the past and predict how you will feel about an experience in the future. You may also use your emotions to understand your likes and dislikes based on what excites you and what bores you. Your feelings take a wealth of information and boil it down to a single indicator of your situation, so they can tell you so much when you learn how to read them.

Most importantly, your emotions help you find your meaning in life by helping you understand what you want and what you believe you can do. For example, imagine how you feel when someone tells you that you are not good at an activity and you either want to be good at it or know that you are good at it. That feeling likely shows you how that person's statement is very different than what you want and know to be true about your potential. If you get angry, it shows that the person is a hurdle to progress and you want to prove him wrong. If you get depressed, it may show that the person's criticism echoes a lack of belief in yourself. Your emotions explain what is wrong—either with the situation or with how you perceive it—and then help you begin to determine what you can do about it.

Once you understand what your emotions are telling you and what is causing them, you now have everything you need to manage them. You need to control your emotions for a few reasons:

- Human emotions evolved to include bodily reactions that may not help you in a civilized society.

- Your beliefs about a situation may be wrong, leading to an emotional reaction that is inappropriate for the actual circumstances.
- You may not be able to take constructive action in response to feedback if your emotions overwhelm you or burden you for too long.

To elaborate on the first reason, bodily reactions in humans are ingrained physical responses that have become tied to emotions through evolution. For example, anger will signal for you that something is preventing you from getting what you want. Your body's natural response to anger is to prepare you for a physical altercation by increasing the heart rate and blood pressure. Similarly, fear signals the perceived presence of a threat that could harm you. Your body prepares you to keep harm away by sending blood to the limbs, heightening your awareness of your environment, and increasing your heart rate so that you can fend off the threat or run from it. Living things for millions of years had to fight or flee from stimuli that triggered anger or fear, so the bodily reaction and emotional reaction are linked.

Unfortunately for humans, these reactions are not appropriate for most modern stresses. Physical violence has lost its usefulness in civilized society when peaceful solutions are available and more appropriate. Similarly, the fear response when performing cognitive tasks can limit your abilities.

Because the physical reaction that comes with an emotion is not always appropriate in a cooperative society, you need to receive the feedback, control your response, and release the emotion. Many athletes, for example, have to deal with the anger, frustration, or guilt of making mistakes during competition. They have to learn from them and then immediately shake off the negative emotion. Otherwise, they risk inhibiting their future performance.

To elaborate on the second reason, an emotional response based on false beliefs can cause you to take the wrong action. Your emotions are always genuine, but your perceptions are not always accurate. Countless tragedies have been written about one person seemingly catching another person stealing, cheating, or killing and enacting retribution before finding out that he or she was actually innocent. If everyone acted on raw emotion before having the full picture, civilization would have fewer marriages, friendships, and business relationships. Given that the human body prepares itself to act on its emotions, a person could get angry and jump into a conflict before being able to think about it.

To ensure that your understanding of the situation and the appropriate response is correct, you need to process the emotional signal, check your facts, test your beliefs, and weigh your options before taking action. The only way to have time to confirm or deny your initial assessment is to control yourself. Use your emotions to understand your perspective, but do not let them dictate how you behave in case you need to respond differently.

You can also question your beliefs to reduce the strength of your emotions. If you are afraid to fly, you can remind yourself of the facts about how safe it is. If you are upset over losing a game, you can remind yourself how well you did, how well your opponent did, and how you can improve. If you begin to weigh facts differently and change your beliefs, your emotions will shift as well. Keeping them in check will stop you from acting in haste, and managing your feelings about the future can prevent you from worrying too much unnecessarily.

To elaborate on the third reason, uncontrolled emotions can overwhelm you to the point that you can no longer act appropriately in your life going forward. An extreme example is victims of tragedies or atrocities who are paralyzed by their fear, anger, sadness, regret, or pain from the event. They experienced a significant loss and reacted appropriately at the time to protect themselves. However, once they are safe again, they have to find a way to pivot their emotions back toward their prior emotional baseline or risk having their entire life overwhelmed by the tragedy.

In this circumstance, their emotions cause them to analyze the situation to see if there is anything they can do to prevent the event from happening in the future. They may replay the event in their heads repeatedly to see if they could have acted differently. Once they have done everything within their control to do, though, they then have to find ways to release the emotions associated with the event. Many people describe this process as "coming to terms with" and "needing to be at peace with" an experience. They are articulating that they have to accept an event once it is over so that it no longer consumes them. Without being able to let go of their emotions, these people will not be able to move forward with their lives.

Your goal after you identify, diagnose, and respond to your emotions is to return to your normal emotional state. If you have already adjusted your desires and beliefs, you now need to change your experience. Engaging in a different activity replaces the emotional residue of your past with feelings reflecting the present.

The most important part of this process is shifting your attention. You cannot let an emotion go if you are consumed by the experience that caused it. The "don't look down" principle is useful in helping shift your emotions just as it is with helping you focus on your desires. When you look at the desired outcome (i.e., "up"), you feel the determination, excitement, and anticipation to continue toward the goal. When you look at the undesired outcome (i.e., "down"), you trigger feelings of fear and paralysis. It is important to know that "down" exists so that you know to avoid the negative consequences, but once that information is understood and your fear tells you about the undesired outcome, you need to focus on the desired outcome and let the fear subside.

The principle's name is intentionally ironic as a humorous reminder that the human brain usually follows the Ironic Process Theory. This theory states that when you tell people not to think about something, it makes them think about that thing (and makes it difficult *not* to think about it).[73] So, when someone tells you, "Don't look down," you automatically think about looking down. Upon actually using the principle, you may want to call it the "look up" principle to remember to focus on the desired outcome and not obsess over avoiding the undesired outcome.

The Ironic Process Theory is the reason why so many people advise others to word their speech in positive rather than negative phrasing. When a person is told not to do something, his or her brain thinks about doing that thing. Instead, talking about doing the right thing and achieving the desired outcome increases his or her focus on the right behaviors and feelings of excitement about doing well. Many people oversimplify the "don't look down" principle by saying it is about always thinking positive thoughts and feeling good as often as possible. This misinterpretation can cause you to ignore potential issues and prevent you from addressing roadblocks.

However, you cannot focus on the goal and see the obstacles in your way if you experience constant, paralyzing fear that you are going to fail. Worrying too much about the negative outcome is debilitating. The "don't look down" (or "look up") approach will optimize your emotional state, as it ensures that you are excited about the goal and interested in getting there without issue. This combination sustains your motivation while allowing you to see and address potential risks and issues.

When you want to shift your focus using this principle, your emotions will tell you quickly when you are encountering issues (e.g., fear, frustration, or anger) and when you are obsessing over them (e.g., worry, despair, or seething) instead of the outcome. You can then adjust your thoughts, actions, or perspective to get back on track and continue making progress in your growth areas. Your emotions will gradually shift in response.

Another approach that has proven effects is classical conditioning, a concept in psychology where one stimulus that naturally triggers a response can be associated with a second stimulus so that the latter triggers a similar response. For example, a dog naturally salivates when it is hungry and perceives food. If it hears a bell ring right before it receives food, it will become conditioned after several instances of the concurrent stimuli to salivate when it hears the bell.[74]

You can use this effect to your advantage by associating a set of activities with an emotional state so that you can perform them when you need to shift away from negative ones. For example, you may have had many positive experiences associated with the outdoors, so going outside can help you alleviate sadness. By taking a walk, you get out of the environment associated with negative emotions and into one associated with well-being. In addition, you get the direct benefits of fresh air and exercise.

This approach works in many circumstances. You can wear certain clothes or scents to bring back happy memories or to get into the mood to go out and have fun. You can go to your favorite restaurant or listen to your favorite song to prepare for a big event. While the experiences themselves will help shift your emotions, they are supported by their associations with other pleasurable activities (e.g., partying, spending time with family). As a result, these activities begin to transform your emotional state so you can regain your motivation and focus.

Once you have adjusted your desires, beliefs, or experiences and released the emotion, you will likely return to your normal state. Regulating your emotions allows you to respond appropriately to life events and recover more quickly from them. Over time, they can improve your long-term emotional well-being, your relationships, and your quality of life.

If you are having trouble understanding your emotions, you can analyze who is involved and when, why, and how you feel them. Everyone processes emotions differently, and your response may change based on a variety of factors. By taking the time to understand the context, you can diagnose and address emotional issues more effectively. When you can manage your emotions, you can respond constructively to any life situation.

Your emotions help you to process and respond to your life experiences. They tell you whether your experiences are contributing to or detracting from your growth potential, and they also tell you about your beliefs and desires regarding the situation. Always be monitoring them, listening to them, and understanding them so that you can make adjustments when necessary.

Without emotions, you could not know what matters to you

Imagine living life without emotions. How would you know if you liked something? How would you know that something was harmful to you and what to do about it? Would you still know how to respond appropriately in any given situation?

There are people in the world who lack many emotions or even the sense of touch and ability to feel pain. The latter group includes those with a condition known as congenital analgesia, which is a condition where a person cannot feel pain (either through insensitivity or indifference to it). These people often hurt themselves and are not able to address the problem because they are not getting feedback.

This physical condition is preventing them from sensing harm, and the pain, fear, and recoil responses do not occur without the sensation. Therefore, they require education on which activities or objects are harmful, and they are frequently getting minor cuts, burns, and bruises. Their injuries are much worse and more frequent than others' injuries because they are missing that unforgettable signal for them to get away and avoid similar painful events in the future.

Similarly, individuals who are devoid of certain emotions also lack critical feedback. Many people who commit terrible atrocities do not experience empathy, guilt, and other emotions that would normally tell them when they are harming others. Some of these individuals may not see why people care about others or commit selfless acts because they do not have the capacity for compassion, shame, or love. Emotions triggered in social interactions provide feedback that a person has harmed the peer group or put it at risk, and he or she would normally respond with cooperative, socially acceptable behaviors. Without the signal, there is no response.

There will be times where you wish you could turn on and off your emotions at will. You may be going through the extreme pain of losing a loved one. You may have slowly lost the strength of love you had when you first met your spouse. Emotions can be overwhelming or underwhelming, but how they work is incredibly useful.

For example, you cannot walk around for the rest of your life head over heels in love when there are so many other things in life to focus on once you have had that initial courting experience. You cannot understand how much someone truly means to you unless you receive the catastrophic feeling of loss. The sayings, "You don't know how much you've got until it's gone," and, "You don't know how much you love her until you let her go," show this in action. Your love emotion has to stop overwhelming you so that you may continue growing in other areas, while the fear and pain of loss has to be possible to remind you how much you really do care.

While some people may have difficulty controlling their emotional responses to behave appropriately in civilized society, emotions are still more beneficial than they are harmful. For every time you have to breathe deeply to let out nervousness before a presentation or take a ten-minute walk to calm down instead of assaulting someone who wronged you, there are dozens of times where your emotions are providing useful feedback that keeps you safe, prevents complacency, and helps you succeed.

Now, instead of imagining not having emotions, imagine having them but completely disregarding them. How long will they stay if unaddressed? Would they return if suppressed? Can you remain psychologically healthy if you constantly bury them?

You may be in a situation where your emotions are not actionable, so you try to ignore or suppress them instead of processing them. While this short-term coping strategy may be your only option at the time, you might then live with those unprocessed emotions for so long that you get used to them or become numb to them. Under these circumstances, you may be so haunted by suppressed rage or overwhelmed with pain, grief, or depression that you just give up on trying to find happiness.

No matter how much you try to ignore them, those emotions are telling you something. You desperately want something, such as friendship, support, financial security, love, or a fulfilling career. Your current experiences and beliefs are suggesting that you cannot have it. Until you can rectify that misalignment, those feelings will remain.

In the long-term, the average person needs healthy coping mechanisms, not fewer emotions. Many people can talk to a friend, colleague, or relative to process those emotions. They can put them to rest by figuring out why they have them and taking small actions one day at a time to move back in the right direction. Others make a radical change such as moving to another country to reset their lives. When you find that right action—that right movement back toward growth—then you will start to see your emotions change with it. Never give up on finding ways to raise your base level of happiness and life satisfaction. It may feel like a blessing and a curse to have emotions, but do not let the difficulty of managing your physical and mental reaction to them make you forget about their usefulness—their practical necessity—in guiding your life direction.

If you are not happy, find the root cause and address it

While feeling blissfully happy at all times would be impractical because it would prevent you from striving for more, you need to feel positive about your desired outcome to continue forward in your life journey. Without a positive disposition, you cannot recover as quickly from setbacks. Regardless of your normal temperament, however, you may accumulate emotional baggage if you experience a barrage of issues, an acute tragedy, or an extended lull in life.

Often people who are unhappy with their current state turn to drugs, alcohol, food, sex, or other temporary sources of pleasure to fill the void they feel elsewhere in their lives. However, people who abuse them know that these options mask the pain and cannot replace the long-term fulfillment of living a life of purpose. With temporary setbacks, such as a bad day at work, simple pleasures help switch your mood back so that you can continue growing. If you are dissatisfied with your life, however, you will need to consider more substantial, long-term changes. Temporarily indulging yourself can quickly spiral into distraction or addiction without healthier mechanisms for dealing with adversity.

To manage unhappy periods of your life more constructively, you can:

- Evaluate your emotions and identify their root causes so you can address the situation and return to normal.
- Identify opportunities to maintain a positive outlook on your future and remain focused on your growth areas.

With the first component, you can benefit from taking time to analyze the sources of your unhappiness. You may need to do some soul-searching to understand your growth areas, experience, desires, and beliefs. During this time, you can make adjustments and recover emotionally so that you can reduce the struggle you feel as you make progress. You should also use this time to reaffirm your resolve to push through adversity.

Below is a sample set of steps for processing your emotions. Through this approach, you can invest the time necessary to identify the true causes of your emotions and begin to address them.

Steps for Processing Your Emotions

1. *Give yourself time to process your thoughts and emotions.*
   Many busy people are at risk of jumping to a solution before understanding the problem. Take at least a few minutes to understand what your emotions are telling you.

2. *Eliminate distractions that you may use to avoid the issue.*
   You can use a temporary distraction such as a phone call or a

movie to calm down and improve your mood, but it will not help you address an issue with long-term emotional impact. Process your emotions in an environment where you can focus.

3. *Keep asking, "Why?" regarding your reaction to an event.* Often, your emotional response to an event is influenced and compounded by your past experiences. You can ask yourself the following questions to identify additional causes or factors that you need to address:

- "Why did I react in that way?"
- "Why did I react that strongly?"
- "Why else did I feel that way?"
- "Why is it still bothering me?"

Each time you answer a "Why" question, ask yourself, "Why?" again to that answer. After a few iterations, you will find deeper issues causing your emotional reactions than just the situation in front of you. Addressing those root causes will have a greater impact on your current and future emotional health.

4. *Review your past experiences for patterns in your responses.* You are more likely to record events with an emotional response into long-term memory[75] and recall them when in a similar environment[76] or situation. Therefore, you should be able to recall previous instances and compare them to your current experience to verify your root-cause analysis.

5. *Identify which causes are within your control or influence.* Because complex problems have multiple causes, you will need a system to evaluate them effectively. Divide the causes into two categories: controllable and uncontrollable. For example, if you perform poorly on a test, you can identify opportunities to improve your study habits or your interest in the subject, but your natural talent is not within your control. Then, break down the controllable factors into manageable parts. In the test example, you can change the frequency, du-

ration, approach, focus, or intensity of your studying.

6. *Accept the uncontrollable factors.*
Obsessing over or trying to control the uncontrollable factors is a waste of time. Check to make sure an aspect of a problem is uncontrollable, then acknowledge your inability to affect it and give yourself permission to focus on the controllable factors.

7. *Create an action plan to address the controllable issues.*
Many people like to vent, which can be healthy, but then they do not act differently after the venting session. For each controllable factor, come up with solutions that you can take to improve the situation or your response to it. Then, create a plan with defined steps and timelines to address the issue.

8. *Let go of the emotion and let the feedback subside.*
You may continue to ruminate over a problem after you have come up with a plan. This emotional state may be a signal for you to act immediately, so let it motivate you if you can be constructive. If something still does not seem right to you, you may want to continue processing your emotions.

Once you understand what you are feeling and do what you can to address the situation, you can then let the emotion go. You release the emotion by reminding yourself that you have done all you can for the moment or by forgiving the source of the problem. When you switch from the stress of having the problem to the relief of addressing the problem, your mood will begin to return to normal.

9. *Move forward.*
When the emotion is released, this step should be natural. If you cannot move on, then you can try the process again to see if you missed anything. While humans have the ability to change their emotional state quickly, most people find that stronger emotions require more time for recovery.

Analyzing and processing your emotions can have a tremendous impact on your long-term growth and well-being. This method becomes even more effective in helping you stay in a state of growth when combined with the second component, emotional wellness techniques.

In addition to addressing problems as they occur, there are many ways to maintain a general feeling of well-being through life's ups and downs. This emotional maintenance prevents stress from accumulating over time. It can also help you return to your normal disposition and move forward more quickly after you have addressed an acute issue.

Below is a list of techniques that you may try to incorporate into your routine. They can help you relieve stress, maintain your psychological health, and persevere through adversity. Most importantly, they enable you to improve your emotional state and control your response to stress in the future.

Techniques for Managing Your Emotional State

- **Exercise** – Exercise releases endorphins that can improve your mood; being fit contributes to overall health and well-being.
- **Deep Breathing** – The relaxing, therapeutic effects of deep breathing can alleviate stress and reduce anxiety.
- **Meditation** – Mental focus can reduce stressful thoughts and negative emotions, relaxing the body and mind.
- **"15-Minute Time"** – Allocating just 15 minutes to life maintenance can be enough time to keep life stress from building up and becoming overwhelming; cleaning your living space and organizing your life can reduce feelings of disarray and provide mental breaks from bigger issues.
- **Time with Friends** – Social interaction and the ability to confide in others can be therapeutic for you if you feel like you are shouldering a heavy burden.
- **Vacation** – The change of scenery and the temporary reprieve from daily responsibilities can help you recuperate if you are feeling weary or stagnant.

- **Saying No** – The ability to choose what not to do is as important as the ability to choose what to do; reducing your burden can improve your ability to maintain your mental well-being.

- **Hobbies** – Taking up a hobby can provide you with an outlet for creativity and skills development if you are not feeling challenged elsewhere; when life stagnates or gets too difficult in one area, you can take up a new activity in another area to continue to grow during this time.

- **Planning** – Planning can help you be more productive if your life becomes chaotic and busy; when you are organized, the same workload will feel less overwhelming.

- **Adequate Sleep** – Having sufficient time for the body and mind to rest, recover, and prepare leads to an improved overall mood; when you are busy, you tend to sacrifice sleep, which causes you to become irritable and moody.

- **Moderation** – The regulation of any activity can prevent it from negatively affecting your mood; many emotional issues are caused by too much or too little of something (e.g., caffeine, alcohol, sugar, work, television, exercise, rest).

- **Gratitude** – Switching your focus to what you have and what is helping you can change your sad, angry, or overwhelmed feelings into more happy, grateful, and hopeful ones; if you focus too much on life's roadblocks, you may lose sight of your assets, support, and potential and feel outmatched.

- **Routines** – Keeping a routine can streamline your life, increase your productivity, allow you to focus on critical issues, and help you maintain a sense of normalcy during difficult situations.

- **Forgiveness** – Giving yourself permission to release negative emotions you feel toward yourself, another, or a situation allows you to move forward in a better emotional state; forgiveness helps you alleviate your pain, resentment, and anger toward past events so that you can focus on the future.

Together, these emotional processing and management techniques help you to maintain a healthy emotional state through daily stresses or major life events. You can continue to practice and develop these techniques to understand your emotions, diagnose issues, and formulate constructive responses.

An example of a time in which these processes can be helpful is the death of a loved one. When someone you care for deeply is suddenly taken from you, you may feel devastated. You need time to grieve, which is why friends, family, and employers may give you space to process your emotions and handle your affairs.

During that time, you can reflect on why that person meant so much to you and whether unresolved issues make the event especially hurtful. You may notice that this event is more difficult for you because the person contributed so much to your well-being and success. You can then decide that since you cannot reverse the tragedy, you can at least console others and provide a proper service honoring that person. You can remember and appreciate the person's life and take a moment to pay your respects.

Once the funeral services have concluded, you can then use daily rituals such as running to recover emotionally. You can dedicate time to sorting through any lingering regret. You can take comfort in friends and family. It takes time, but you can slowly recover and move on with your life even through the darkest of tragedies.

By adopting emotional wellness and processing practices, you should have more control over your emotional and physical reactions to life's challenges. Practicing activities that maintain your well-being will allow you to handle stress more effectively. Processing your emotions, taking action to improve situations you can influence, and letting go of your frustration over the uncontrollable factors can help you become more emotionally resilient. While you cannot control all things in your reality, you can control how you respond. Let your emotions tell you when something is right or wrong, good or bad, or needing attention or not, then hold yourself responsible for your reaction.

As you practice taking appropriate actions in response to your emotions, remember that your response can be as simple as a change in what you want or a change in what you believe to be true. Many people are angered, saddened, or annoyed every time they encounter a situation because of their beliefs about it, and changing those beliefs can change their reactions in the future.

If you are testy at every perceived slight against you, for example, you may believe that others are out to get you. However, it is more likely that they are ignorant, forgetful, in a hurry, or preoccupied with a personal issue. Most people are focused so much on their own problems that they do not notice that they said or did something to offend you.

In such circumstances, it may benefit you more to believe in an understandable and excusable reason because it leads to more constructive behaviors and less wasted time seething over the problem. If you exude anger and bitterness, your life will begin to be more influenced by your emotional state than by the original offense. Change your beliefs about the situation, and your emotional reaction will change as a result.

Even if another person intentionally insulted you, it does not benefit you to hold that anger for too long. You cannot rid the world of all jerks, and over-the-top revenge stories like *The Count of Monte Cristo*, where a wronged person dedicates his whole existence to revenge,[77] make for great entertainment but do not serve as a blueprint for finding constructive meaning in your life. Letting the anger, sadness, depression, or frustration hold you back will allow the wrong to harm you even more.

You may master these emotional management techniques and still not know what will make you happy in life. In this situation, you can use your emotions as a guide for what your direction, decision, or action *should be*. As a human being, you have the unique ability to imagine and visualize situations without actually experiencing them. You have foresight and planning. You can mentally construct a scenario and then emotionally react to a possible (but not yet realized) scenario.

Your brain's prefrontal cortex is responsible for providing the planning and executive functions that allow for complex analysis of hypothetical situations. It is a large part of what makes humans the most cognitively advanced creature on Earth. However, this function is even more useful when used in conjunction with the limbic system—specifically, the amygdala—that processes emotions. With these two capabilities combined, you can now imagine future events, fill in gaps in knowledge with various assumptions, and then see how your emotions change in response to the hypothetical scenario.

No other living creature on Earth has this advanced relationship between their emotions and their imagination. **Use it.** If you are not sure whether something in life will make you happy, you can always test it first by imagining yourself being, doing, or having it. Your thoughts will trigger an emotional reaction that will give you immediate feedback as to your opinion. You may not have the right information to judge the situation fairly, so gather that information, update your beliefs, and reassess your feelings.

You will inevitably feel differently than others do about the same experience, such as when others like food that makes you queasy. Differences of opinion are normal, as everyone has different desires, beliefs, and experiences. Therefore, you do not have to let others' feelings influence yours. If they are trying to discourage you from doing something that contributes to your growth, they could be leading you astray. They may believe that they have your best interest in mind, but you may not agree.

When being influenced, you have to determine whether to listen to others or follow your emotions. Given the same information and assumptions, your emotions will be more accurate because they also factor in your desires and experiences. If they have information that you do not have, however, then that knowledge may change how you feel about the situation. You ultimately decide whether your desires, beliefs, and experiences are accurate, leading you to the appropriate emotional response, so you have control over your emotions and others' influence on them.

For example, you may have someone tell you that you should not draw because it is a waste of time (experience). You may love to draw (desire) but also care about her opinion (belief). As a result, you feel upset (emotion). This feeling will only go away by changing one of these three factors. If you hated drawing (desire), you would not feel bad when someone spoke negatively about it. If you believed that the person's opinion was worthless (belief), you may feel indifferent. If you avoid her or change her mind (experience), you will no longer be exposed to the stimulus that caused the emotional response. Your ability to control these three aspects of any situation gives you the power to influence your own feelings and accept or reject someone else's influence.

This effect applies when you are trying to persuade others as well. While you may have plenty of facts and anecdotal evidence, they have to decide between your argument and how they felt before you spoke. For this reason, salespeople and marketers will tell you to tap into people's emotions when you try to attract buyers. If you can make someone feel strongly, then you have appealed to their deeply held desires and beliefs that trigger an emotional response and drive them to act. Therefore, you can effectively guide someone toward growth and away from harm with a factual argument that stirs someone's emotions.

Others' emotional feedback is helpful for you as well. Humans evolved to be able to express their feelings non-verbally so their peers could quickly tell if something was wrong and respond appropriately. You can use others' non-verbal cues to understand their emotions, desires, and beliefs, which can help you improve the way that you interact with them. You may even find that the way in which you are approaching a situation is making the situation worse and not better. Pay attention to their feelings to gather that information and improve your relationships.

Emotions help you understand yourself and others, and they give you deep insight into what truly matters in life. People who tell you to "be yourself" or "be true to yourself" when you ask them for guidance are telling you just that: you feel like yourself when your behaviors and experiences are in alignment with your beliefs and desires. If you try to act like someone you are not or do something you do not want to do, your feelings will signal the resulting misalignment to you. When you tell someone else to follow her heart, you are telling her to search her feelings for direction and meaning.

Your emotions are a powerful tool in your pursuit of growth and fulfillment in life. They signal what is beneficial or harmful to you, what is important to you, which experiences you enjoy, what you want in life, and what beliefs you hold. While they can be manipulated, you can manage them effectively when you know how and why they are signaling to you. Monitor and assess your feelings to get a better understanding of your current state and your progress in life.

QUESTIONS

Questions That Help You Understand Your Emotions

Your answers to these questions will help you understand your emotions. When you are done answering them, you should be more in tune with what your emotions are telling you about your state so that you can use them to diagnose problems and identify solutions. This chapter's content provides guidance on how to think about these questions, but only you can supply the definitive answers for your life.

1. How do you feel when:
    * you achieve a goal or obtain something you really want?
    * you are on the path toward achievement?
    * you are learning something new?
    * you believe that you can achieve something?
    * you strongly desire something?
    * you are disinterested in something?
    * you are struggling to understand or do something?
    * someone blocks you from attaining your goal?
    * you believe that you are failing at something?

- you fail at something?
- you quit at something?
- you believe that someone will harm you?
- someone harms you?
- you do not even want to get up in the morning?

2. What are your emotions telling you about an experience when you feel:

- love?
- joy?
- excitement?
- contentment?
- boredom?
- annoyance?
- frustration?
- anger?
- fear?
- sadness?
- depression?

3. How effective are you at understanding and diagnosing your emotions when you experience them? How can you improve?

4. What can you do to improve how you react to negative emotions?

   Examples: I can perceive failure as a learning experience; I can handle frustration by reminding myself that it signals how much I want to attain the outcome

5. What can you do to improve your emotional state when you hold negative feelings?

   Examples: I can go for a run, talk to a friend, or watch a movie

6. What can you do to maintain emotional health and wellness?

   Examples: I can meditate regularly, get enough sleep, and keep my workspace free of clutter and distractions

EXERCISES

Activities That Help You Understand Your Emotions

Completing these exercises will result in improved emotional awareness, management, and response.

Thought Exercise: Identify emotions that you wish to understand and manage more effectively. For each emotion, evaluate its cause and your response by answering the following questions:

- Which events trigger those emotions?
- What actions do you take in response to those emotions?
- Having learned what your emotions are telling you, should you respond differently?

The goal of this exercise is to understand how you can use the feedback that your emotions are providing to take more effective action. If you are responding in ways that contribute to your growth, then you are making the most of your emotional feedback. If you are responding destructively, see what you can do to change your reaction.

Brainstorming Exercise: Identify a difficult or stressful situation that you are currently facing or have recently faced. For this experience, brainstorm ways that you can process your emotions effectively.

How can you:

- give yourself time to process your thoughts and emotions?
- eliminate distractions that you may use to avoid the issue?
- keep asking, "Why?" regarding your reaction to an event?
- review your past experiences for patterns in your responses?
- identify which causes are within your control or influence?
- accept the uncontrollable factors?
- create an action plan to address the controllable issues?
- let go of the emotion and let the feedback subside?
- move forward?

Example: I am currently dealing with a major setback at work. My project is failing, and I feel frustrated.

- **Give yourself time to process your thoughts and emotions** – *I can talk through my problem with a friend or go for a walk outside where I can think.*

- **Eliminate distractions that you may use to avoid the issue** – *I can turn off my electronic devices and get away from other issues.*

- **Keep asking, "Why?" regarding your reaction to an event** – *I can keep myself honest by asking, "Why am I so bothered by this situation? Is that the real reason why I feel that way?"*

- **Review your past experiences for patterns in your responses** – *I can ask others if they have ever felt the same way or have seen me react in the same way in similar situations. If so, I can look for a theme; if not, I can determine why my response is different this time.*

- **Identify which causes are within your control or influence** – *I can review which parameters of the project are set and where my actions can influence its direction going forward. If I believe that the timeline is rigid, I can confirm with the project manager.*

- **Accept the uncontrollable factors** – *I have to take a deep breath and realize that there is nothing I can do now to change the past. I can identify and set aside the things I cannot change, such as my colleagues' personalities and the project budget.*

- **Create an action plan to address the controllable issues** – *I can take my action items, which are to communicate project issues to leadership and recommend changing its scope, and I can schedule dedicated time to follow through with my plan.*

- **Let go of the emotion and let the feedback subside** – *I have to tell myself that I have done what I can and then give myself permission to detach when I go home. I can then distract myself or focus on what I appreciate in my personal life to shift my emotional state.*

- **Move forward** – *I can take action now where I can, commit to avoiding these issues in the future, and switch my focus to other areas of my life when I am satisfied with my response.*

This exercise improves your emotional resilience, which is your ability to handle stress and return to a healthier emotional state. Acknowledge and feel the emotion, then practice ways to act constructively when something is within your control and accept it when it is uncontrollable. With improvement, you should be able to address issues more effectively and recover more quickly from setbacks.

Creative Exercise: Take the collage that you were working on in the Desire and Belief chapters. Starting with the Appreciation area, look at each item and think about how these things make you feel. Shut your eyes and remember experiencing these events or having/using/consuming these things. Feel both the positive emotions and the appreciation that comes with these memories. When you are done, write down your emotions in a section with the heading "How I Feel about What I Have" placed to the left of the Appreciation column. Alternatively, you may find and paste pictures of facial expressions that reflect your emotions.

Next, view each item on the Desire side and think about how it would make you feel to have that thing or experience. Look at the qualities you listed having and think about how those qualities will allow you to attain these things. Now, shut your eyes and imagine the moment when you attain what you want. How does it feel? Write those feelings down (or paste pictures of those emotions) in a section with the heading "How I Feel about What I Want" placed to the right of the Desire column.

If you are having trouble imagining attaining what you want, imagine taking that first step and making progress toward your goal. If you seem to have a clear view of what you want and do not feel a strong emotion, it may just be what you think you should want and not what you actually want. You may see how it feels when you imagine not getting it to confirm. In any case, use the emotional feedback to identify opportunities to adjust your desires and beliefs accordingly.

In this exercise, your feelings either validate your desires and beliefs regarding your stated growth areas and experiences or signal a misalignment between them. Make sure to be as accurate as you can when imagining a potential future state so that your emotions properly reflect what it would feel like if it happened.

Negative emotions indicate misaligned beliefs or inaccurate desires, so adjust them accordingly. Also, check for unrealistic beliefs about your emotions; assuming that you will be happy forever after the attainment of a goal or miserable forever if you do not attain it are both inaccurate. There will always be something new after you attain or fail to attain each desire. Finally, note any mixed feelings that may arise if you have desires that compete for time and resources. Your belief that you may have to choose between them and make tradeoffs may feel unsettling.

Note: You may wish to leave space on, next to, and below your collage for future chapters' creative exercises.

Writing Exercise: Take your list of growth areas with their associated experiences, action items, desirability scores, and feasibility scores from first four chapters' writing exercises. For each growth area, write down how you feel about your current state and score your happiness on a scale of 1 to 10 (1 being depressed; 5 being bored; 10 being fulfilled). You may wish to sense and describe your current state first to elicit an emotional response. Then, for each experience or action item, write down how you expect to feel afterward and rate that state on the happiness scale. Again, you may wish to visualize your future emotional state first.

This exercise will signal whether your goals, experiences, desires, and beliefs are in alignment and serve as a reminder of how your deliberate action can improve your well-being. If you surface issues with your beliefs or desires, you may make changes or reprioritize your list. Note how changing your desires and beliefs influences how you feel. Your emotions will help you determine whether the list you have created to this point is right for you and prioritized correctly.

If your happiness score is still lower than you would like, you can then adjust the goal or experiences to see if they are too much or too little for you. Raising the goal can increase your desire but decrease your belief, and lowering it does the opposite. This adjustment keeps you from feeling bored or overwhelmed, respectively. Not everything has to put you in a state of bliss, but optimizing these four components can put you in the best state of mind to take action.

At the end of the exercise, you should have calibrated the list so that the items on it bring you excitement, joy, hope, or optimism for what you will do, be, or have in the future.

Example:

Growth Area	Current Feelings & Happiness Level	Experiences	Action Items	Future Feelings & Happiness Level
Physical Growth	Feeling: Stagnant, unhealthy Happiness Level: 5	Exercise	Sign up to a gym	Feeling: Energetic, fit, healthy Happiness Level: 8
Social Growth	Feeling: Sad, lonely Happiness Level: 2	Club activities	Mark meetings on calendar	Feeling: Optimistic, appreciated Happiness Level: 7

Note: The above example does not show all of the information you will bring from the previous writing exercises; it is possible that this chapter's teachings may cause you to refine that information.

OUTCOME

After reading this chapter, you should have a clear understanding of how your emotions act as indicators of whether your experiences are helping or hindering your growth. You should have gone through your list of growth areas and used your emotions to verify that you are focusing on the right things and going in the right direction at the right pace. You should also have evaluated the alignment between your experiences, desires, and beliefs to make adjustments that will improve how you feel. Finally, you should monitor your feelings for changes in those variables.

When you have your updated list, you are ready to proceed to the next chapter.

Ethics

Ethics are principles for your growth within a society

> *"Do unto others as you would have them do unto you."*
>
> — The Golden Rule[78]

> *"Let me give you a definition of ethics: It is good to maintain and further life; it is bad to damage and destroy life."*
>
> — Albert Schweitzer[79]

PRINCIPLES OF ETHICS

- Ethics are rules that allow life forms to grow safely together
- Ethics help humans grow effectively without harming others
- Your ethics factor everyone's well-being into your behavior
- Without ethics, you could not grow peacefully in a society
- If the ethics of an act are unclear, evaluate its consequences

ETHICS AND THE MEANING OF LIFE

Live and let live. Ethics are the moral principles that life follows to allow for safe, mutually assured growth with other life. The only way for civilized life to coexist peacefully is to have ethics. Along with evolutionary advantages such as an advanced brain, an ability to communicate with language, and opposable thumbs, ethics are key to enabling humans to grow and develop more than any other species on Earth.

Ethics are rules that allow life forms to grow safely together

All life forms generally behave in ways that enable growth and prevent harm. Natural selection will filter out organisms that do not act in the best interest of their genes, while the ones that follow the best rules of conduct toward that goal will survive. Instructions on how to behave are built into life forms' deoxyribonucleic acid (DNA). All cellular life on Earth, from microscopic organisms to complex animals, contains DNA-based instructions. These rules instruct organisms to consume nutrients, repel harmful material, replicate, and perform other life-sustaining functions.

As organisms become more complex and have greater capabilities for survival, they have more behaviors at their command. Given these conditions, the rules for optimal living get much more sophisticated. Inherent rules for how animals behave are known as instincts, and they will inherit the instincts that kept their ancestors alive. As diverse organisms evolve in the same environment, they will fiercely compete for space and resources, learning to fight, eat, or avoid each other. Predators that evolved to eat other animals have instincts for hunting, while animals that evolved to evade predators have instincts for blending into their surroundings.

In such a competitive environment, multiple organisms that followed rules not to harm each other while pursuing their own goals would have an advantage. Commensalism and mutualism are forms of symbiosis between two species where the incentive for both parties is to let the other pursue its growth objectives unimpeded. In mutualism, both parties benefit from the interaction and would be worse off if they tried to hurt one another. For example, a shrimp may eat algae growing on a fish for energy, while the fish is cleaned and protected from disease. In commensalism, one party benefits and so has an incentive not to harm the other. The other party is not harmed and so has no incentive to discourage the interaction. An example of this relationship is when a vulture follows a lion to consume the remains of its prey. Natural selection favors these interactions because neither species is harmed while at least one benefits.

All interactions between organisms are a delicate balance of the probability of being better off (i.e., the benefit) compared to the risk of being harmed (i.e., the cost). For carnivores and parasites, harming other organisms means staying alive, so the risk of being killed is lower than the risk of dying if they do not eat. For prey, being near food and water keeps them alive, but they are likely to encounter their predators in those areas. Organisms of the same species compete for the same resources but also are more likely to acquire and defend those resources as a group.

It is within the same species and between kin where the benefits are the greatest and risks are the lowest. Species have similar communication capabilities, intelligence, and goals, while close relatives share the most DNA and are most likely to share instincts to trust, care for, and protect each other. Cooperative groups succeed, so their genes thrive. In contrast, organisms that were too trusting would have died if they confused competitors or predators for allies, so evolution favored kin-based relationships and cohabitation.

Advanced organisms developed more effective ways of influencing each other's behavior safely. These social species could live harmoniously within larger groups and achieve more success if they adopted more sophisticated rule systems. These social animals evolved nuances in their behavior toward kin, elders, children, friends, strangers, and transgressors.

When life transitions from an every-organism-for-itself environment to a group environment, its rules must change. Organisms now have to factor in the welfare of the group as well as themselves. Rules to behave in ways that factor in the growth or harm to the self and others are known as ethics. Ethics are the foundation of all cooperative behavior and are necessary for a social animal to maximize its potential for growth and minimize its risk of being harmed.

Ethics are not divinely provided, universal, or unchanging. Life needed billions of years to evolve into social species (e.g., dogs, birds) that could demonstrate ethical values such as loyalty, cooperation, and reciprocity. These behaviors were not naturally right or wrong; they just tended to lead to a higher likelihood of reproduction.

Unfortunately, animals also inherit harmful behaviors that keep the group alive. For example, female mantises will bite their partners' heads off after copulating when food is scarce,[80] and male lions will kill the cubs of a competing pride and copulate with the females.[81] Again, these behaviors do not have an inherent morality; they just have a positive (or neutral) effect on the ability of species to pass on their genes.

Of course, groups would not survive if their members killed each other frequently enough. Instead, rules that evolve within groups are more likely to involve cooperation and non-fatal competition. These rules are set via instinct or education and include staying in groups, following group norms, and behaving in ways that benefit or protect the group. While deviant behavior will inevitably manifest in members of the group, mechanisms such as peer pressure and reciprocity are also developed within social species to encourage animals to adhere to group norms.

Once a group is formed with its own set of rules and enforcement mechanisms, it can then apply its moral code to all members. Animals then have to be able to determine which individuals are in the group or outside the group to apply the proper ethical standards.[82] Different groups follow different rules, so identifying the group that another organism is a part of allows the animal to know how to treat it and what behaviors to expect of it.

Unfortunately, there will never be a point at which all living things can adopt shared ethics to stop harming each other. This in-group/out-group dynamic necessarily evolved due to the dependency of life on other life for food, the competition for limited resources, and the inability of most species to follow a shared rule set consistently at scale. These three reasons prevent life from having a set of ethics that can be universally applied.

First, living organisms have evolved to the point where they are completely interdependent. Herbivores eat plants to survive. Carnivores eat animals. Omnivores are flexible enough to consume either. Microorganisms decompose dead organic matter, and animal waste fertilizes the soil for plant nutrition. Most life requires the death of other life to survive. In addition, all life forms compete with each other for space, so one's existence prevents other life forms from existing in that space. Any cooperation between advanced life forms would, therefore, be to their own benefit and to other species' detriment. Lastly, not all organisms have the advanced cognition to overcome their innate programming, and not all organisms evolved the advanced social capabilities that enable cooperative behaviors.

The combination of intelligence, communication, and other skills enables animals to learn, teach, and follow rules of behavior that are best for themselves and the group. While all life follows rules to survive, only advanced social animals have the capabilities necessary to acknowledge, agree to, and follow the ethical rules of the group. With the ability to override instinct with learned behavior, advanced organisms engage in deliberate cooperation.

The core requirement for social animals to cooperate deliberately is to agree not to harm each other in pursuit of their individual goals. For maximum group benefit, they would agree to help each other. Ethics are critical to life because one life form is limited in its ability to grow and protect itself. By agreeing to a shared set of ethical rules that benefit all involved, animals have a higher probability of (and potential for) safety, growth, and well-being.

Cooperation is a risky proposition for life forms without advanced methods of communication and cognition because their rules and punishments are almost never understood without experiencing the consequences. In these situations, anyone can misunderstand the rules, take advantage of the lowered defenses, or not reciprocate. Life forms with advanced methods of communication (e.g., humans) who try to communicate and cooperate with other life (e.g., snakes) expose themselves to similar risks.

Humans, however, can cooperate with other humans to imagine potential future scenarios, set rules in advance, and agree on consequences. As a result, ethics in society can prevent harm from occurring before it ever happens, which is one of the most effective ways to keep the species alive and thriving. Ultimately, human ethics are the most sophisticated mechanism for minimizing harm to a group and maximizing its potential for growth. While other social animals demonstrate morality, humans have improved reasoning, language, planning, and self-control that enable their rules to be more clear, nuanced, and comprehensive.

Even with these advantages, humans are still influenced by both "nature" (i.e., genetics) and "nurture" (i.e., the environment) when developing ethical social behavior. Studies in psychology, neuroscience, and behavioral economics, for example, have shown that humans have an innate sense of fairness and a natural tendency to reciprocate.[83,84] Having these ethics be instinctual makes it safer to trust and help others because they are more likely to respond in kind.

Additionally, scientists believe that the evolutionary advantage of cooperating as a group is what led to social emotions such as shame, embarrassment, and guilt.[85] These emotions are triggered when a person commits what he or the group considers to be an unethical act, and they are projected nonverbally to both encourage the offender to apologize and allow the offended party to forgive. This natural ethical indicator system is missing in sociopaths, so they have more trouble behaving ethically and require more social and moral education to fit into society. Empathy, sympathy, mirroring/mimicking behavior, remorse, apologizing, and forgiveness are all examples of how most humans are genetically optimized for interpersonal interactions. Due to their emotional impact, ethics have a strong influence on behavior.

Ethical predispositions can be overridden by experience, however. Traumas, brain damage, or improper moral education can all lead to unethical behavior. The instinctual bias toward fairness and reciprocity that people have can be conditioned out of them. If the world treats them harshly, they may treat strangers with a cold distance even after benefiting from their generosity. In these cases, past experiences of being mistreated or manipulated can lead them to be so distrusting that they always have their guard up and are never generous to anyone again.

These exceptional examples show how important ethics are to growth. Ethics are critical for humans to be able to focus on growth activities instead of protection activities. They cannot make as much progress in their desired growth areas if they believe that others might harm them. Therefore, when one person can agree with another to follow the same rules, the optimal way for her to pursue her growth is to do so in a way that does not encroach on the other person's right to grow. This approach provides the best chance for everyone to fulfill his or her dreams.

Because ethics require a person to determine what is best for herself while not being harmful to others, deciding the best action in any situation is much more complicated than pure self-interest. After years of study, social scientists factored these group dynamics and social considerations into economics and psychology through concepts such as game theory. These approaches do not assume that people only care about maximizing their own utility, so they more accurately reflect thought processes that consider what is best for the individual and best for the group.

A well-known example of considering the actions and consequences of multiple parties is the Prisoner's Dilemma.[86] In this scenario, two prisoners are being interrogated in separate rooms and cannot communicate with each other. Each prisoner has the option to testify against the other or remain quiet, which creates a few possible outcomes:

- They both keep quiet and receive a short prison sentence.
- They betray each other and receive a moderate prison sentence.
- One of them testifies against the other in exchange for no time in prison; the other stays quiet and receives a long prison sentence.

The best outcome for the group is for both prisoners to keep quiet, but each individual's best outcome is to get the other person to keep quiet while he or she testifies against the other. If they betray each other, they are both worse off than if they keep quiet.

In real life, there are many situations where the best outcome for a group is for everyone to follow the rules even though each individual has an incentive to break them. For example, society could maximize its collective wealth if no one stole from anyone else, but an individual citizen would benefit from stealing if he knew that no one would steal from him. However, humans would not have survived for very long as a species if no one had qualms about harming each other or the group for personal gain. As a result, society does establish a common set of rules and norms that most people follow for the benefit of the group.

Real life is, of course, much more complicated than the basic Prisoner's Dilemma scenario. This model assumes that people are perfectly rational and that there are no external factors or considerations influencing their decisions. If this situation were real, there would be many ethical considerations involved. The severity of the crime would influence their decisions. The level of trust and the role of each person in the crime would have effects. Both parties' ethics and loyalties toward themselves, each other, their peer group, and the public good would be taken into account. The best decision for each party would be based on much more than just the jail time and the other's decision. Ethics and decision making become very complex very quickly.

Fortunately, humans' ethics and decision making get more complex over time as their mental models more accurately represent the real world. Most people start with simple rules such as treating others how they want to be treated as an initial guide. Then, they have to evolve these absolute principles to more nuanced ethics that inform precise decisions and actions impacting many parties in both positive and negative ways.

The weakness of simple rules is that they do not consider all factors and cannot account for the variability of ethics between individuals and cultures. While broad ethics such as "do not harm others" sound easy to follow, they can be very difficult to implement since everyone has different growth areas and different definitions of harm. These complexities make ethical behavior impossible to exhibit at all times from all perspectives.

One of the complexities making absolute rules difficult is that the same act may be helpful in one situation and harmful in another. A person may light a fire to keep someone warm, and that fire may get out of control and cause harm. A couple could ask to cut in line ahead of others because they are running late, but then someone else in that line might miss a job interview. It is not always easy to determine whether a behavior is ethical because it is difficult to understand the intent and predict the consequences.

When lighting a fire, society would typically agree that warming a cold, sick person and preventing the fire from spreading are both ethical. The person lighting the fire has to weigh the benefits of the warmth against the risks of property damage to make the best decision. In the line-cutting incident, the person who is in line has to analyze whether it is ethical to deny the couple permission because it was their responsibility to be on time or unethical because she knows the negative consequences of that decision.

Because people have different genetics, past experiences, motivations, and incentives, they will perceive and evaluate circumstances differently. Any situation, therefore, is open to multiple ethical interpretations. The couple asking to cut in line may believe that their lateness was unavoidable and that their request is ethical since it will benefit them and not hurt anyone else. The person allowing the line-cutting may remember that she has been late before and has had kind people help her. The person denying it may believe that the couple was probably not really late, that their lateness was their fault, or that their plight is no worse than others who have waited patiently in line. These perspectives could all be valid based on the person's knowledge of the situation, her past experience, and the weight she gives each factor.

Unfortunately, this room for variation leaves people susceptible to rationalization. Because humans want to see themselves as ethical and will experience shame and embarrassment when they are not, they may change their perception of the situation to avoid a negative self-image. They also need to make sense of the world and their own motives. As a result, their brains are incentivized to find a good reason for their behavior after the fact. Even someone with strong ethics can find an excuse for their own behavior while condemning another person in a similar situation. Anyone can rationalize and justify their actions.

Ethical differences are difficult to reconcile, which complicates the defining and enforcing of shared ethics. People usually look for and associate with others who match the ethics and values that they have. While no two individuals will agree on absolutely everything, a person will typically pick a set of values, such as political, religious, or familial beliefs, and identify with groups that share them. Shared ethics are critical to establishing trust and rapport, and they also help make the group safer as a whole. Breaking a rule—even if it does not cause direct harm—can cause a person to be ostracized from the group entirely because of how it can affect the group's long-term well-being.

To reconcile these differences, humans self-organized into societies and established a sophisticated rule system based on those shared beliefs. These rules first seek to prevent harm and then attempt to balance the growth and well-being of the individual with the growth and well-being of the group. These rules are extremely complex to weigh various factors and account for a multitude of situations. Laws, rights, codes, bylaws, regulations, and standard procedures are all examples of rules that groups agree upon and set to guide people toward appropriate behavior. There is often no perfect answer, so society has to define rudimentary rules and evolve them as they learn from experience.

To ensure that everyone follow the rules, the group (or a subset of the group representing its interests) has to establish, understand, and agree upon punishments for violating them. An ethical justice system seeks to apply rules and punishments as consistently as possible. Humans have a few mechanisms to try to garner compliance from all parties, including social pressures, rewards, and penalties. The degree of benefit or harm of an act usually determines how strong the reward or punishment is.

To evaluate whether an act complies with the rules, the group factors in the person's intent, his or her behavior, and the result of the behavior. For example, a person may have an intent to harm, act in a harmful way, and achieve a harmful outcome. These acts, such as premeditated murders or planned robberies, are clearly unethical and receive the harshest punishments. Alternatively, a person may intend to cook someone a meal and accidentally burn her with the pot when serving the food. Because the harm was unintentional and the act is normally beneficial, punishments are usually less severe or non-existent. Finally, if a person attempts a crime and fails, they are punished less severely for the less harmful outcome but are still culpable for the negative intent and behavior. The intention, action, and result all factor into the group's ethical judgments.

Once these punishments are set, people have greater incentive to follow the rules than break them. As a result, gaining at the expense of others occurs less frequently. Some unethical behavior will remain, however, such as when people cheat at a small, diluted cost to the group. An example is the Tragedy of the Commons, where individuals overexploit community resources for personal benefit without considering how their behavior at scale would harm the group.[87] In response to people who exploit the system, the group will continue to adjust the incentives so that the lowest number of people behave to the group's detriment as possible.

Setting rules involves a trade-off between simplicity and universal applicability. Simpler rules are easier to follow, but adhering to simple rules in complex situations may not be the most ethical approach. Because of this trade-off, laws are not always perfectly matched to ethics. A person may do something that is ethical but not legal, such as disobeying traffic laws when there are no other cars on the road to get a dying person to the hospital. Alternatively, he or she may do something that is legal but not ethical, such as using the law to overwhelm a business competitor with litigation until it discontinues operations.

Even when the rules and societal ethics do align, not everyone may want to enforce or follow them under certain circumstances. If the violator is a friend or relative, for example, the enforcer may not want to punish him. If the rules inconvenience people, they may risk the punishment to avoid the personal sacrifice.

Because the rules are prone to exceptions and disagreements, sub-groups may subvert them or establish and enforce their own set. An example is organized crime, which offers illegal goods (e.g., alcohol) or services (e.g., gambling) to citizens when they are prohibited by law. Because mobsters are subverting the rules, they then cannot rely on official law enforcers to help them when violators of their rules need to be punished. New ethics, such as "snitches get stitches" (i.e., retaliate against people who talk to law enforcement) and "honor among thieves" (i.e., criminals should not betray each other), spread within these sub-groups to protect themselves from the punishments of the overall group. These ethics come with associated penalties, such as broken bones or torture, to ensure that members of the sub-group comply.

Humans will continue to strive for a perfect, universal set of ethics that everyone can agree to and follow. Many people, for example, look to a deity to provide them with universal rules and a post-life reward and punishment system. Religions include exact sets of rules for everyone to follow with a divine incentive to follow them. Followers believe that their deity can monitor everyone's behavior at all times and deliver the final judgment of each person's lifetime character. It is the ultimate incentive to behave ethically even when no humans are watching.

Invoking divine authority may increase the likelihood of adhering to the rules, but it also reduces the flexibility to change ethics as circumstances change. This trade-off is unnecessary, however, as people do not have to appeal to divine authority to have an ethical society. Most people adhere to the rules because they are educated on their importance, incentivized by consequences, and genetically predisposed to cooperate. People who do not are usually miseducated on the rules, incentivized by the benefits of violating the rules, or genetically predisposed to deviant behavior. By not implying that ethics are universal and unchanging, society can best mature its ethical system.

Life establishes rules to maximize its potential for growth. Social animals set rules for their groups to ensure cooperation toward that same end. Ethics are agreements that life forms adhere to when taking actions that may affect others. Societies establish an extensive set of complex rules to maximize the potential for human growth and well-being, and they punish unethical behaviors to offset the benefits of non-compliance and ensure adherence. The ways that groups set and enforce these rules will substantially influence each individual's life journey.

Ethics help humans grow effectively without harming others

In modern human society, ethics serve two important functions:

- They set boundaries to prevent people from hindering others' growth. (Negative Ethics)
- They provide guidance as to what people should or

should not do to live virtuous, fulfilled, and meaningful lives. (Positive Ethics)

In a world of practically limitless possibilities for how people can live and grow, ethics provide a framework through which people can determine which approach is best for themselves, the people they care about, and society at large.

First and foremost, ethics help humans minimize issues within a group by setting rules that define when one person is hindering someone else's ability to grow. There are two core methods that modern societies use to do this: rights and laws. Rights are protections that humans have as members of a group (e.g., citizens of a country, members of the human race) that cannot be violated by other specified parties (e.g., the government). Examples include the right to vote, assemble, speak out against the government, or practice a religion. Laws are rules that discourage people within a group from behaviors that are harmful or could be harmful to others. Examples include laws against killing others or stealing their property.

These rights and laws are agreements among people in a civilized society to maintain peace and order by punishing certain behaviors. These rules are mainly intended to prevent harm, but they also encourage growth. People who are afraid of loss will try to protect what they have; people who feel safe will strive for success and contribute more to society.

The agreement to follow the rules is not sufficient, as the incentive for any member of a group is to break the rules while others follow them. To offset the benefits of exploiting others, the group enforces penalties on individuals who violate laws or rights. Once punishment has been established, the perpetrator risks his own freedom and well-being when he harms others. The result is a system that encourages everyone to follow the rules so that the group can thrive.

This legal system will contain a multitude of laws and penalties regarding its citizens' conduct. The system has to govern how individuals act toward each other and how their actions affect the group. It also has to determine how to weigh various factors and apply rules and punishments as consistently as possible under a variety of specific circumstances.

Rules and incentives are both important because there are many instances where one person can gain at the expense of another. Just like plants fight for sunlight and animals compete for resources, one human's growth trajectory may compete with, conflict with, or prevent the growth of others. For example, one may grow their wealth by taking it from someone else or by convincing a customer to buy his product instead of competitors' offerings.

This potential conflict in human interactions is why ethics and laws are necessary. The goal of ethics is to provide humans with a moral compass of what is and is not the right thing to do in any given situation. Whether humans are cooperating or competing, they agree to rules of conduct that ensure that these activities are beneficial to the group and fair to each individual.

Laws focus mainly on harming or inhibiting someone else's growth. If there is clear physical harm, there is usually a law against it. Murder is an example of clear physical harm, as the murderer intentionally causes the death of another person without justification. There is general agreement that this kind of behavior cannot be accepted in civilized society, so it is illegal. If an act causes harm that is not tangible or provable, however, it is often part of a moral or ethical code but not necessarily a law. Examples of morals that are more difficult to make laws are lying, sexual infidelity, swindling, or reneging on a promise. These acts are considered to be immoral, but their legality is conditional.

While most laws and ethics are about the treatment of others, often self-harm or abnormal behavior is considered immoral because it is self-destructive. Laws against self-destructive activities such as taking drugs or committing suicide are very controversial because many individuals believe that they have the right to do what they want with their own lives as long as they do not harm others. There are also blurry lines for what constitutes self-harm, as drugs and foods can be beneficial in the right amounts.

As a consequence, many laws will try to respect a person's right to harm himself while trying to regulate harmful substances that pose a risk to the group. One law may allow someone to tattoo or brand themselves, but another law may require healthcare professionals to notify authorities when a person is a danger to himself or others. One law may protect the recreational use of alcohol or tobacco, while others may ban explosives, automatic weapons, or narcotics such as cocaine and heroin. These laws are constantly evaluated to balance personal freedom with public safety.

In addition to regulating harmful acts and substances, many laws exist against behaviors that have a high risk of leading to harm. A law against jaywalking, for example, reduces the number of pedestrian deaths and automobile accidents. This law is passed to let people know that the behaviors are risky. The penalty encourages pedestrians to cross at crosswalks and not in the middle of the street. This law is expensive to enforce, so its value is in establishing social norms for human behavior. Because the act is not directly harmful, law enforcement often only applies penalties when it results in harm or excessive risk of harm.

Risk-mitigation laws also help determine fault and establish appropriate penalties when harm does occur from the risky behavior. For example, a pedestrian being hit by a vehicle while legally crossing the street is protected under the law, but a pedestrian intentionally obstructing traffic on a whim is violating the rules and will receive less protection. In these examples, jaywalking laws factor into how the legal system enforces other laws. This approach discourages risky behavior without necessarily penalizing every instance of it.

The government also uses taxes to reduce the negative impact of harmful products. It may tax tobacco and alcohol to reduce consumption and then fund programs that provide nicotine replacement therapy or support victims of alcohol abuse. The legislators who levy these taxes find them to be a fair compromise to preserve the personal freedom to consume these substances while reducing and addressing their negative public impact.

Any system has limits in its ability to protect people. Assuming that everyone who understands and agrees to the rules will follow them, the legal system can still only stop people from knowingly and willingly engaging in behaviors that cause harm to others. Individuals without full mental capacity, without intent to harm, or without knowledge of the rules can still violate them. Understanding that these people are not deliberately engaging in malicious behavior, the law often treats them differently. Even in an ethical society, accidents will still happen.

Through establishing rules, communicating them, accepting them, enforcing them, and identifying exceptions, humans can grow together as a group in the most effective way possible. The first goal of ethics is to prevent harm, and these social structures protect people from the risky, detrimental behavior of others.

The second function of ethics is to provide recommendations for how to approach life in the right way for the best outcome. This function is, in essence, the inverse of the first function. Negative ethics usually establish what **not** to do to minimize harm, costs, and pain. Positive ethics recommend how to approach something in the right way to maximize growth, benefits, and happiness.

In a free society, positive ethics are usually documented and communicated by knowledgeable, successful citizens or societal sub-groups (e.g., companies, clubs, teams) instead of being set and enforced by legal entities. While the whole group has to agree upon and abolish harmful behaviors, individuals are free to determine the most successful approach in their own endeavors.

In this model, members of the group will begin to provide general ethical guidelines, such as, "Never stop learning," "Respect your elders," and, "Help yourself first so that you have a greater capacity to help others." These recommendations suggest ways to behave that are beneficial to the follower without harming the group. Unlike laws, there are no legal penalties for not following them. As long as people are not hurting anyone, they can refuse to take in new ideas, despise authority, and repeatedly make personal sacrifices for others. Without a legal mandate, people choose to adopt positive ethics for their benefits.

Positive ethics can help guide someone toward meaning and fulfillment, but no universal set exists that applies to all people in every situation. The best approach will differ based on the person, the context, and the goal. For example, the "measure twice, cut once" mantra of carpenters is a good general rule to follow, but someone may only have time to measure once or may need to measure three times to reduce risk further. Similarly, exercising for an hour per day, three days per week may be enough for the average person to stay healthy, but an athlete training for a championship may need to practice for hours every day. Despite this variance, role models will often identify rules that apply to most people in most situations so that they may help as many people succeed in life as possible.

When these individuals have to generalize their ethics or recommend ethics to someone they do not know, they have to make assumptions about the person, the context, and the goal. Often, they assume that others' goals are similar to theirs, so they recommend ethics that are right for themselves. For example, people with a strong work ethic have career goals or find meaning in their employment, so they recommend hard work. Others may see it as just a paycheck to make a living and fund their leisure time. Ethics for social interaction often assume that a person is an extrovert, so they may not apply as well to introverts. This tendency is not merely egocentric; people are more credible and confident in recommending a practice to others when it worked for them. Given this risk, the giver and receiver of advice need to understand each other's goals, values, and situations to ensure that the recommended approach applies.

When combining positive and negative ethics, any human can

find the optimal approach to grow in life without harming others in the process. However, identifying these ethics in a group setting is difficult because everyone places different degrees of importance on different forms of growth. The importance that a person places on different parts of their life is also known as the values they hold.

Values define what is significant and meaningful to a person (e.g., goals, objectives, ideals, resources, life) and are the source of all ethics. Negative ethics exist to protect what someone values, and positive ethics exist to promote the right way to get, maintain, or adhere to what he or she values. Rights and laws protect shared values, such as life, liberty, the pursuit of happiness, and private property. Recommended approaches to success enable people to obtain or achieve what they value, such as friends, family, property, time, money, fame, marriage, world records, and status. Guidelines and recommendations help others behave in the best way toward their objective but are often not legally enforced unless not doing so will cause harm. People with different values will have different ethics, and ethics will change as values change.

Ethics vary significantly between people because everyone values different growth areas to different degrees. Most people will value their friends' and families' lives over strangers' lives, and some cultures place a higher value on children, the elderly, or women during emergencies. Some people care about money more than friends, family more than fame, or professional success over leisure time. Some citizens may value freedom above all else and are willing to sacrifice their own lives to defend it. Which values a person has and how he or she weighs them will influence his or her ethics and decision making.

A simple example of how values translate into rules is when a father has a valuable coin collection and sets a rule for his children not to touch it so that they do not damage it. The father values the coins and finds meaning in collecting and preserving them, so he sets the rule to protect them. He would also have advice for aspiring coin collectors for how to keep them in mint condition to promote his hobby. Together, those rules and recommendations form the best approach to coin collecting. If the coins become worthless or he stops valuing them, he may change his rules and ethics for handling them.

These ethics and values may influence others as well. Over time, his children may place great sentimental value on the coins. Alternatively, they may resent the coins if they were punished harshly for touching them or if they felt that their father valued the coins more than his family. Because ethics apply to group behavior, they cannot help but affect the group's relationships as well. Applied at a societal level, a nation's shared identity and values shape its ethics and laws, which can then influence the ethics and values of future generations.

The process of adopting shared values can take a long time, so it is often faster and easier for the group to ensure that new members follow the rules than it is to get them to understand why they are in place. Not surprisingly, then, many children first learn about values through the rules set to uphold them. There are many stories of children being forced to participate in family time only to realize how important family is later in life. According to research, the elderly cite, "I would have spent more quality time with my family," as one of their biggest regrets.[88] With this knowledge, parents may have ample cause to enforce "family night" or other shared activities. Though children may not be grateful at the time, they are likely to be when they are older.

From this perspective, it would seem to be prudent for people to learn and follow the general rules while trying to understand why they exist. Then, they can ascertain the nuances of when the rules should apply. Strictly following the rules will minimize early issues, but understanding their intent can help people achieve better outcomes if the system is not perfect.

Unfortunately, the literal language of rules may not convey their intent, and most people care more about whether others follow them than they do about whether they understand them. As a result, people can have difficulty connecting a rule to the reason why society follows it. Still, someone in the group should know the reasons why a rule exists in case conditions have changed in a way that makes it unnecessary.

The group needs to monitor conditions and make adjustments when appropriate so that it can continue to follow the best set of ethics for everyone involved. For example, if a group of early humans set a rule not to go into the woods because of the danger involved, it would need to revisit that rule if its main food sources became barren. If no one tested the rule to see whether it was more beneficial than harmful to go into the woods, the group could starve. Given the new conditions, someone could check to see if the danger was still present and prepare for it as he searched the forest for new food sources.

Monitoring rules becomes more important when groups establish them to reduce the probability of harm or increase the likelihood of benefit. These rules are more likely to be based on assumptions that could become invalid as conditions change. For example, society may have rules for how to treat people with a specific mental disorder to prevent them from being a harm to themselves and others. If a more effective approach with better outcomes becomes available, then those rules should be changed accordingly. If they are not changed, the old rules may be unfairly restricting the freedoms of these individuals now that their risk to society has been mitigated.

Understanding how negative and positive ethics can be set, monitored, and changed, society can now establish an effective governmental model. First, the group as a whole can identify the rules that must apply to everyone to prevent harm. Then, individuals can experiment with approaches, identify best practices for achieving certain goals, and recommend them to others. Finally, sub-groups can form and set arbitrary rules that its members must comply with as long as anyone can voluntarily join or leave. Collectively, this system will give every individual a firm list of "don'ts" to avoid harming others along with the freedom to discover the best "dos" for his or her optimal growth.

At the societal level, the group focuses on its shared values. Because everyone in society values human life and growth, the group can set general rules to avoid harming another unless it will immediately stop an equivalent or greater harm in progress. These rules establish peace and allow people to live without the constant fear of being harmed.

Once those societal laws are set, all rules of conduct are each person's ability to determine based on what he or she uniquely values. Successful people may recommend some common "dos" such as eating a balanced diet, getting plenty of sleep, exercising regularly, and being kind to others. Anyone can choose to follow them or choose to eat candy, get only two hours of sleep, avoid all forms of exercise, and refuse to help anyone. While some of these actions arguably cause self-harm over time, legal systems usually have higher thresholds for when self-destructive behavior requires government intervention.

Finally, individuals will almost always choose to form subgroups because of the power of working together in harmony toward the same goal. These sub-groups form around shared goals and values that may differ from the overall group, and they enforce both positive and negative ethics to ensure that they succeed. For example, a business, which is a group of people willfully working together to deliver a product or service to a customer, may set rules for all employees to follow a defined process for making a hamburger. The standard procedure enables the team to serve more customers, provide more value, and make more money. Everyone benefits from following this positive ethic. In another example, a university may enforce standards for submitting an academic paper.

In these situations, the business and the university can set positive ethics as rules because individuals have the freedom of association. If members of the group disagree with these rules, they can petition to change them or leave the group. They can also subversively violate them at the risk of having their employment terminated or being reprimanded by the university. Sub-groups that individuals voluntarily join have much more leeway to set positive ethics as rules than governmental bodies.

Even though each person can generally choose his or her own positive ethics in a free society, many people follow the sociocultural norms of their sub-groups. Humans' genetic predisposition toward social behavior benefits the group overall but may result in unconscious, thoughtless compliance with its norms. They will work the same number of hours as their peers or wear clothing that matches their professional or social situation. They could violate these norms without legal penalty, but they may pay a social price of being seen as lazy for not working enough or being asked to leave an event for not wearing the right attire. At worst, the sub-group may exclude them for not adhering to the norms.

While this three-tiered ethical system (society, self-organizing sub-groups, and individuals) is the most effective that humanity has found to foster growth among a group, it is not without exceptions. Jury duty, for example, is one of the positive ethics that may be required to enforce negative ethics in a justice system of the people, by the people, and for the people. However, voting may not be mandatory despite being an equally important civic duty. In either case, the societal tier has to determine which positive ethics are necessary for civilization to function.

This tier also has to determine the definition of harm and what constitutes a sufficient risk of harm to be unethical enough to warrant a law. Physical harm is most tangible and measurable, so that type is the easiest to translate into laws. Any non-consensual physical harm or direct, visible threat of violence can be legally punished. However, even these laws vary and change over time based on new innovations, such as when knowingly giving someone an untreatable illness could be considered a capital crime until a cure is found that prevents it from being fatal.

Ethical lines are even blurrier and more volatile with psychological and emotional harm. Bullying and harassment are examples of offenses where the rules have evolved to punish sustained psychological and emotional trauma in addition to any physical harm caused. As these forms of harm become more measurable, the rules may continue to evolve to discourage them.

The most difficult of all ethical lines to establish is when a person's behavior offends another. Someone who takes offense is feeling insulted when another person crossed his or her ethical boundaries. Throughout history, humans have tried to prevent behavior that they do not like. There have been laws against performing certain consensual sex acts, selling alcohol on Sundays, being naked in public, and using profanity. These laws were instituted because enough people in the group found them offensive enough to add disincentives and punishments.

Because harm is so difficult to define, anyone fighting for these laws will use intangible harm or potential harm as a rationale. Citizens looking to ban certain sex acts may cite the increased rate of sexually transmitted diseases. Opponents of public nudity will cite health concerns. Profanity law advocates may cite the effect on children's behavior. By identifying potential harm in acts that would otherwise be only considered offensive, objectionable, or indecent, activists can secure greater support for their causes.

People attempt to make positive ethics seem like negative ethics because society hesitates to mandate positive ethics as laws. In a free society, a lawmaker would be quickly rebuffed if he or she justified laws regulating sexual behavior by explaining that the only ethical form of sexual intercourse is the one that leads to reproduction. To maximize freedom, laws focus more on stating harmful behaviors to avoid than mandating proper behavior.

Society is best served by not making too many laws based on positive ethics, as generalizing what is best for everyone is impossible. People have different wants, needs, and interests, so they will follow different ethics in their pursuit of them. Those differences will lead to disagreements, and those disagreements will lead to some people being offended by or condemning others' behavior. Without harm, though, disagreement or offense is not an excuse to enforce positive ethics via laws. Instead, those individuals should follow ethics that work for them and exercise their freedom of association to join sub-groups with shared values.

Out of the behaviors that could cause harm, offensive speech is probably the most difficult to legislate. Most societies will place laws against verbal commands that cause violence because of the direct connection to the act. Threatening violence also causes someone to feel in imminent danger, so laws will also restrict that speech. However, people commonly say, "I could kill him!" in anger and have no intention of committing the act. The law now has to evaluate the situation, the intent, the act, and the result to lay judgment. Otherwise, law enforcement would have to imprison anyone who uses slang, figures of speech, and hyperbole.

There are many statements that may or may not violate the law depending on the situation. Repeated, unreciprocated verbal abuse is identified as harassment and is against the law for the emotional trauma. However, one insulting comment is usually not. How many insults or how long one needs to continue engaging in the act before it becomes a crime is up for debate.

In another example, a law might prevent people from making derogatory comments based on someone's immutable characteristics (e.g., race, sex, age), but this law has to account for legitimate reasons to discuss genetic differences. Scholars can have civil, scientific discussions about the variation in facial features, hair, skin, susceptibility to diseases, or other factors. Limiting this conversation to avoid causing offense would hinder the research.

Society has to make significant decisions as to whether it can and should legislate offense consistently and fairly, whether it can measure the emotional harm of offense, and how much emotional harm constitutes a crime or tort. It has to decide whether someone can legally defend themselves physically against emotional harm. Because a person can be offended by anything that contradicts his or her beliefs, treating positive ethics such as stating what a person believes (i.e., speech) like negative ethics (i.e., violence) has many complications. While these legal questions may never be perfectly answered, the fact that humanity has advanced to the point of determining whether causing discomfort deserves punishment is indicative of how ethical society has become.

Ethics will continue to evolve as society grows. Playground equipment and vehicles are examples of products that receive stricter regulations over time to reduce the risk and impact of harm to users. However, these rules also restrict the freedom of individuals to choose whether to accept the risk of a product, as society has made that decision for them.

These laws are difficult to define perfectly because they put people who hold the "as long as it does not harm anyone" philosophy against people who hold the "there ought to be a law against that" philosophy. The former group wants society and the government to stay out of its life decisions, while the latter group wants to align laws with its ethics, manners, and risk tolerance. The point at which a behavior transitions from being distasteful to causing fear, burden, or harm is not exact and changes based on one's values, perspective, and situation. This burden or harm can be physical, emotional, financial, or even spiritual (if it encroaches on religious freedom).

Just as some philosophies can conflict with others, ethics and rules can conflict with each other. For example, a country's mandatory requirement to participate in the military may conflict with deep religious ethics against all forms of violence. A country's right to free speech may conflict with laws against inducing panic and ethics against hateful rhetoric. There are no easy answers when rules come into conflict with each other, but societal leaders try their best to balance the needs of the individual and the group to determine the best approach.

Because of the conflicts, disagreements, and evolutions regarding ethics, the rules around the correct way to behave are complex, nuanced, situational, and subject to change. There is no perfect set of rules that can apply to everyone in all situations forever. Fortunately, most systems understand the need for nuance and change, so they incorporate them into lawmaking processes. If the rules are appropriate and fair, most citizens willfully abide by them without needing to be threatened with punishment.

As there are so many different ways of growing (and, therefore, many different ways to prevent someone from growing), new ethics and laws are being identified every day. For example, it was long considered to be ethical for children to take on the occupations of their parents in a family business. In modern times, however, many cultures value the freedom to pursue happiness more than the obligation to sustain familial occupations. As a result, it became unethical for parents to try to force their children to pursue their careers.

In this example, new social norms changed the "right" way for parents and children to interact. While many people will argue that it was never ethical to force people to do what they do not want to do, others will argue that the ethical approach changed as the world changed. In either case, the ethics of society have to be open to change to improve the rules over time.

Despite this need for ethics to differ between people and change over time, many people try to find the perfect set that can help anyone lead a meaningful life. For example, many philosophers conflate ethics and meaning when they focus on how to live "the good life" or "a life well-lived" in their studies. A similar conflation shows up in the English language, as "good" can mean either beneficial or moral.

There is no doubt that having a strong moral code can reinforce a sense of purpose in life and that cheating can take the fulfillment out of an activity. However, there are also plenty of people with a purpose in life to destroy something or people who follow the rules but feel unfulfilled because they forgo growth opportunities in the process. Ethics are simply rules to live by to help people get the most from their life journey. Therefore, anyone who is trying to find meaning through ethics alone will be left wanting. The only way that ethics can lead people to the correct life path is when they realize why it is the right way to approach the situation. Ethics are the "means" to the goals' "ends" in life, not the meaning itself. As long as people have different ends and debate over the best means, they will differ greatly in their ethics.

Because of these differences, someone could read ten books on "how to live a meaningful life" or "how to be successful" with ten different combinations of goals and rules and still not find a formula that works for them. Many books on "success" focus on financial success. Many books on "living a good life" provide recommendations for enabling others' growth. Many books on "finding meaning" offer a path to achieving spiritual enlightenment and a higher purpose.

The authors of these books assume that their readers' goals and paths toward those goals will be similar. For specific, well-defined goals with common steps, these assumptions are relatively safe. When providing life recommendations, however, assuming that certain values, goals, and positive ethics are universal will inevitably become less accurate given the human race's great diversity of interests. Few liberal arts professors will apply the same principles as government officials or corporate magnates. Few religious leaders will have the same recommendations as anarchists or nihilists. Different cultures have different values, and different countries have different laws.

Certain writings, however, try to give a master list of goals and rules to unify all people under one ethical framework. Famous attempts to combine meaning and ethics include Islam, Judaism, and Christianity. These religions provide clear direction for how to live a moral, meaningful life, and members believe that everyone would benefit from following their teachings. Their texts cover negative ethics, such as telling people not to lie, steal, or kill, and positive ethics, such as making recommendations regarding relationships, diet, daily rituals, and attendance at places of worship. Some ethics are requirements to remain members, whereas others have means of asking for forgiveness and receiving punishment if someone violates them.

The risk of these divine master lists is that they are less subject to change as societal ethics. Many religious rules are based on ancient beliefs about how the world works, and the rituals often remain after science identifies superior methods. Following these practices may still contribute to a more fulfilling life, but benefitting from them usually depends on the faith of the individual.

In early human civilizations, religious beliefs were often the basis of laws. That model slowly ceded to secular, science-based rules and governance. In modern societies with diverse belief systems, there is no need for the legal system to enforce one religion's positive ethics because there is no harm to others if non-believers do not follow them. On the contrary, restricting a person's freedom or punishing someone who has not harmed another is a breach of widely accepted ethics. Modern systems assert that every person should have the freedom to engage in any behavior as long as it does not cause nonconsensual harm to another. In this worldview, past rules regarding sexuality, relationships, gender roles, religious participation, and other behaviors become unnecessary and gradually stop being enforced.

Knowing how these types of philosophies combine meaning, values, goals, and rule sets, individuals can choose to follow the ethics that align to their meaning, values, and goals and ignore the others. They may have to follow certain ethics to be part of a specific sub-group, but they always have a right to disassociate. They should always check to see whether others' recommendations are the optimal ways for them to approach the situation and then respond accordingly.

Without a perfect list of universal ethics that everyone must follow at all times, many people may wonder which ethics could serve as the foundation of civilization. The three ethics that are most widely recognized and agreed upon are reciprocity, fairness, and minimal harm:

- **Reciprocity** is when a person responds in kind to another person's behavior. This ethic underlies the "live and let live" and "do unto others as you would have them do unto you" principles. It serves as a core guideline for human interaction because a system that rewards beneficial behavior and punishes harmful behavior leads to greater cooperation.

- **Fairness** is when a person treats everyone consistently, equally, and appropriately given the circumstances. This ethic underlies the statement, "The punishment should fit the crime." It permeates rules for how to provide rewards, punishments, and opportunities because people are more likely to cooperate when they are treated in the same way as everyone else.

- **Minimal harm**, a concept encapsulated in the famous statement, "First, do no harm" ("Primum non nocere"), is a general rule to prevent people from impeding on others' growth while they pursue their own life paths. People will not cooperate if they believe that it will harm them or their loved ones.

These ethics are so critical to civilization's survival that they form the basis of cooperative living in modern societies.

Many other principles are pervasive ethics within a community or applicable for most situations but have more exceptions than reciprocity, fairness, and minimal harm. For example, some may point to ones that seem universal such as, "Thou shalt not kill," but there are exceptions where killing is legally and ethically justified, such as when a terrorist is in the process of killing hundreds of other people. Humans also have to protect themselves from harmful organisms and consume other living things to survive, so that rule cannot apply to all life. Agriculture involves killing weeds, pests, and insects, and staying healthy requires killing innumerable bacteria and other microorganisms.

Rules that can apply in most cases could become near-universal in practice as long as they had exceptions for when the violating acts were fair, reciprocal, or minimizing harm. This adjustment allows people to kill a murderer if he or she is actively trying to kill others because they are reciprocating deadly force, using force fairly, and minimizing harm to law-abiding citizens. It also allows people to deceive others who are trying to deceive them, and it enables them to restrict the freedoms of convicted criminals.

Most general rules apply as long as they are fair, harmless, and reciprocal. The rules allow for fair reciprocation against wrongdoing while the act is in progress as long as it does not cause undue harm. Once order is restored, the legal right to reciprocate directly is revoked, and an objective party (e.g., a law enforcement officer) is used to prevent further harm to the victims and excessive, unfair retribution against the perpetrator.

A behavioral trait that may seem to be universally ethical is honesty. Honesty is generally ethical because it is key to trust. A person will not agree to a set of rules if he or she does not believe that others will follow them, and few people will believe a person who lies frequently. Society accepts honesty as a synonym for moral to the point where they will describe a virtuous friend as a "good, honest" person. The reality, though, is that the ethics of deception depend on the situation. Few people would consider lying about a surprise birthday party to be unethical. Similarly, almost no one would denounce lying about the location of family members during a burglary. Lying about job qualifications in an interview, however, would be unethical to most people.

Being honest is not inherently ethical; the reasons behind and consequences of being truthful or deceptive factor into its morality. There are plenty of games, competitions, and life circumstances in which deception is necessary and ethical. Because everyone agrees to the rules, players engage in fair, reciprocated deception and accept the possibility that others' deceit could negatively affect their performance. There are also cases where being honest and forthcoming would be considered rude and therefore inappropriate. In those situations, being open and honest is not an ethical imperative.

Much of the time, however, people lie for personal benefit at others' expense. For example, someone may deny damaging or stealing property so they do not have to pay for it. Lying is considered to be unethical in those situations because it violates the minimal harm, fairness, or reciprocity principles. Therefore, people will often tell the truth as a general rule so that they avoid telling unethical lies. There are too many examples of ethical deception, however, for honesty to be a universal virtue.

Most rules have exceptions: killing, lying, stealing, trespassing, imprisoning, harming, and threatening others all have situations where the acts could be considered the right thing to do. Those exceptions are almost always due to the three near-universal ethics. Even the three core ethics have exceptions, though, because they may conflict with each other. Reciprocating against someone who breaks the rules, for example, requires at least some harm to be added to the damage that has already occurred. Some people want reciprocal punishments to be slightly unfair to prevent future harm. Some laws minimize harm by requiring that people do not reciprocate even if it would be fair. The rules set by society are meant to balance these competing ethics so that people can live together as cooperatively as possible.

The reason why the three core ethics are the most commonly held across societies is largely genetic. People who cooperated survived. The only way to cooperate is to trust, and the only way to trust is for someone to believe that the other party will, in fairness, reciprocate that trust and cooperation. If either party harms the other, that trust is broken. As a result, natural selection favored these ethics in human instincts as the basis for social interaction.

Those biological drivers for ethical behavior are then expanded upon by the need for a group to have shared values, rules, and incentives to live together peacefully. With the genetic predisposition to cooperate, families and communities are able to spend time socializing, bonding, and adopting shared values. Those shared values lead to shared ethics for how to behave for everyone's benefit. With the combined influences of nature and nurture, humans established an ethical foundation for society.

The final factor in establishing and applying ethics is determining which attributes a being must have for rights and responsibilities to apply to them. While all social species follow rules to live within a group, humans' advanced nature requires both a higher level of ethics as well as a higher bar for what capabilities are required to be held to those ethics.

This high level did not evolve overnight; ethics expanded from families to tribes and societies over a long period of time. Along the way, humans have applied different ethics based on biological relatedness, potential as a mate, age, gender, race, marital status, parental status, religion, political beliefs, sexual orientation, mental capacity, physical capacity, and physical attributes. Ethics have evolved so much over that time that many past ethics may seem barbaric in comparison.

Ethics will always vary by some of these attributes, as people will never treat strangers exactly like they treat their parents, children, or spouses. However, society has pushed for as many negative ethics to be applied as equally as possible. Some have pushed for negative ethics to apply to as many life forms as possible. To resolve this dispute, society has to identify the attributes that directly determine a being's ethical accountability.

Through centuries of legal and ethical disputes, societies have either implicitly or explicitly defined five key attributes required to hold any living organism accountable for breaking the rules:

Required Attributes for Human Ethical Accountability
- The ability to comprehend the rules (e.g., intelligence)
- The ability to communicate the rules (e.g., language)
- The ability to agree to the rules implicitly or explicitly (e.g., will)
- The ability to follow the rules (e.g., self-control)
- The ability to decide on or be aware of the rules in advance (e.g., planning)

Most humans satisfy these requirements, so one set of rules can apply to the majority of society. However, people who do not meet all of these requirements are not held to the same standards. For example, people who cannot differentiate right from wrong are often placed in a psychiatric facility instead of a prison after committing a crime. Foreigners who are not familiar with the local language and customs are often granted more leniency when they violate social etiquette. Religions may have exemptions to a law if it prevents followers from performing their rituals. Children who behave inappropriately do not receive the same punishments as adults. Society makes these adjustments to which rules it applies or how it enforces them because it understands that people without these five attributes are exceptions to its standard ethical system.

Applying ethics to interactions with other things—e.g., living things, the environment, or property—can get even more complicated. The legal system considers property damage to be a transgression against the owner of the property. Harm or damage to the environment is usually evaluated based on the necessary harm done to survive, such as cutting down a tree and leveling the land to build a shelter, compared to the unnecessary harm done, such as polluting a water source with sewage. Ethics applied to other organisms are usually based on the degree to which humans can co-exist peacefully and the degree to which the organisms have the five required attributes for ethical accountability.

Determining how humans should apply their own ethics when interacting with other species is one of the most difficult and controversial aspects of ethics. No other animal has all five attributes of ethical accountability to the degree of humans, so they will never be treated in the same way. Humans also must consume other living organisms to survive, as do all animals. However, people have a much greater understanding of and control over themselves and the world around them, so they may agree to the ethical obligation of allowing other organisms to live as long as they do not impede on human growth.

Under this model, microscopic organisms such as bacteria are killed when they pose a danger to human lives despite the scientific evidence that they have the ability to communicate and co-operate. Plants are useful to humans for oxygen, shade, erosion prevention, and food, so they are harvested for consumption, preserved for environmental protection, and kept for their benefits. However, trees, weeds, and other plants are controlled or killed for their danger to humans and other organisms if they fall, grow into a building's foundation, or prevent other plants from accessing water, nutrients, or sunlight.

Wild animals are treated similarly to plants, where they are hunted for food, protected for environmental preservation, and reared for their benefits while being controlled or killed for their danger to humans and society. Domesticated animals, such as dogs, cats, and farm animals, are more capable of co-existing peacefully with humans, so society generally affords them additional protections as long as they do not harm others. The degree to which the rules apply to them is limited, however, based on the degree to which they can understand, communicate, agree to, and follow complex, nuanced rules ahead of time.

The extension of human ethics to other living creatures will have to end at some point, as giving the same rights to lions, zebras, and grass would mean that a lion could not eat a zebra and a zebra could not eat grass. Taken to its logical end, insects could not bite humans, Venus flytraps could not eat insects, plants could not block other plants' access to sunlight, and humans could not eat plants. Ethics are only a means through which advanced organisms can cooperate for greater growth; they are not a means through which all harm to all life on Earth can be eliminated.

Because of the limits of ethics, the goal of broadening their scope to other life forms is to ensure the sustainability of the ecosystem. When humans had a small population and limited technology, they could hunt and gather like any other animal without the risk of mass extinction. In modern society, humans are the dominant species and must hold themselves to a higher ethical standard or face self-destruction through squandering their sources of oxygen, nutrition, shelter, medicine, or income.

No matter what conclusions society comes to regarding the establishment and application of ethics, its rules are set for a very specific purpose: to live peacefully together and promote the best individual and collective growth. Those ethics can and should change as society changes, and they will differ across fields, types of relationships, and personal goals. People must hold themselves and others accountable to agreed-upon negative ethics while allowing others to pursue their own goals in their own way. As you consider the ethics that you should hold, you will see that you can and must factor your own well-being and the well-being of others so that you can maximize your growth without inhibiting the growth of people around you.

Your ethics factor everyone's well-being into your behavior

Ethics are complex and difficult to optimize for your life. With every decision you make or action you take, you can measure the degree to which it benefits or harms yourself and others. Someone who acts out of pure selfishness would try to maximize personal benefit regardless of how it affected others, while someone who acted out of pure altruism would try to maximize benefits to others regardless of the self-sacrifice. Either extreme is self-limiting. Harming others will eventually result in reciprocation, and sacrificing yourself limits your ability to help others in the future.

Optimally, you would pursue your life goals in a way that is best for yourself while considering how it affects those you care about and society as a whole. Helping yourself prevents you from being a burden to others and makes you better able to help others; helping (or not harming) others makes them more willing to help (or not harm) you.

If you wish to determine how you can behave ethically in your life journey, you need to understand:
- your goals and values
- the rights, laws, and negative ethics of society
- the positive ethics that you currently follow

First, trace your goals and values to the actions that you need to take to achieve or uphold them. Then, apply the rules that you must follow to avoid hurting others as you work toward your goals. Finally, ensure that you adopt positive ethics that optimize your approach. Through this process, you will uncover the best set of rules to succeed in your journey without harming others.

For example, if you have a goal of winning a race and value your honor, then you would need to train to complete the course faster than your competitors within the rules of the competition. While you could win by cheating, that approach would go against your values. You could train more if you stopped going to school or working, but that would hurt your intellectual or financial growth. You may also be violating a law requiring children to go to school or breaking an employment contract with your company, so you would want to incorporate what is best for your parents, employer, or co-workers into your decision. In the end, your optimal ethics are to train hard while meeting other obligations and to win fairly by following the race's rules.

You can use this approach to determine the ethics for any part of your life. If you value life, freedom, honesty, fairness, and faith, then you can identify ways that you can act in accordance with those values without encroaching on others' right to live by their values. You can then also determine what is the appropriate, legal response if someone else violates your values. Finally, you can delineate between the negative ethics that you must follow to live in society and the positive ethics you choose to follow to live the best life possible. This approach enables you to establish a foundational set of ethics, but you want to add and adjust rules as your goals and values change over time.

If anyone else suggests rules or ethics that you should follow in your life journey, make sure that they are aligned with your values and goals. For example, someone may suggest that you do not have a good work ethic if you do not work at an office job from 9 a.m. to 5 p.m. every Monday through Friday, but you may have a situation where you prefer to work in the evenings with flexible work hours to support young children. In your case, that standard work ethic would not apply to you.

However, if you do not work at all and place an undue burden on your family or cohabitants, then your action (or lack thereof) would become unethical. The same would apply if you did follow the traditional office work schedule but contributed the bare minimum at work while other employees worked harder to make up for your lack of effort. Again, that places an undue extra burden while you receive the same compensation.

When you have identified and begun to follow ethics based on your goals and values, make sure that you do not try to force your personal ethics onto others if they do not share them. For example, if you value family, you may try to pressure your family and friends into having children. If their path focuses on financial, emotional, spiritual, and social growth, they may not wish to take steps toward familial growth.

To confirm which ethics you should apply to all others and which you should keep for people who have your goals and values, identify the behaviors that are harmful or unfair compared to the ones that are a matter of personal preference. In this model, your society may ban non-consensual, non-defensive violence but grant a person the freedom to choose his or her occupation based on personal preference. The ethics that you apply to yourself, recommend to others, and enforce on the group will differ from the ones that others apply because everyone has different goals, values, and perceptions of what is harmful.

These differences in ethics that people choose to follow are why your manners and rules of conduct are not just "common sense" for everyone. While there are many commonalities across people as to what is harmful and helpful, prosperous growth for you may not be the right path for another. People will like and want different things; it is only when it crosses the line of being harmful that you can ethically intervene.

Unfortunately, there will always be differences of opinion as to what constitutes harm and to what degree it is harmful, so that is why you cannot logically derive an incontrovertible set of laws and punishments that everyone can follow and enforce perfectly. As such, you will have to determine which actions are harmful or risky enough to warrant restricting others' freedom, and you will have to determine which laws are so unnecessary or restrictive that people should change or ignore them. Decisions of this magnitude have far-reaching consequences, so you should not take them lightly.

In addition to reconciling ethical differences, you will often have to address ethical conflicts. These conflicts include:

- making trade-offs between short-term and long-term goals
- applying multiple competing ethics to the same situation
- causing short-term harm for a long-term benefit
- choosing options that benefit some and harm others

A common ethical dilemma is a trade-off between what feels good in the moment, such as staying up late and watching a movie, and what is best for you in the future, such as completing an assignment and getting enough sleep. Another common ethical challenge is when you have to decide how to balance the needs of your family with the demands of your job. These two growth areas compete for your time and attention.

Perhaps the most traumatic of these conflicts are the two that require harm for a benefit. For example, you might have to cause excruciating pain to cauterize a wound or amputate a leg to save a person's life. You might have to choose which people to save on a sinking ship. You might have to choose whether to steal from one person to help another in immediate danger, to tax one group of people for the benefit of another group, or to refrain from defending someone who is under attack because of the risk to yourself. These situations may have no "right" answer, and you may not be able to avoid all harm. The best you can do is try to find the optimal solution that provides the most benefit with as little harm as possible.

These extreme examples show that you cannot easily follow simple "do not harm others" or "always do the right thing" ethics. Harm may be inevitable, and the right thing may be unclear.

These absolute rules would eliminate "tough love" approaches, drug recovery programs, and other help that may seem to make the situation worse before it gets better. Also, since everyone has different needs to enable their growth, what is "right" for one person might be "wrong" for someone else. Eating strawberries could be part of a healthy diet for one person, but it could kill a person with a strawberry allergy.

Because the right thing can be unclear, you have to be careful not to obfuscate it—intentionally or unintentionally. The most common ways that people who see themselves as ethical behave unethically are that they either only look at it from their own perspective or rationalize their actions. A particularly egregious example is slavery, an act that is unethical but was legal for a substantial portion of history. Slavers would rationalize to themselves and others that the slaves were less than human, that they deserved it, that it was what was best for them, that it is common practice, or that they were receiving food, clothing, and shelter in exchange for their labor.

As despicable as it might be by all commonly accepted ethical standards, a slaver's rationalized and willfully ignorant perspective invoked the near-universal ethics in their explanations. He would discount or ignore the fact that he was restricting their freedom and right to grow on their terms in their own way. He would rationalize the harmful treatment he was doing as corrective punishments that someone would use to teach a child or dog to behave.

You may dismiss people who commit heinous acts as evil and scoff at the notion that you could do anything that unethical, but scientific studies show that anyone is capable of atrocious behavior under the right conditions. The Milgram experiment on obedience to authority figures and the Stanford Prison Experiment on the interpersonal dynamics between guards and prisoners show that normal people can rationalize despicable acts. In the former, people administered what they thought were potentially dangerous electrical shocks to another person because an experimenter asked them to continue and said that he was responsible for any harm done.[89] In the latter, participants who were asked by experimenters to play the roles of tough prison officers escalated how they exercised their authority to psychologically abusive levels within days of the start of the experiment.[90]

Behind the unethical acts of otherwise ethical people will usually be rationalizations based on the near-universal ethics. Because of the ambiguous nature of ethics, the distinction between rationalization and justification is not always clear. While almost everyone would describe slavery as abhorrent in modern times, they would have a less severe reaction to indentured servitude, prison labor, and mandatory community service. Even though all four are examples of restricted freedom and forced labor, the latter three involve people working to pay their debt to another person or society. Whether a society banishes all forms of compulsory labor or allows certain forms as reciprocity against unrepaid debts or crimes is up to the group as a whole to decide. Some might believe that forced labor is not a harsh enough punishment for many crimes since prisoners receive taxpayer-funded food, clothing, shelter, heating, and entertainment in exchange. Each person may calculate the ethical tally slightly differently.

Because of these ethical quandaries, you will have to use your own judgment as to how you ultimately define your ethics. Right and wrong are not as obvious as they seem. This reality is why two people who hold themselves to the highest ethical standards can have completely different opinions on what laws to pass. Opposing political parties, for example, can have well-meaning people on both sides with what can sometimes seem like polar opposite ethics. No matter what one side might say about the other, both parties can have valid ethics because they have different goals, values, and priorities.

Contentious political topics are based on this difference in priorities. Abortion, for example, pits the right of humans to make their own bodily decisions without government intervention against the right of an unborn child to have a right to grow and be protected from harm. If asked about each right separately without context, the majority of people would agree that both of them are important. Because these rights conflict, society has to decide which one outweighs the other when establishing the law.

Many advanced societies identify a compromise between the two ethics: give women the right to make decisions for a period of time to terminate a pregnancy, but give the unborn child the right to be protected from harm after that point. Some individuals believe in one of the extremes, such as no abortions allowed or abortions allowed until birth, and may fight for those ethics to become law. In the former case, the reasoning is that harming a baby is never allowable, even in complex situations such as when the baby's existence is killing the mother or when a pregnancy as a consequence of rape could be psychological torture for the mother. The latter stance discounts the fact that the child could live on its own later in the pregnancy and therefore may need to begin to receive the same protections as a newborn baby.

The options are unenviable: enforcing one extreme would imprison teenage girls and rape victims for murder, and enforcing the other extreme would kill unborn but fully developed babies. The most common compromise essentially allows women to destroy the developing organism before it becomes viable and then requires a woman to protect the child once it reaches that point. There is no universal consensus in these cases; there are only rules that society or its representatives can agree to set, enforce, and follow. Between those two extremes are a multitude of potential opinions, such as banned abortions except for rape or incest or allowed abortions up to the point that the fetus can feel pain. Society does the best that it can to do what is best for the individual and the group, and it is up to you to determine which ethics take priority in your final decisions regarding these moral conflicts.

In addition to prioritizing ethics, you will have to determine when, how, and how far ethics apply. Society, for example, has to decide which rules apply to humans, animals, plants, insects, and microorganisms. Because only humans have the five requirements for full ethical accountability, it has to determine which ethics apply and how they apply when dealing with any living thing that does meet those requirements. The minimum level of ethics necessary in a civilized society is to have a set of laws that apply to all of its (human) citizens. At that level, being socially responsible for the environment, plants, and animals would be optional. At the maximum level, universal ethics would exist for all living things, and harming any living being—plant, animal, or microscopic organism—would be wrong.

Both extremes—having no care for the environment or causing no harm to other living creatures—are unsustainable. Because humans rely on other living things for food, oxygen, and resources, humans have to have at least some ethics regarding their environment or risk killing themselves in the process. On the other extreme, humans are examples of life forms that must consume other life forms to live, and they must harm other living things in the process of living. Humans eat living organisms for food, prevent them from growing by taking up space where they could live, kill them to protect themselves and their property, or accidentally kill them while walking, sitting, or (in the case of microorganisms) just existing. Carnivores, herbivores, omnivores, and parasites all must harm or kill other living things to live, but they also must allow other things to live for them to have food to consume.

A society that killed nothing or killed everything would end up killing itself. In between those extremes, there is just no clear line that you can draw that is divinely or naturally correct; it is a matter of both what humans can agree on and what personal rules you choose to live by beyond ones that require agreement. Humans do not naturally have a greater right to live than other animals because of their intelligence, and animals do not naturally have a greater value than plants because they show intelligence and emotion. Humans agree not to harm each other so that they may live peacefully together, and they agree to treat animals, plants, fungi, bacteria and other life forms in ways that are best for themselves, society, and the ecosystem. People must have ethics regarding other creatures to sustain their own existence, but those ethics will differ because most creatures are unable to plan, communicate, understand, agree to, and follow human rules.

How far you can extend the boundaries of your ethics will depend on the point at which it harms or restricts the freedoms of other people. You cannot avoid harming microorganisms, as you would die quickly. You cannot get your necessary nutrition from inorganic matter such as rocks, so you have to consume organic matter to live. You have to keep harmful or unsanitary creatures away from where you sleep, so you may have to (rely on others to) harm or kill creatures to keep yourself safe and healthy.

Where you choose to set your ethical boundaries is up to you. However, organisms on Earth have been consuming each other and competing for resources long before humans developed the minimal harm ethic. Therefore, a degree of harm and prevention of growth is required by yourself and your fellow humans to stay alive and prevent other organisms from harming or killing you. Societies have modern ethics to avoid harming each other; there is no divine or enlightened rule never to harm another living creature for a person's entire existence. When you define the ethical line for yourself or your group, it does not automatically make it universally wrong for all people in all circumstances; there are many exceptions of people having to protect themselves or get the nutrition they need to grow and thrive.

Once you have defined your ethics and worked through their ambiguity, conflicts, exceptions, and limitations, you will want to monitor and adjust them over time. To improve your ethics, make sure that you continue to learn more about what others' wants and needs are and what might encroach on their growth or their right to grow. Check for direct physical or emotional harm as well as indirect forms of harm such as discrimination, oppression, prejudice, and violating others' rights. Because it is difficult to know when something that may seem harmless to you is undermining others' growth from another perspective, you have to be willing to learn from your mistakes and change your approach.

No matter how vigilant you are, you will probably not get your actions right every time. Because of these inevitable mistakes, contrition and forgiveness are two essential components of social interaction. To live together in long-term harmony, you have to be willing to apologize when you unintentionally hurt someone and forgive when they apologize to you for unintentional harm. You also have to be willing to apologize or forgive when the harm was intentional and seemingly justified at the time but later turned out to be wrong.

There will be times when people will intentionally harm you without remorse, and you should respond to these situations based on society's laws and your personal ethics. Society's legal system will do its best to dispense the appropriate justice. Without forgiveness, however, you may hold anger, resentment, and pain that can keep you from progressing on your life's journey for a long time. Especially in extreme circumstances such as the murder of a loved one, you need to learn to forgive for your sake, not theirs.

Apologizing is a tool to communicate to others that you regret the harm that you have caused and that you have learned a new ethic. Forgiveness is an even more powerful tool to show that you accept their apology (if they gave one), are ready to let go of the negative emotions holding you back, and are beginning to shift your focus back toward growth. Together, these two mechanisms act as a de-escalation tool to counteract the potential for two parties to respond to each unfair act between them with a greater unfair act that they rationalize as being a fair punishment. Use them to stop the never-ending escalation of reciprocal acts that each party will believe is justified until irreparable harm is done.

Finally, when monitoring and adjusting your ethics, make sure that you are treating yourself and others with the same respect. While there are plenty of examples of people who hold their needs much higher than everyone else, there are also examples of those who belittle themselves and treat themselves with much less respect than they do others. If you treat yourself poorly, talk down to yourself, and otherwise tell yourself that you do not have worth, ask yourself whether that is an ethical thing to do. Do the same if you treat others poorly.

You may rationalize your behavior, saying that you or they deserve it or that others put you or them down first, but maybe those previous actions were not ethical and should not be perpetuated. If you frequently put yourself or others down, you will quickly find yourself surrounded by people who frequently put you, themselves, or others down. If you frequently sacrifice yourself for others, you will eventually be exploited and, as a result, inadequately equipped to help others in the future.

When you are done with the whole process of establishing, monitoring, testing, and adjusting your ethics, you should have an effective list that will guide your life decisions going forward. This list should include rules to minimize harm to yourself and others as well as principles that you should follow to best progress toward your goals. You may choose to listen to others for guidance while keeping in mind that many different paths to success could work based on the situation. Review proposed rules to see if they are best for you without being detrimental to others. Then, apply them to your approach going forward.

Your ethics are your rules for living. While there are laws and social pressures that provide incentives to keep you from deviating from societal standards, you ultimately choose to live life on the terms that you set. You can make a conscious effort to be loyal, respectful, kind, polite, helpful, generous, lawful, and cautious, or you can choose to be rude and obnoxious toward the people around you. You can live and let live, or you can apply a "might means right" approach and force your will upon others.

Whichever you choose, remember that successful people will often note that their ethics were essential to living a rewarding, meaningful life. Your goals, experiences, desires, beliefs, and emotions will point you in the right direction, but your ethics will determine how you approach that path in the best way possible.

Without ethics, you could not grow peacefully in a society

Imagine a world without ethics. Most post-apocalyptic tales hypothesize what would happen to ethics if society crumbled and left every person to fend for himself or herself. In these scenarios, people cooperate less, fight over limited resources, and are continuously monitoring their surroundings. Trust breaks down, so the boundaries of ethical behavior shrink to one's core group. Rules significantly diverge between groups, and physical conflict and harm increase substantially from pre-apocalyptic society.

Similarly, life on Earth prior to those with advanced cognition was unforgiving. Environmental conditions were harsh, and early animal life had to be vigilant as it fought among countless organisms to live and grow. In both scenarios, the lack of agreement on behavioral rules between living things makes it difficult to thrive.

Technically, it is impossible to live without any rules because all living things have a survival instinct built into their DNA that instructs them to eat, drink, protect themselves from harm, and reproduce. Life forms value their own lives, so they will consider any action that sustains their existence to be appropriate for them. Similarly, it is impossible to live without any ethics because all social animals have or develop rules for group interaction. Therefore, these scenarios are describing a lack of advanced ethics that humans have established over the history of civilization.

Advanced human ethics would not exist without the species' larger brains with a frontal lobe, language, and social nature. Advanced brains and language enable the establishment and communication of ethics. Living in groups requires cooperation and ethics for the species to succeed. Humans without these capabilities could not form the advanced ethics necessary to organize effectively to achieve societal and technological advancements.

While human capabilities enable sophisticated ethical systems, ethics still exist without all of these attributes. Any social animal shows the ability to work in groups and to set rules for how the group should behave through instinct, rewards, and punishments. Packs of wolves, flocks of birds, schools of fish, and herds of bison all have systems for organizing and managing their groups that evolved with their unique skill sets. The reason for these ethics is the same: to live cooperatively to increase the probability of the group's survival. Even though animals' rules may involve harm or other behaviors that would be deemed unethical in modern human society, they exhibit instinctual and learned ethics that resemble the social behavior of humans.

For example, *On the Origin of Species* identifies many organisms, such as peafowls, that have developed extensive rituals to prove that they are worthy mates.[91] Because the male's fitness and ability to provide protection, shelter, and food have value to the female and offspring, the optimal mating behavior for the male would be to demonstrate his proficiency in these areas during his courting process. Given the importance of successful reproduction and the limited number of ova, the female's optimal mating strategy would be to select the best suitor from both a genetic standpoint and a survivability standpoint. In these cases, the best way to live is in line with how natural selection works, so ethics become both instincts and learned social behaviors.

Humans still retain some of that instinct in their mating rituals. Classic human courting processes involve males finding females that are attractive to them and showing off how worthy they are as mates (e.g., indicators of ability to provide such as wealth, status, talents, or power) to attract them. Females maximize how worthy they are as mates (e.g., indicators of fertility such as body shape, skin clarity, and rosy cheeks) and determine which of the courting males is most suitable for them. While human approaches are naturally similar to the courting systems of other animals, these instinctual ethics are supplemented or overridden by modern social ethics to find a compatible mate through shared interests or complementary personalities.

"Nurture" ethics (i.e., social rules) override "nature" ethics (i.e., instinct) in modern society because what maximizes social animals' ability to survive in the wild is not the same as what is necessary to grow in a civilized environment. Gender roles that maximized survivability early in human history can now lead to oppression, discrimination, and stereotyping. Enforcing gender roles today would hinder a female's ability to support herself financially and a male's freedom to devote himself to child-rearing. As ethics evolve, humans have to learn to supersede instincts with well-reasoned social agreements if they wish to thrive.

Making these adjustments is difficult, as nature and nurture influence social behaviors such as reciprocity and cooperation as well as social emotions such as guilt, embarrassment, and shame. Humans evolved to have these attributes because they would otherwise never have been able to live together safely and securely. By feeling bad when they violate social rules, they will try to avoid harming or alienating others. This biological system does not work appropriately, however, unless they are taught the rules to know when and how to cooperate, reciprocate, and feel in various situations. Because nature and nurture are both involved in determining and following the best set of ethics, people will struggle to act appropriately when they conflict with each other.

Ethical conflicts between biology and social rules are plentiful. People face ethical conflicts between vigilante and legal justice, the polyamorous sex drive and the monogamous relationship structure, and the age of biological readiness to rear children and the age of resource readiness. These conflicts can be the most difficult to manage because people have to consciously reject behavior that served humans well as a species for millennia to live a more civilized life.

The ethical norm that epitomizes this conflict between instinctual and social ethics is the aversion to incest. This aversion evolved as instinct because of its evolutionary advantage: genetic diversity increases the probability of survival. Inbreeding puts the species at risk because genetic weaknesses, such as susceptibility to a certain condition or disease, are more likely to carry on to the children and threaten their survivability.

In addition to the instinctual disgust, the practice is taboo in modern society for two rational reasons: it has a much higher rate of congenital disorders, and there is a power imbalance in the case of older family members with younger family members. However, there is no direct harm or added risk of harm to anyone in the case of birth-controlled incest between consenting adults. After weighing these factors, society has to come to an agreement on how this behavior should be treated under the law. They can follow their instinctual disgust and create a law against all forms of incest, or they can follow the agreed-upon harm-based system that requires some (risk of) harm to become illegal.

Systems differ on the approach, but many of them make incest illegal and do not allow close relatives to have sex or get married. In these cases, they have to define incest, which might include sexual relations between parents and offspring, siblings, or cousins. Some may determine that it should be legal in theory but oppose it because there is still a risk of pregnancy when using birth control. Even people who might be open to applying a "no harm, no crime" view to birth-controlled incestuous relationships between consenting adults might still see them as morally wrong because of their instinctual disgust. Although this aversion to incest is almost universally, instinctually held, it is still up to society to agree upon whether they should make a law against it. The group will decide based on whether they prioritize freedom and privacy or safety and the prevention of suffering.

Society may never resolve all ethical conflicts perfectly, but it keeps changing and improving them. For example, humans have held different ethics based on age, race, gender, sexual orientation, physical and psychological ability, and socioeconomic class. Some variations, such as holding children to a different standard as they mature cognitively, are supported by instinct, science, and reason. Others, such as variations by race, are not appropriate and restrict people's right to autonomy. Upon seeing the issues with these variations, society's members propose to remove them so that these factors do not affect someone's ability to live freely and be treated fairly in society.

These changes are just a part of the long, arduous transition from a world where people had to fight over resources to a world where society establishes rules for people to exchange or share resources through peaceful, cooperative means. This process involved overcoming millennia of restrictive, oppressive governments and laws to reach free societies where each individual was allowed to live as he or she saw fit without harming others. Without the need to protect themselves constantly from the environment, other creatures, diseases, and other people, humans can adjust their ethics to a level where they can further reduce harm and enable growth. With its continued advancement, the human race can continue to raise the ethical bar for all of its members.

After millennia of ethical evolution, the modern quandary for human interpersonal ethics is the degree to which people should be required to help others and not just refrain from hurting them. When the goal is maximizing individual growth without harming others, the most effective approach combines a political system based on individual liberty with an economic system based on the free exchange of goods and services for mutual benefit. This system elegantly allows people to pursue their own self-interest by requiring them to provide value to others in the process and incentivizing them to provide as much value as possible.

However, many people will argue that the goal should be to ensure the safety, health, and well-being of the group first and foremost. Systems that prioritize group welfare require citizens to contribute to the group before pursuing personal growth and to take care of the people who cannot contribute. This approach sacrifices individual liberty and growth for the sake of the group.

This debate balancing the freedom of the individual and the safety and welfare of the group will likely never end. People who prioritize freedom will resent others who try to limit it for safety reasons, and people who prioritize welfare will resent others for not contributing as much as they could toward the public good.

Each side has ethical concerns. Collectivists will ask why anyone ever has to live in poverty when there are enough resources for everyone. They believe that people will not be generous or organized enough if they are given the freedom to choose whether to sacrifice their time, money, and effort for others. Individualists will question why people who work should be forced to give a large portion of their income to people who choose not to work. They point out the counterproductive incentives of systems that entitle people to basic life necessities if they do not work and force them to give much of the benefit of their labor to others if they do.

The same core ethics of fairness, reciprocity, and minimizing harm can and will be used to argue for either position. Helping people who cannot help themselves minimizes group suffering; having to contribute to society while other capable citizens do not is unfair. Because the core ethics conflict with each other in this debate, society may strike a balance between providing basic necessities to people who cannot provide for themselves and requiring people who are able to contribute to earn their income.

The ethical conflict between individual liberty and group safety will continue indefinitely because people value both freedom and safety. They want the right to choose their own paths in life, and they also want to help the less fortunate and serve the greater good. The ultimate debate will be over the degree to which it is ethical to impede on personal freedoms for group benefit. Game theory shows that the best outcome for a group may be one that is not best for the individual, but the minimal harm rule prevents unjustified harm against the individual to achieve that group outcome. Because there is no perfect answer, society will account for both values in every ethic they establish.

Even though there will always be questions around which ethics are best, there is no doubt that a lack of ethics will severely limit your growth potential and inhibit your meaning in life. In his book, *After Virtue*, Alasdair MacIntyre said that the loss of a language of virtue, grounded in a particular tradition, makes it difficult for us to find meaning, coherence, and purpose in life.[92] While ethics are not the same as meaning, they do help you find the right or best way to approach a path and can enhance the meaning you have in your pursuit. Succeeding through unethical means takes away the value and meaning away from people who consider themselves to be good, moral people. Without a purpose and a set of values, ethics seem unnecessary; without ethics, it is hard to find meaning in what you are doing.

Ethics enhance meaning because humans tend to find more value in their actions when they benefit others as well as themselves. Through ethical behavior, they can show that they care and serve as role models for others to follow. In contrast, people who act without regard to others will often find that their lives lack the fulfillment of succeeding in harmony with them. They will also face the consequences of acting unethically: retaliation against their acts and unavailability of help when they need it.

Unethical attainment of goals can limit other forms of growth. For example, wealth and power are just two ways to grow, so attaining them unethically could limit social or familial growth. People may see only the benefit of the unethical behavior until they find out later that they committed a risky, undesirable tradeoff with other desired forms of growth.

Alternatively, making a personal sacrifice because it is ethical to help others can make a person's life more meaningful. For example, psychological studies have shown that people with children are less happy due to the added stress, but they also derive an added sense of meaning from parenthood.[93] Parents find value in seeing to their children's well-being and helping them grow.

Because a person cannot live without following rules, humans will never know what it is like to live without ethics. Humans do, however, know what it is like to live without agreed-upon ethics and without consistently applied ethics. They know what it is like to have certain individuals be devoid of commonly accepted ethics and act in very unpredictable, harmful ways. They know how civilization can quickly devolve into cutthroat, hypervigilant scenarios with little safety or cooperation.

While it may feel unfair for some people to act unethically while others act ethically, it may be of some solace that people who have no values and no rules for living well usually find themselves lacking in meaning and fulfillment. People who harm others may or may not see that harm repaid—despite most people's instinct to hope for themselves, others, a deity, or karma to reciprocate. However, few find long-term fulfillment and meaning in harming and destroying others. If they do, they probably believe that their actions were justified. Without that sense of justice, the harm caused is usually considered "meaningless" violence.

Society will never define rules that satisfy and protect everyone perfectly, but it usually attempts to optimize everyone's opportunity to grow on their own terms without encroaching on another's right to grow. Because humans live in a world with ethics, the biggest threat to the system is that people may not follow the rules. Any system put in place can be gamed or violated to one's advantage, and sometimes the only thing that keeps some people behaving ethically is the greater incentive to comply.

Despite society having an ethical system in place, it can quickly break down if the people who see the first manipulation or violation decide to ignore the rules themselves to restore fairness. To preserve ethics, the group has to retain them even when individual members abandon them. While some people will always be harmed in an ethical society by people who violate the rules, humans would quickly revert to the behaviors of their animal ancestors without them. Your primary role in helping maintain societal order is to act in the best way possible for yourself while factoring in how your actions may impact others—even if others do not care how their actions affect anyone else.

If the ethics of an act are unclear, evaluate its consequences

You may become exhausted just thinking about the complex relationships that determine your ethics. Many people feel the same way and so try to simplify life down to basic rules so that they do not have to get lost in the nuance. The ten commandments are an example of ten simple rules for living. "Thou shalt not kill." "Thou shalt not steal." "Thou shalt not bear false witness against thy neighbour."[94] These rules are simple, but there are plenty of circumstances in which they fail because the right thing to do in a situation may be to lie, steal, or even kill.

Before you try to set simple, universal rules, remember the exceptions. Mass shootings are situations where the best outcome to minimize harm to the most people would be to neutralize the shooters by any means necessary before they can kill more people. Confiscating someone's supply of drugs might be the right thing to do to prevent them from accidentally overdosing and dying. If you were hiding Jews in Nazi Germany or slaves in the Confederacy and soldiers came asking you where they were, the best outcome to minimize harm could be to lie or to omit information.

Ethics are too complex for pithy, absolute statements of what is right or wrong. Long, detailed law books better represent how nuanced ethics can really become. Blanket statements may be easier to remember, but they fall short when your unwillingness to harm a person in defense of others or unwillingness to hide the truth leads to people's deaths.

With this caveat, the closest to a blanket principle that is simple enough to remember and flexible enough to apply in most situations is the Optimal Outcome Principle. The Optimal Outcome Principle states that you should find and choose the option that maximizes growth and minimizes harm. You can achieve the optimal outcome when you make the decision or take the action with the best consequences after factoring in all potential parties' points of view and needs. With an objective, accurate evaluation of the impact of your decisions and actions on yourself and others, you can find the best option.

Many will equate looking for the optimal outcome with looking for a compromise or a perfect outcome, but there are some distinct differences between them. The optimal outcome is not the same as a compromise because it does not necessarily require concessions. For example, if a group of friends has a disagreement over which movie to see at a theater, a compromise might be for the group to watch one movie today and the other in the future. Both parts of the group see the movie they want to see, and both parts see the movie they do not wish to see. However, an optimal outcome could be for them to have dinner together, to break up into two groups to see the movie they want, and then to meet afterward to talk about the movies over dessert. Because people should not be talking in the theater during the movie, that option could benefit all and have no downside for the group.

The optimal outcome also differs from a perfect outcome because not all situations will have a solution that will benefit everyone and align with all parties' personal codes of ethics. For example, a soldier who falls on a grenade to protect the soldiers around him is clearly not achieving a perfect outcome for all parties. However, he is choosing the action that leads to the optimal outcome of minimal harm to the group. In that no-win situation, this selfless, honorable act protects dozens of people from harm and enables them to continue defending others. Unfortunately, this sacrifice is the best possible outcome given that no action could prevent all harm at that exact moment.

In the above two examples, the optimal outcome is neither a perfect outcome nor a compromise. In the former example, the perfect outcome would be for the group to find a movie that everyone wants to watch. A compromise requires concessions on both sides. The optimal outcome is to please both parties given that they cannot agree on which movie to watch. In the latter example, there is no perfect outcome and no compromise between parties. Instead, the optimal outcome given the tragic circumstances is to minimize the damage. The optimal outcome might be the perfect outcome or a compromise, but a compromise or a perfect outcome is not necessarily the optimal outcome.

Most laws set by objective parties aim for this optimal outcome because they can rarely benefit everyone without any negative consequences. They cannot create welfare programs without taking money from people who earn it through work, and they cannot set restrictions on immigration to a country without preventing people who might be better off in that country from entering it. Conversely, they cannot eliminate welfare programs without putting people who are unable to support themselves at risk, and they cannot allow unlimited immigration without risking negative cultural, economic, and social impacts.

Knowing these inherent trade-offs, lawmakers have to weigh various factors and make difficult decisions on controversial topics such as mandatory enlistment in the military and the use of mind-altering substances. Laws on both of these topics need to factor in the need of the country to protect its citizens, the right to practice a religion, and the freedom of each person to make his or her own decisions. With all factors considered, lawmakers will set laws that prioritize safety when the risk is too high, set limits to avoid encroaching too much on individual freedoms, and include specific exemptions to prevent people from violating their religious beliefs.

The end result may be to have an all-volunteer military unless the nation is under attack and a list of banned substances that are too dangerous for consumption. The exemptions in the law may allow conscientious objectors to opt out of a military draft on religious grounds or permit members of a religion to use certain banned substances in their rituals. These legal complexities enable society to balance the needs of the country and its citizens. The final outcome factors in the needs of a diverse population to let everyone grow optimally based on his or her beliefs and ethics.

The hardest part of following the Optimal Outcome Principle is ascertaining how your actions will influence the world around you and how other parties will perceive them. The best outcome given a multitude of variables is so difficult to determine that it is the subject of an entire field of study. Game theory studies the conflict and cooperation between rational decision-makers, and many scenarios take into consideration what is best for themselves and best for the group. In these models, the Nash equilibrium and the cooperative equilibrium describe when all parties in a scenario have set strategies that lead to the best possible outcome after factoring in the other decision-makers' strategies. Governments, corporations, and other organizations use these models to determine the effect of rules on human behavior so that they may establish the best structures possible.

You can perform similar analyses when you are unsure of the best decision in an ethically ambiguous situation. Fortunately, you do not need years of experience or complicated models to begin. To use the Optimal Outcome Approach, look at any decision you make or action you take from your perspective as well as from the perspectives of others who may be affected (e.g., family, friends, society). Check to see whether anyone is physically, mentally, or emotionally harmed by your decision or action. If so, check to see whether you could avoid that harm by adjusting your approach. Finally, check to see whether you could change your approach to benefit more people than you initially expected without any additional harm.

You will notice when evaluating a situation for an optimal outcome that you will factor in the amount of benefit, the amount of harm, the number of people affected, and the importance of those people to you, family, friends, and society. The final decision will not be the same for everyone, as everyone will have his or her own perception of what harm is, how much is acceptable before it crosses an ethical line, and which decision criteria are the most important.

A common line is human lives lost, where societies will undertake options that cost millions of dollars more or lead to much less benefit to its population to prevent the loss of life. Organizations will remove millions of bottles of their medicines from store shelves if a couple of contaminated ones kill people. Governments will spend a substantial amount of money to stop a serial killer or terrorist from harming more people.

Some will draw the line that no harm is worth any benefit, but then there are also different types of harm, such as physical, emotional, psychological, and financial. Most will say that hurting someone's feelings cannot be protected by law, but then there are laws against continued harassment that can significantly disrupt a person from living his or her life. You have to be able to offend people, though, in the process of correcting their behavior or exercising your right to be who you are. Damage to people or property are also pretty strictly against the law, but there are exceptions for when the people or property pose an immediate threat. While it is up to you to draw your own ethical lines, it is generally understood that harm for a greater good can be okay under extreme circumstances.

There is also harm caused by inaction to consider in ethical decision making. The optimal outcome, for example, may require you to call the police if you witness an emergency or a crime. The cost of your action is minimal, while the cost of your inaction could lead to great harm or death. Some criminal organizations raise the cost by threatening harm to people who call the police, so law enforcement responded by allowing people to report crimes anonymously. The phone call involves time, effort, and risk, but the benefits far outweigh the costs. Therefore, inaction is usually unethical under these types of circumstances.

Remember that unethical and illegal are not always the same, so it might be morally wrong not to get involved but not against the law. Unless you are in a position of authority with a responsibility to act, inaction is usually not illegal because you were not the person causing the harm and may not have been able to help without exposing yourself and others to risk. On the contrary, people may think that it is unethical to punish innocent bystanders. You will have to determine the best option for everyone involved given the situation, but your decision should factor in the law, the risk and impact of harm, and the potential benefit.

Because no one can foresee every possible consequence of any decision or action, remember to consider the intent, behavior, and outcome in your decisions and your evaluations of others' decisions. Many tragedies that occur are not necessarily matters of poor ethical decision making. If a person swerves his vehicle to avoid hitting a child and ends up hitting another vehicle, he may not be charged with a crime. In this situation, the driver intended to save the child's life and accidentally harmed another driver in the process. However, if it turns out that he staged the act and intended to harm the other driver, it could be considered attempted murder. Because the same act can result in multiple different ethical judgments, you have to take the circumstances into account.

The set of ethics that you establish using the Optimal Outcome Approach will be complex, nuanced, and continuously improving. It has to factor in agreed-upon societal rules along with individuals' rights and freedoms to choose their own life experiences. It has to factor in the benefits and drawbacks to multiple parties. It has to factor in types and degrees of harm. It has to factor in uncertainty and unknown variables. You have to balance these competing forces and arrive at the best decision. There may often be an optimal outcome that involves little to no concession by all parties, while others will be tough decisions between several options that will each negatively impact parts of the group.

This process of evaluating the impact of decisions and actions on all parties involved may completely change your perception of how you should act. Sometimes, it may involve being more socially responsible and acting to protect others or the environment from harm. Other times, it may involve allowing others to behave in ways that you do not agree with because their freedom to think, speak, and act without direct harm to others is more important than your disdain for their opinions.

You may experience difficulty in finding where the ethical line is for you. You may extend the definition of harm to include forms that you had not previously considered, or you may realize that too much protection encroaches on people's freedom to make their own life decisions. For example, you may find that using derogatory terms to describe people may have direct, clear emotional harm, so you decide to eliminate it from business settings. However, you may also notice that trying to suppress speech that you do not like in public settings because you disagree with it or find it to be offensive restricts others' rights. Your perspective will change as you learn more, and you will continue adjusting your ethics for the rest of your life.

Ultimately, it is up to you to determine where your line is and how you react when someone who has a different ethical boundary crosses your line. There will always be trade-offs between freedom and security and differences between what is moral and what is legal. Moreover, there will always be a balance to strike between what is best for yourself, others, and the group as a whole. Most importantly, your ethical behavior will not necessarily ensure others' ethical behavior.

Whatever your ethical line may be, remember that you should apply it as fairly and consistently as possible. Hypocrisy and favoritism are objective violations of the fairness ethic. In general, you should not hold others to standards that you cannot uphold if you wish to be seen as an ethical person. You may believe that your behavior is appropriate given the situation, but others are usually quick to call out any perceived unfairness.

Once you figure out what the optimal outcome is based on everyone's point of view, you have to be prepared for others to disagree. They may not consider others' needs in their decisions, or they may just not see the situation in the same way that you do. When this happens, you will have to decide whether you will stay with your ethics or adopt theirs out of reciprocity and fairness to their behavior. You also have to be ready for someone to have a moral line that is stricter than yours that you violate, and you have to determine whether you think their rule is just and apologize or disagree and dismiss their protests.

Relationships between people with significantly different negative ethics are difficult to sustain. The fairness and reciprocity ethics are so strong that they drive you to adopt their ethics, hold them to yours, or disassociate from them. With positive ethics, however, a "live and let live" approach is attainable if your life choices are not affecting anyone else and vice versa.

You may notice that the process through which you identify and adjust ethics is similar to the one for beliefs. There are beliefs based on facts that achieve general agreement, and then there are your personal beliefs. Similarly, there are agreed-upon ethics governing group behavior, and then there are your personal ethics. The reason is that ethics **are** beliefs. Specifically, they are beliefs that people hold about what is right or wrong behavior. As such, you should continually test your ethics just as you test your other beliefs to ensure you have the best set to maximize growth.

Additionally, trying to force your positive ethics onto others is just as much of a recipe for resentment, hatred, conflict, and even violence as it is for beliefs. For example, your view on which career paths are worth pursuing may have served you well in helping you make the right choices for your growth, but they may not be appropriate for someone else. Telling someone that a particular path is a waste of time may seem like good advice, but you may also be inhibiting their growth if they strongly desire to pursue that growth area. If they are not hurting anyone, try to respect their life decisions.

Finally, you must continuously monitor your ethics just as you monitor your beliefs for when they might be wrong. There is a fine line between justification and rationalization as well as justice and revenge. It is not always clear where a good reason becomes a bad excuse. It is not always clear where the protection of one person becomes the unfair restriction of another. Your retaliation in response to harm against you will seem fair at first, but there will be a point where responding to unethical behavior with escalated unethical behavior will no longer be justice. There will be a point where taking away certain rights and freedoms for safety reasons will cross the line into oppression.

Therefore, you should regularly test your ethics for rationalizations of your actions. Anyone can justify an unethical act by convincing themselves that it is only fair, reciprocal, or not that harmful. You might convince yourself that you are not harming anyone when you use aggressive sales tactics on someone that you know cannot afford what you are selling. You might tell yourself that other people are not following the rules when they cheat on their taxes, so it is unfair if you continue to pay your full share. You might explain that rules are for everyone's safety when they provide disproportionate personal benefits. Rationalization can make almost any act seem appropriate.

This flaw in human ethics explains most unethical behaviors by otherwise moral people. Wars, economic crises, terrorist attacks, and oppressive governments are almost always caused by people rationalizing their actions. People do not walk around actively trying to be immoral in every single act to every single being around them for no reason. Instead, they believe that their actions are justified, do not have the capacity to care, prioritize themselves or their in-group members over others, have been improperly educated on social behavior, or do not understand the harm they cause. Your biggest risk, then, is not of knowingly committing atrocious acts but of not realizing that you have crossed the line until it is too late.

The list of behaviors that most would consider objectively unethical but can seem subjectively ethical is practically infinite. Many people who steal or pirate property may justify their actions as fair given their current financial situation or as retaliation against the unethical acts of corporations. Many people who cheat in sports to gain a competitive advantage may use the fairness rationalization. The first person might use performance-enhancing substances because he believes that it is not fair that others are naturally stronger or less injury-prone, and others who follow may then believe that it is now fair for them to use them.

If those companies go out of business or cheaters beat non-cheaters, though, those people will not point to themselves as part of the problem. Instead, the diffusion of responsibility will allow them to rationalize to themselves and others that everyone does it and that their actions did not wholly, directly cause the harm. They may then blame others for not joining them or not trying hard enough to stop them.

With the exception of a few random, senseless acts, most ethical offenses risk compounding by either spreading or deepening. Behavioral economics research has shown that the majority of people cheat a little bit, rationalizing it to themselves in various ways to maintain their moral self-image.[95] It then just takes one person witnessing unpunished cheating, though, to then use the fairness or reciprocity rationalization to spread and escalate the cheating. It will quickly get out of hand, leading to major ethical violations that no one would have thought were possible at the beginning. If unchecked, the cycle will lead a game, economy, or society on a path toward self-destruction.

To avoid going down the path of rationalizing unethical behavior, beware of the common excuses. Social acceptability—real or perceived—is one of the most common excuses: "If others do it, it must be okay to do." Another is the perceived unfairness and injustice of the universe: "Some people are born stronger, taller, smarter, or wealthier than others, so it is okay to be unfair toward them to correct for that unfairness." Another is the belief that an unethical act's harm is negligible: "This is nothing compared to what others do." The most dangerous, arguably, is escalated reciprocity: "Someone performed an unethical act, so he or she must be punished disproportionately to his or her violation to discourage anyone from doing it again."

These excuses may feel right at the time, but they have significant flaws. The first assumes that what other members of a group do is ethical, which is not always the case. The second erroneously applies human fairness ethics to the universe and conflates fairness (i.e., applying the same rules) with competitiveness (i.e., having the same potential). The third is highly subjective, so you are prone to discount the harm you are doing to feel better about your actions. Finally, the last has the highest risk of people invoking a never-ending stream of unethical acts out of vengeance, not justice.

If you find yourself falling into this rationalization trap, look at your behavior from the perspective of the people who are not breaking the rules. Through this lens, you will be able to see how your behavior is harmful or unfair to them and how they will likely feel justified in reciprocating against you. It may be wrong for someone else to break the rules at your expense, but your response of also breaking the rules is probably just as unethical. In essence, you are joining them in being unfair to individuals who choose to follow the rules.

If you want to be ethical in everything you do, you have to be prepared to do so despite others not being ethical. If you choose to be unethical in response to someone who is being unethical, you have to be prepared for the unintended consequences. Most likely, you will accidentally harm an innocent person with your behavior or beget more unethical behavior. If you find yourself with a good reason to perform an act that is normally unethical, thoroughly verify that reason to avoid regret and other worse consequences in the future. Groups' justice systems are established to prevent people from rationalizing increasingly unethical behavior, so try your best to address issues within them before resorting to vigilantism to punish others' behavior.

Once you are clear on the ethics that you should follow and how to stay true to them, you need to apply them accurately. You can assess ethics' applicability by ascertaining why they exist and determining whether they are appropriate for the current situation. All rules are set for a reason, whether it be to increase growth, decrease harm, improve efficiency, reduce risk, or ensure fairness. The best way to apply ethics is to trace them back to the value or intended outcome and then verify that following them is the most effective approach given the circumstances.

In an example using negative ethics, laws against murder are intended to prevent people from killing each other. The reason is clear, but there are circumstances where these ethics do not apply. Soldiers following agreed-upon rules of engagement against enemy combatants are generally not considered to be committing murder, nor are citizens killing in self-defense. Assisted suicide is more controversial, as ethics against killing conflict with ethics supporting an individual's freedom to choose what to do with his or her own life. In that case, you may ultimately believe that it is always wrong or that it is not legal but is ethical under certain conditions. When you combine the reasons and the circumstances, you can determine how to apply your ethics appropriately.

In an example using positive ethics, someone may follow a rule to go to the gym to exercise before she gets home from work. Because she may lose the motivation to work out once she enters her house, this rule ensures that she exercises. If you do not have that problem, then you should follow a different approach. She also might run every day because she is training for an athletic competition, whereas you may run three days per week to maintain general health. Your ethics will change based on why you are exercising and what the best way is to keep you committed.

You can use this method for negative ethics to determine where your boundaries are. For example, you may conclude that lying is never ethical or that it is acceptable if you are sparing someone's feelings or protecting someone. You can also use it to find the suitability of positive ethics for your life. You may find that some approaches to diet, exercise, work, relationships, or learning work for you and others do not. When you understand why and how a rule works, you can understand how to apply it.

Many ethics are estimates, guesses, or even just a continuation of what others have done for no known reason. Analyzing and challenging the rules you follow to make sure they are right and applicable for your path in life is a necessary, constant activity that you should continue throughout life. Through this approach, you can make sure that you have the best set of ethics that will allow you to succeed in your life while allowing others to have the opportunity to succeed in theirs.

If you are still unsure of whether a specific act is ethical, there are many techniques you can use to help you determine the best approach. For example, you can imagine how proud or ashamed you would be if your behavior was the top story in the news. This technique, the Front Page Test, allows you to view a decision from society's perspective and helps you to determine whether your act is socially acceptable. You can also use the "What If Everyone Did This?" Test to evaluate whether your act has great harm at scale. This approach counteracts the common rationalization that a small act has negligible impact. One of the most popular methods is the Golden Rule Test: "Would I be upset if someone did this to me?" This check allows you to assess the negative impact of your actions on others more objectively.

Checks are arguably most important to have in place for circumstances where your moral compass is likely to waver. You need to be ready when the incentives are so strong that you may be willing to sacrifice your ethics to achieve the outcome. Make sure that you have techniques in place to keep yourself in compliance with your personal code of ethics.

For example, you have a high risk of rationalizing unethical behavior when you are interacting with people you disagree with or dislike. When someone states a fact, belief, or opinion that you think is wrong, you may become angry or upset because this experience does not align with your beliefs. You may also conflate them being factually wrong with being morally wrong and therefore unconsciously feel justified in reciprocating with insults or harm. Being on the "right" side of the argument, however, does not justify unethical behavior toward the other side.

If you find yourself in this situation, tell yourself the following phrase to moderate your behavior: "Just because you're right, doesn't make it right." This test can help you stop yourself from participating in the vicious cycle where disagreements escalate into name-calling, harassment, bullying, death threats, and violence. It is a common persuasion and argumentation tactic to demonize the opposition, but people too often use that rhetoric to rationalize unethical behavior toward their opponents.

These methods of evaluating the ethics of your behavior help you to view the situation objectively and find the best approach.

Use these techniques to keep your moral compass in line with what you believe to be right or wrong. It is hard to be impartial when you are likely to overemphasize personal benefits and discount the negative consequences. Do everything you can to get an objective view of a situation before making an ethical decision.

When you are finally clear on your ethics, you may find that they are different from the group's established rules. In those cases, you can follow the rules, petition to change them, join a group with different rules, subvert them, or ignore them. Whichever action you take, you need to be prepared to face the consequences. While everyone's ethics do not have to be the same, the laws of society should avoid inhibiting any person's growth unnecessarily. Sub-groups have more leeway to set the rules that they like, and you have the freedom of association to decide whether to continue to be a member or to leave if your ethics do not align.

After adhering to the shared laws of society, you need to find the ethics that work for you, apply them consistently, and continually test and improve them. Always remember why you follow them and consider the context in which you apply them. When you have the right set of ethics, you will be taking the best path toward success.

Ethics are a critical component of optimal growth in society. Without them, life is chaotic. With them, life becomes safer and more constructive. However, there is no perfect set of ethics for everyone; there is just a set of rules that everyone can agree to follow. Humans tend to oversimplify to teach others or make decisions more efficiently, but formal decision-making rules such as law books are much more nuanced. To be as ethical as possible, you must do your best to understand how your decisions and actions affect yourself and others. Using this knowledge, you can identify an ethical framework that achieves the optimal outcome given the rights and needs of all parties involved. Your ethics will conflict and change over time, especially as your wants, needs, and beliefs conflict and change.

Most will summarize ethics with the concise phrase, "Live

and let live." As you live, you will determine what values, goals, and ethics work best for you and what you should do to maximize growth. As you let others live, you will determine the rules that everyone must follow to prevent harm and the freedom that all people should have to pursue their own growth in their own ways. With ethics, everyone can live life in the best way possible.

QUESTIONS

Questions That Help You Find Your Ethics

Your answers to these questions will help you find guidelines for how to pursue your life's purpose ethically. This chapter's content provides guidance on how to think about these questions, but only you can supply the definitive answers for your life.

1. What do you believe are the fundamental human rights of individuals?

   Example: The Declaration of Independence lists "life, liberty, and the pursuit of happiness" as unalienable rights

2. Which rules need to be followed by everyone to prevent harm to others? Which rules do not need to be followed by everyone because they are right for some and not for others?

   Example: Killing and stealing are generally wrong for anyone to do; although I like to maintain a stylish, professional appearance, others may not be concerned with how they look

3. In your areas of growth, which rules should you follow to maximize your potential? Why?

   Example: To learn and be a successful student, I should attend classes, complete assignments, and study for tests

4. Are there unethical ways of attaining that growth? How would otherwise ethical people rationalize these actions?

   Example: Competitors may use banned substances or techniques to enhance their performance; people who use them may justify their actions by telling themselves that everyone does it

5. Can you achieve your goals without being unethical? How?

   Example: I can win without cheating by training within the rules

6. Are any of your ethics preventing you from pursuing or achieving your goals? How can you adjust them?

   Examples: I think that being wealthy or successful is wrong because it prevents someone else from being successful; I think that treating myself well is selfish and that I always have to put others first

7. In a relationship, what are your principles for a good marriage/partnership/friendship?

   • Does your spouse/partner/friend share these principles?
   • Can you agree on relationship ethics so that you will avoid hurting each other in the future?
   • How might your ethics change as you grow together?

8. How do/should you handle yourself when someone violates your ethics? How do/should you handle yourself when you violate someone else's ethical standards?

9. What could happen to you if you use someone else's behavior as justification for your behavior? How do you make sure your response to unethical behavior is appropriate?

10. How have your ethics changed over time? Were these changes because you improved or because society evolved?

11. How do you test your ethics in ambiguous situations?

12. Who sets a high standard of ethics for their personal or professional lives? What can you learn from their approach?

13. Do you disagree with any of the rules you must follow? How can you reconcile or address these ethical differences?

EXERCISES

Activities That Help You Find Your Ethics

Completing these exercises will improve your ethical model so that you approach your life goals in the best way possible.

Thought Exercise: Think of an ethical dilemma in your life that you are unsure of how to approach. For each option that you are considering, imagine how you would feel if your decision or action was reported as the top story in the news the next day. How do you think that others would view it, and how would you feel if everyone knew what you did?

This thought exercise is a quick way to get instant feedback on whether something is ethical from an objective perspective. It amplifies the feeling of shame and embarrassment from minor unethical acts like cheating on tax returns or littering that you may not feel when no one is watching. It also helps you recognize rationalizations that would not survive public scrutiny. Use it whenever you think that you might be discounting the negative consequences of your actions.

Brainstorming Exercise: To determine your ethical boundaries on an issue, draw a continuum (i.e., a horizontal line with points at each end) and place competing ethics at each end. Then, brainstorm where various scenarios would fall on the continuum and draw a line depicting the point at which one of your ethics encroaches too far on the other one. Alternatively, you can use this continuum to identify the point at which an act becomes unethical. In that case, label the ends Ethical/Just and Unethical/Unjust, plotting various scenarios based on how ethical or unethical they are, and drawing the line where right becomes wrong.

Example 1:

Objective: *Determining the optimal line between two conflicting ethics*

Topic: *Balancing privacy and security – data gathering for police and national defense use*

Task: *Draw a line where you think the right balance between privacy and security is.*

Label on the left side of the continuum: *Security*

- *The government can monitor citizen activity at all times for any reason*

- *The government can monitor individual citizen financial, call, and internet history without a warrant*
- *The government can monitor non-citizen financial, call, and internet history without a warrant*
- *The government can monitor aggregate financial, call, and internet data*
- *The government can monitor travel information for suspicious activity*
- *The government can monitor public or tax information*
- *The government can monitor citizens only after having valid probable cause and a warrant*
- *The government cannot monitor citizens unless there is overwhelming evidence of a crime and a warrant*
- *The government cannot review any citizen information for any reason*

Label on the right side of the continuum: *Privacy*

When you are done finding your ethical line, note the criteria you used to determine that line and consider where others would draw it.

Note: you may believe that items on the list are partially or conditionally ethical; if so, draw lines to delineate the obvious ethical and unethical items and note what is ethical and unethical about the debatable items.

Example 2:

Objective: *Determining for society when an act is ethical/legal*

Topic: *Killing another human*

Label on the left side of the continuum: *Just (e.g., Self-Defense)*

Label on the right side of the continuum: *Unjust (e.g., Murder)*

Task: *The following list is in a random order. Plot the actions on the ethical continuum based on how (un)ethical you believe each act is.*

- *Killing someone unprovoked after months of preparation*
- *Mass genocide of a large group of people*
- *Killing someone after finding out that he or she was unfaithful*

- *Killing enemy soldiers while defending the country from an unprovoked invasion*
- *Killing someone who has a gun to another person's head*
- *Killing someone who is raping another person*
- *Killing someone who is reaching for a gun*
- *Assassinating a leader who has threatened the world with nuclear war*
- *Killing someone who was assaulting a person but is now fleeing*
- *Killing soldiers of a country that was threatening to attack*
- *Killing someone who just killed someone else in front of you*
- *Killing someone who killed others the day before to avenge them*
- *Killing someone accidentally while performing life-saving surgery*
- *Killing someone accidentally while drunk driving*
- *Bombing enemy soldiers holding innocent civilians hostage*
- *Killing someone who is dying a painful death with no hope of recovery*
- *Killing a mass shooter during their attack on a group of people*
- *Assassinating a leader who ordered the killing of 10,000 citizens*
- *Killing a person who is burglarizing a home and might be armed*

When you finish plotting these actions, draw the line where ethical acts become unethical and note the criteria you used to determine whether the act was ethical and how ethical or unethical it was.

This method helps in three ways: to find the line between right and wrong, to determine the relative severity of an unethical act, and to find the appropriate balance between two conflicting ethics. The first example above plots the trade-off between citizens' privacy and national security to determine where a government's actions would be violating individual liberties. Safety and freedom are both important for growth, so the goal is to understanding where one reaches a point where it excessively inhibits the other. The second example takes an action that may be right or wrong depending on the situation and helps to clarify the evaluation criteria used to judge whether it is ethical and how ethical it is. This form of the exercise can help you define rules and their punishments more appropriately.

You may find through this exercise that even something that seems so simple can become very complex. In imagining yourself in these situations, you may see a difference between what you would be able to do yourself compared to what is objectively ethical. For example, you may be a pacifist and refuse to kill under any circumstance while respecting the social acceptability of killing in self-defense. In those cases, you can mark your ethical line compared to society's to see how they differ.

After completing the examples, perform this exercise for any situation in your life that has a fine line between right and wrong or ethical trade-offs to figure out where the line is for you or where the best balance is for your needs.

Creative Exercise: Look at the collage that you created through the creative exercises in the previous three chapters. When you envision achieving your desired outcome, make sure that you are attaining it in the most ethical way possible. Envision that you legitimately earn or obtain the items that you want. Imagine that your personal success comes from fair practices. Picture yourself upholding your values as you become the person you wish to be.

Next, adjust your Desire column to include pictures, words, or symbols that represent taking an ethical route toward your goal. These items can represent direct behaviors, such as working hard or waking up early, or intangible ethics, such as honor, loyalty, respect, fairness.

Thinking about acting ethically can help you identify the best approach and prepare you for difficult decisions. Taking the ethical approach gives you the best chance to achieve the optimal outcome and feel fulfilled by your actions and decisions.

Note: You may wish to leave space on, next to, and below your collage for future chapters' creative exercises.

Writing Exercise: Take your list of possible experiences and action items from the writing exercises of the first five chapters. For each experience or action item, write down how you could do this ethically or unethically. Then, write down how you can avoid the unethical route while still achieving your goals.

This exercise helps you surface ethical scenarios that you may encounter so that you can mentally rehearse responding in the most ethical way possible. For example, you can prepare what you would say to people who ask you to cheat or how you will handle others who use unethical means to win or succeed at your expense. Ethics are extremely difficult to uphold in high-pressure athletic, scholastic, political, and business situations, so rehearsing and preparing for these situations is the best way to overcome obstacles without sacrificing your principles.

At the end of the exercise, you should have calibrated the list so that the items on it and the means of attaining them are right for you while not being harmful to others.

Example:

Desired Outcomes	Experiences	Action Items	Ethical Approach	Unethical Approach	How to Avoid Being Unethical
Attractive physique	Exercise	Sign up to a gym	Go three days per week	Use gym without paying	Get a part-time job
Make close friends	Club activities	Mark meetings on calendar	Be honest, friendly, and caring	Lie about self	Find people who will like me for me

Note: *The above example does not show all of the information you will bring from the previous writing exercises; it is possible that this chapter's teachings may cause you to refine that information.*

OUTCOME

After reading this chapter, you should have a clear understanding of how your ethics guide you to live life in the best way possible for yourself and others. You should have the rules, values, code, or principles you will live by in pursuit of your growth areas. You should then have made sure that you know how to attain your goals ethically and that your desired experiences and planned behaviors are consistent with your ethics. You may have noted items on your list where you need to learn more about the best way to attain your goal. Continue to monitor your ethics over time, as they may need to change as you and the people around you evolve.

When you have your updated list, you are ready to proceed to the next chapter.

Support

Support enables you to realize your life's meaning

"Alone we can do so little. Together, we can do so much."

— Helen Keller[96]

"If I have seen further, it is by standing on the shoulders of giants."

— Isaac Newton[97]

PRINCIPLES OF SUPPORT

- Support is the ability of life to cooperate for greater growth
- Humans who cooperate make more progress more quickly
- Your support system helps you maximize your potential
- Without support, you will be less likely to succeed
- If you lack support, look for it, ask for it, accept it, and give it

SUPPORT AND THE MEANING OF LIFE

Humans are a social species. To be social, they have to engage in activities that contribute to each other's success. Support is the act of one life form helping another life form to grow. Contributing to others' growth allows humans to achieve more than what they could attain alone. While ethics ensure that people can grow in harmony, support enables them to reach their full potential.

Support is the ability of life to cooperate for greater growth

"No man is an island," wrote John Donne.[98] No living thing can exist among other living things without affecting or being affected by them. In early organisms, those interactions were random and unintentional. The harmful interactions made other organisms less likely to survive, while the beneficial interactions increased their survivability. As a result, natural selection favored life forms that could engage in mutually beneficial interactions.

Through that process, single-celled organisms over their billions of years of existence began exhibiting cooperative behaviors. These behaviors evolved from random beneficial acts between single-celled organisms into the coordinated actions of multicellular organisms. In modern times, studies have shown that microorganisms can communicate and cooperate to perform many multicellular activities. These activities include the ability to acquire or produce resources for the group, the ability to gather around those resources (e.g., biofilm formation), and the ability to signal other group members to coordinate behavior (e.g., quorum sensing).[99]

Similarly, early cooperation between multi-cellular life forms, such as mutualistic and commensalistic symbiosis, was coincidental and serendipitous. Over time, some of these creatures, such as wolves and birds, evolved an instinct to cooperate within their species. Groups of organisms can protect their members, share food, and take care of their sick and injured. Some animals developed cross-species relationships, such as when dogs provide protection and companionship to humans in exchange for food and shelter. In some instances, individuals will even help others to their own detriment.

As Richard Dawkins explains in his book, *The Selfish Gene*, organisms developed selfish, cooperative, and altruistic behaviors based on how they affect the probability of gene survival. While altruism may seem to reduce an organism's own survivability, this self-sacrifice for others' benefit increases the survivability of the group as a whole by preserving its shared genes.[100] As a result, natural selection favors these social behaviors.

Cooperation has clear advantages. Groups have greater visibility of threats in the environment and can more effectively defend against predators. Individuals within the group can also specialize, which allows each person to excel in specific skills to strengthen the group's collective capabilities. These capabilities eventually allowed social animals' populations to grow at higher rates and thrive in large numbers.

This type of cooperation requires more than just the willingness not to harm others. Members of a group with specialized roles become interdependent and must support each other. If one role is a hunter and another is a caretaker, then the hunter needs to provide the group with food while the caretaker nurtures offspring. Without the hunter, the group does not have enough food; without the caretaker, the group's territory and offspring would not be cared for and protected while the hunters were hunting.

Social species have developed many capabilities that make them willing and able to help each other meet their needs, thrive, and recover from harm. Three of the most important capabilities are language for communicating a want or need, empathy for understanding and internalizing it, and compassion for caring about it. These traits genetically equip and predispose social animals to provide care, support, and assistance for each other.

Humans have advanced forms of communication, empathy, and compassion. Their evolved facial expressions enable a variety of nonverbal signals, including blushing, smiling, laughing, grimacing, wincing. Their evolved empathy allows them to feel the same emotions that they are seeing someone else express. Their evolved compassion drives them to help others in need and support their life goals. To reinforce the supportive behaviors that people with empathy and compassion exhibit, the brains of humans involved in social interactions release chemicals such as serotonin and oxytocin.

Together, these functions influence people to behave in ways that are best for the group. Because humans also have the core ethics of fairness and reciprocity, they will also feel the urge to repay help given to them, creating a virtuous cycle of support. Combined with humans' physical and intellectual advantages, this set of characteristics and behavioral traits gives humans a greater capacity to help each other grow than any other species.

Human cooperation has excelled so far that all humans may benefit from the group's acts. In modern society, for example, even hermits who are seemingly cut off from society are directly benefitting from the existence of police, fire, and emergency services. Scientific advancements spread around the world and help people to live more safely and productively.

Support is such an important component of the universe beyond life. Any mass combined with another mass becomes stronger. Any person can snap a twig in half or tear a sheet of paper in half with his or her bare hands; snapping a wrapped bundle of twigs or tearing a large book bare-handed becomes impossible because of the force required to break it apart.

Similarly, support in life generates a whole that is greater than the sum of its parts. Groups of people can solve problems faster, complete more difficult tasks, survive threats, and manufacture products more effectively than individuals. Support allows humans with their individual advantages and disadvantages to contribute to the group so that they collectively maximize their strengths and minimize their weaknesses.

Unlike inanimate objects, life can support other life in more ways than just physically. Humans provide many forms of support, including emotional, intellectual, social, and financial, to help each other grow well beyond what any single person could attain alone. Being able to contribute to others' growth or a group's mission is often the best way for people to give their own lives purpose.

Humans who cooperate make more progress more quickly

Support can be the difference between success and failure for any individual on his or her life journey. For example, human babies need constant care and protection because the size[101] and metabolic requirements[102] of their brains require them to be born before they are capable of autonomous movement. Other mammals are more developed and can perform more independent tasks at birth, so humans need additional support to survive until they are able to take care of themselves.

Given their helpless state, human children instinctively trust their caretakers. Adults instinctively protect and nurture children. These instincts influence how they interact with each other. Adults view babies' physical attributes (e.g., being small, having big eyes relative to their faces) as cute so that they take care of them. Mothers pull small children close to their chests when encountering danger. Children cry when they lose sight of their parents. Adults speak in a slow, loud, and enunciated manner—i.e., "baby talk"—so babies can learn words more easily. Adults hug, kiss, and tickle children to bond with them. These behaviors are critical for the children's survival and development.

Support is also critical between parents. For example, scientists have found that adult couples develop a strong romantic love for between 18 months and three years,[103] and that duration helps the father partner with the mother to protect and provide for the child through its fragile infancy.[104] This bonding secures physical and emotional support for the parents and the offspring, increasing the survivability of the whole family.

Support helps to keep large groups safe and prosperous as well. Societies have set up support systems that protect the community from criminals, wild animals, fire, disease, natural disasters, and unexpected financial hardship. These systems reduce individuals' risk of harm and enable them to recover from tragedies more quickly. Society has also established institutions to foster growth and development, such as schools, community centers, continuing education programs, coaching services, mentoring programs, and tutoring sessions. These organizations accelerate growth compared to learning in an unstructured fashion.

Collectively, these support systems allow humans to reach their full potential. Without having to worry about being harmed, members of the group can focus on growth. Without having to figure things out on their own, they can both learn from and build on the group's collective knowledge.

The multiplicative effect of support is clearly demonstrated in the productivity impact of working in organized groups. Multiple people can work to complete a project that no single person can do alone, and role specialization allows the group to accomplish much more than if each person performed every task. In communities or marketplaces, one person who cannot complete a task by himself may receive assistance from or may trade with another person in exchange for work that he is able to do.

There are examples where each form of cooperation is necessary for maximum growth. A group joining forces can lift a heavy object that is too heavy for any single person. A team with specialized roles can assemble a car in hours with the proper knowledge and technology, whereas one person would take weeks or months to complete the work. Finally, some tasks, such as surgical procedures, haircuts, or orthodontics, are more effective when one person performs them on another than when someone tries to do them on herself. Anyone moving to a new home, trying to solve a difficult problem, or starting a business knows that having support can help her achieve her goals faster and more effectively.

The best non-human example of support's impact on growth is technology. Humans invent new technologies to increase their productivity, and they accomplish multiple times more when their efforts include machine or computer assistance. They can even program technology to learn and grow on its own, increasing its ability to support people's objectives to an even greater degree. Add in the ability for machines with artificial intelligence to build and teach themselves, and humans have practically infinite growth potential.

Support, however, includes more than productivity improvements. After catastrophic events, people can help others recover from physical, emotional, or financial harm. They can help others manage setbacks and improve their probability of success in the future. They can help others make new friends, connect to job opportunities, find potential mates, and push for social and political change. The ways to support others in their growth is as numerous as the options for personal growth.

Helping others can be one of the most rewarding experiences life has to offer. The feeling of fulfillment through support has its roots in biology, as both the giver and receiver of help experience positive emotions and receive neurochemical rewards from the interaction.[105] Additionally, the tangible improvement achieved together brings with it a feeling of pride and accomplishment in both parties. Finally, the beneficiaries of that support will reciprocate with gratitude, reward, or recognition, which validates the helper's contribution. These consequences provide incentives to continue helping and lead to greater satisfaction with life.

Many political, spiritual, and community leaders will cite service to others as a key to finding meaning in life. Indeed, it is arguably the best option for people who desire to have a "higher purpose" or "greater meaning" in life. When asked to define what "higher purpose" means, most people will state that they want to contribute to something greater than themselves. An individual's meaning multiplies when she lives not just for herself but also for her family, friends, community, or society.

As a result, the maximum value that a person can deliver to a group is practically unlimited when compared to focusing on one's own interest. The potential meaning that he or she can find in supporting others is going to be greater as well. Fortunately, people do not have to choose between one and the other; they can take actions that have mutual benefit. If they better themselves and then use their abilities to benefit others, their overall impact will be much, much more significant to everyone affected.

While much of society may seem to be selfish and competitive, most of society is designed for mutual benefit. In capitalistic economic systems, people provide products and services that benefit others in exchange for money that they then spend on products and services provided for them. Because people specialize for maximum productivity, members of society are interdependent and need to provide value to others to receive everything that they need to survive and thrive in return. In a seeming paradox, systems based on self-interest and fair competition make everyone contribute more and ensure that transactions are mutually beneficial. Even systems based on altruism and non-competitive cooperation, such as socialism, require everyone to contribute to society for them to work. The compensation received in these models is just tied to time spent exerting effort or degree of need rather than the value of goods and services provided.

While support is necessary for humans to survive and critical for them to maximize their growth, it can be abused or taken too far. Evolution instilled humans with an inherent need to be accepted in a group because it kept them alive. The need for companionship can be comparable to the drive to eat, sleep, drink, or reproduce. If that need combines with having low self-worth, many people may neglect their own needs to please others. They may even begin to resent the people they help for accepting their offer (often known as "playing the martyr" or "being taken advantage of"). Taken to an extreme, providing too much support can take a toll on any person. People who are prone to self-sacrifice need to remember that the stronger they are, the more and better support they can provide.

In addition to sacrificing oneself too much for others, people can become too dependent on others. As a person receives more support without contributing to the group, he becomes less willing and able to support himself and others. Additionally, people who see that they can receive more assistance if they appear to be less capable have a disincentive to strengthen themselves. This combination can create a downward cycle of becoming less capable and requiring more support, thus no longer growing but instead maintaining a stagnant existence. It is just as necessary to support oneself as it is to give and accept help to ensure the sustainability and growth of the group.

The right amount of support for optimal growth is difficult to determine. Each person has different nutritional, educational, financial, social, and emotional needs that require different levels of support to have the best quality of life. Too much support for someone can lead to unnecessary dependency, while too little support can lead to unrealized potential. The right amount of support allows people to push through challenges, improve themselves, and help others.

Because each person will have their own needs for what will help them grow, helpers have to learn what the right amount of support is and adjust accordingly. As a general rule, additional support is beneficial if it helps people to grow more, overcome hurdles, or deliver more value to others, and it is harmful if it enables self-destructive behavior, fosters codependency, or allows people to avoid their problems. The goal of support is to accelerate and maximize growth, not to prevent and inhibit it.

Support is critical for human progress. Others can increase your growth potential significantly, and helping others can increase your impact on the world around you. This greater capacity for achievement and impact gives you greater meaning. When you cooperate with others to achieve a goal, you significantly increase your growth potential and your probability of success.

Your support system helps you maximize your potential

Life is difficult, and it is practically impossible to avoid all obstacles in your path to growth. While you can accomplish almost anything with enough desire, belief, time, and effort, support enables you to overcome those obstacles and achieve a greater outcome more quickly and efficiently.

Cooperative work is so powerful that most of what you own, do, or become involves other people. You likely wear clothes made by someone else, use utilities that others set up for you, and perform a job that someone needs you to do to earn income. Any new invention or venture is supported by the inventions and ventures that have come before. Any achievement has years of education, nurturing, and protection behind it.

Humans have specialized to the extent that most of your activities throughout life will involve other people. Sexual reproduction is a primal example, as you cannot continue the species without another person's help. More recently, businesses have created production methods that involve thousands of parts and hundreds of specialized roles, making it impractical or impossible for you to try to replicate their output alone. If you attempt to live "off the grid" and become completely self-reliant, you will accomplish a fraction of what you could by partaking in some trade or division of labor.

If you wish to attain the greatest outcome, you are better off maximizing your productivity in a specialized role and leveraging others to multiply the overall output instead of trying to do everything less efficiently by yourself. Corporations, armies, governments, sports teams, and schools all show the power of what can be accomplished through organized, specialized cooperation. These cooperative groups all help you reach your full potential, and you can maximize the potential of other individuals and the group as a whole by contributing as much as you can in your role.

When you specialize and engage in reciprocal support, you can focus on what you do best and can rely on others to help you with what you are unable or unwilling to do. As a result, you will have clothes to wear, food to eat, water to drink, a safe community to live in, and medicine to treat you without having to sew, farm, pump water, police your neighborhood, and study pharmacology. If you had to do all of these things yourself, your productivity would plummet, and you would have no time to help others. By leveraging your strengths and getting support for other tasks, you spend less time doing the necessary work to stay alive and more time focusing on your prioritized growth areas.

While there may never be enough time in a day, month, year, or lifetime to do everything you want to do, support allows you to make the most progress. For example, if you have physical, emotional, intellectual, and career goals, support multiplies your productivity so that you make fewer trade-offs and sacrifices. With help, you can have a full-time job, go to school, exercise three times per week, and spend one or two nights per week with friends and family. Get help with activities related to your goals so that you are more likely to achieve them, and get help with unrelated activities to prevent them from distracting or inhibiting you.

In addition to accelerating your progress, support is critical when you are facing harm, adversity, or difficulty. You are safer in a group of friends than alone when encountering a threat. After experiencing setbacks, you recover much more quickly when someone helps you address both the issue and its emotional impact. Friends and family may go to great lengths to help you through trauma, but even support as simple as a hug can release chemicals in the brain that can relieve stress and help you cope.[106] Your ability and willingness to get help when you are struggling can be the difference between persevering and admitting defeat.

Social connections are especially important to humans' emotional well-being. Without them, the resulting loneliness can be depressing. Being alone is not the problem; feeling lonely is. If you are properly supported at the moment and do not need anything or anyone, you will feel fine. Feeling lonely—even when you are around people—means that you believe that you are not getting the social or emotional support you need to thrive.

Fortunately, humans are evolutionarily wired to support each other. Your empathy, bonding, friendship, and nurturing instincts will activate when you see someone who needs help, and people who care about you will try to support you when they see you in need. There will be variations on how much social interaction is necessary, such as introverts needing less exposure to large groups than extroverts, but most people need at least some support and are willing to reciprocate.

With everyone being incredibly busy in modern times, it may seem that people are primarily focused on themselves. However, most people are busy fulfilling their duties to others, including their children, parents, spouses, companies, communities, and friends. You may also not notice the unsung actions—donations, gifts, thoughtful actions, and courtesies—that help others who may be struggling or just having a bad day. People often want to help, and they do the best that they can with their limited time to care for the people around them when it is needed.

As such, if you need help, you often do not have to look too hard for it. Many people go to family to get the support that they need. Others go to friends or colleagues. In some cases, however, your goal might be so far removed from the ways that these individuals can help that you have to go elsewhere. In that case, social clubs, support groups, leagues, seminars, trade associations, and other groups may have people who can help you.

In difficult situations, you may have to completely remove yourself from your current conditions to find the support you need. You may be recovering from a disastrous situation such as an abusive relationship or a major career setback and have to move to a new area and make new friends. Fortunately, these dire circumstances are exactly when people who have been through similar rough times will want to make themselves available to help you. If you have the desire for the necessary support and the belief that you can get it, you will seek and find it.

When determining the support you need, start with a reminder of the support available. No matter what your current state is, you currently have a support system. Your government has a military, sets laws, and spends money to protect your rights as a citizen. Community service organizations work hard to improve people's lives without asking for anything in return from the people they help. Schools teach children and prepare them to contribute to society. Police, fire, and medical services protect you from harm and help you recover. Friends, family, support groups, trade associations, guilds, clubs, teams, fraternities, sororities, religious groups, political parties, and suicide prevention centers all exist to protect, nurture, or empower people.

You may not have all of these systems or may want to point out the selfishness and corruption of these institutions. They may not have worked or helped you in the past. These organizations are not perfect, nor are people. Everyone has to support themselves first before they can help anyone else, and they may prioritize one person's plight over another's. Unfortunately, that may make it harder for you to receive help than you wish it was.

No matter how bad it seems, though, you are not alone in the world. There are people and resources available to help you. Someone out there is either going through a similar challenge and wants to commiserate with you or just wants to help. You have it within your power to identify and seek the appropriate parties for support, and you can even set up a virtuous cycle by helping others first and allowing them to reciprocate.

In finding support, you probably have at least one person who has your interest in mind by default: a parent, guardian, a child, or a close relative. If they are not appropriate for the support you need, you then have your friends, acquaintances, classmates, extended family, or co-workers who also care about you because of your shared history or interests. If those sources are not appropriate, then you can look to groups outside your network that have shared values or specifically help with your situation. If you are still finding difficulty, many groups, such as crisis centers, clergies, and support groups, are willing to listen.

These sources of support could help you, but it is difficult for them to know that you need help before you make it known. Government institutions cannot take action unless they are notified through official channels, and your friends and relatives may be so busy with their own issues that they might not notice when you need help. If you really need their support, make sure that you ask. No one is so independent that they will never need anything, but they might be too proud or scared to ask for it.

On your life journey, when you identify and pursue your growth areas, you should look for what help is available to accelerate your progress. Your support system can go beyond people to include animals, artificial intelligence, insurance, financial savings, books, music, videos, tools, buildings, food, water, land, and other resources. No matter what your goal is, it is your responsibility to get the support you need and, optimally, to set up your own support system for when you will need it.

If you have a strong desire to succeed in your objective, you can increase your probability of success by taking every controllable factor in your life and optimizing it for how it will enable you to achieve that goal. Starting with your resources, you may find that a private study area allows you to focus on your homework, a special diet optimizes your health, music gets you into a productive mindset, or insurance mitigates the financial risk of unexpected setbacks. You can then set a schedule to help you dedicate time to your goal, surround yourself with like-minded people who can motivate you, and identify people to call when you are struggling. You can even help others to build goodwill for when you are in need.

It is very important to set up a support structure even if you do not foresee needing it. For example, you may feel that private, personal goals may not require help until you discover how difficult they are to complete if your environment is working against you. If you are preparing for a marathon, your family may complain about the number of hours that you put into training. If you are dieting, it can be difficult to eat a healthy meal when everyone around you is eating unhealthy food. If you are starting a business, it is not easy going it alone while everyone around you is telling you that you are going to fail. You can accomplish much by yourself, but most goals are easier to attain when you build support and eliminate obstacles.

When receiving support, remember to be grateful and show your gratitude. You will bring meaning to others when you recognize and appreciate their contribution to your success. Just as important, however, is that recognition helps to ensure that you continue to receive support in the future. Gratitude strengthens the bond between the giver and receiver and increases the positive feelings they have toward each other.[107] Recognition does not belittle your own accomplishments; instead, it brings others up with you in your success.

Knowing how important gratitude is, successful people emphasize how critical support was to their success. For example, award acceptance speeches often contain lists of people who were significant contributors to the winners' accomplishments. One winner may recall a mentor saying something that changed her life, and another may explain how he was on the verge of giving up when a friend gave him the renewed strength to continue. Few people would refrain from thanking anyone and then go home alone with their award. When people are at the pinnacle of achievement, they usually take a moment to appreciate their support system.

One of the best parts of success is sharing it with others, and the biggest accomplishments involve people united around a common goal. When you succeed, remember your support or inspiration: parents, siblings, spouses, children, peers, colleagues, mentors, coaches, partners, leaders, and even competitors. Celebrate with your teammates, friends, or colleagues when you achieve shared goals. Remember the moments when someone was a source of strength or a savior in a time of need. Those people and those moments are the ones that will make the difference for you, and they are the ones that will have the most meaning and significance in your life journey.

The most successful people in the world have a support structure that enables them to achieve their dreams. While the majority of meaning is about finding the power within yourself to grow in ways that are significant to you, support from others is critical to finding and achieving that purpose. Without that support, your potential will be severely limited.

Without support, you will be less likely to succeed

Imagine one person trying to build the Great Pyramid of Giza. Think about how long it would take to construct Stonehenge by yourself. Imagine if all knowledge and media on Earth disappeared and a person with no resources or expertise wanted to create a self-driving automobile.

One person inventing the math, science, engineering, and technologies necessary to build such marvels—and then building them—is clearly an impossible task. Even with desire and belief, efforts like that would take longer than one person's lifetime to do alone. Ignoring the time required for pre-requisite technologies, it took a great number of people over a millennium to construct Stonehenge, over a decade to construct the Great Pyramid, and over a century to equip a commercially available automobile with self-driving features.

Humans can only accomplish these feats by working together toward shared goals. Parents work hard to secure their children's futures. Competitors bring out the best in their competition. Organizations make intellectual, social, technological, political, and scientific progress through large-scale cooperation. Support makes us powerful as individuals and unstoppable as a society.

Without support, your individual potential is severely limited. Your individual strength is much less than a group's. Your doubt, fear, and frustration may hold you back without emotional support. Without the benefit of others' knowledge, you would have to learn everything on your own.

Fortunately, a world without support cannot exist; anything that is beneficial to you supports your growth. With that broad definition, there are many sources of support for any form of growth that you pursue. If you do not currently have what you need to succeed, identify resources and people that can help you. Below are examples of how others can foster your growth as well as ways that you can secure the help you need:

Examples of Support by Growth Area

- **Physical Growth** – Receiving food, water, clothing, shelter, coaching, training, physical education, or medical treatment
- **Intellectual Growth** – Being taught, tutored, tested, mentored, or provided with books
- **Emotional Growth** – Being counseled, receiving therapy, joining a support group, taking a personality test, or talking to friends
- **Social/Interpersonal Growth** – Being introduced, joining a social club, going to group events, or volunteering
- **Familial Growth** – Visiting relatives, procreating, organizing family trips, hosting a reunion, or receiving family counseling
- **Financial Growth** – Consulting a financial advisor, conducting business with suppliers and customers, receiving a loan, fundraising, securing investors, or receiving a salary increase
- **Professional Growth** – Being coached, trained, or mentored, networking, receiving job offers, pursuing a certification or degree, or speaking with industry experts
- **Spiritual Growth** – Joining congregations, religious or spiritual groups, meditation activities, or relevant internet communities
- **Relationship Growth** – Double-dating, receiving marriage counseling, or scheduling relationship-building activities
- **Asset Growth** – Bartering, attending trade shows, posting

ads, browsing catalogs or stores, or meeting collectors

- **Capability (Skill) Growth** – Receiving coaching, training, teaching, mentoring, competency models, opportunities to practice, seminars, demonstrations, or success stories
- **Technological Growth** – Building or receiving tools, devices, computer applications, inventions, or materials
- **Artistic Growth** – Taking an art class, joining a band, collaborating with peers, receiving critique, or visiting a museum
- **Organizational (Company) Growth** – Reading management, leadership, or entrepreneurship books, attending seminars, hiring experienced managers, or facilitating meetings
- **Martial (Defense) Growth** – Collaborating with other nations, working with defense contractors, or soliciting advice from scientists and experts in military strategy
- **Political Growth** – Partnering with and learning from other governments, listening to citizens' feedback, or monitoring the news for emerging trends and issues in society
- **Communal Growth** – Volunteering, participating in community events, engaging politicians and business leaders, or collaborating with neighborhoods or homeowners' associations
- **Cultivation (Enabling Others' Growth)** – Participating in fundraising activities, encouraging organizations to sponsor service events, or recruiting for mentoring programs

Progress in these growth areas is significantly limited without help. When you garner support from others, you will accomplish much more in your lifetime and can share your success with them. Seek and provide support if you want to reach your maximum potential and help others to reach theirs.

If you lack support, look for it, ask for it, accept it, and give it

Everyone needs and almost everyone receives support when they are born. Early in life, children are "liabilities" in that they require significantly more help than they can provide. The necessary care is usually so significant that many adults are involved in child-rearing activities.

As children grow, that role is expected to change. Older children have chores, young adults have extracurricular activities and part-time jobs, and adults work, take care of families, or volunteer. Over time, people become "assets" in that they provide more support than they require. They are trained to be self-sufficient and to contribute to society, and they learn cooperation and ethics. This shift allows them to grow more independently, and most of them then prepare the next generation to advance even further.

However, that training often goes wrong. People with difficult childhoods might believe that people are untrustworthy and selfish, so they only rely on themselves. Unfortunately, they severely limit their own potential with that mentality. Similarly, people who were not taught cooperation, sharing, or friendship will often not understand the value and importance of helping others. Those individuals may be able to garner some support through charm, manipulation, or other means, but they will find it challenging to thrive in the long term without meeting others' needs.

Alternatively, others respond to difficult childhoods by being the stable individual who keeps the family afloat through the turmoil and dysfunction. They may become accustomed to selfish, abusive behavior by their parents and come to believe that these interactions are typical of a relationship. They will sacrifice themselves for their families, even if it means abandoning their education, careers, friends, and leisure activities. These individuals are in tragic situations with heartbreaking decisions to make, and their growth may be severely inhibited.

Exploitation or codependency can occur when two family members, friends, or partners have not learned to form healthy, supportive relationships. A self-sacrificing person may have a selfish individual take advantage of her or may form a codependent relationship with a self-destructive or abusive individual.

In both examples, the relationship is unsustainable, and the two parties will never attain what they could by helping each other. Reciprocity and mutually beneficial support are required for long-term growth and success, and these harmful relationships show how not supporting oneself and others will leave everyone worse off in the long run.

These are not the only two unhealthy attitudes toward support. Some people learn to exploit entire societal systems. Some people are trained to help people based on nationality, ethnicity, or social class. Others are trained not to help anyone or, conversely, not to accept any help. Some are taught that they have to sacrifice themselves for others. These teachings can lead to some extreme beliefs. "You're either the predator or the prey." "Stick to your own kind." "Anyone who asks for help is weak." "I could never prioritize myself over others, as that would be selfish." People with these kinds of beliefs will likely neither ask for help when they need it nor give to others and let them reciprocate.

If you have beliefs that prevent you from asking for help or helping others, you may need to change them before you can multiply your growth through support. You might not ask for help because you distrust others or because you are afraid of rejection or judgment. You may have good reasons to be distrustful or afraid, and you may want to be careful where you go to for support. Eventually, though, your desire for success must outweigh the fears and risks if you are going to get the support you need. If you need help, ask for it; if someone offers help, accept it. You will probably not get help if you do not ask, and you will probably not receive help if you do not accept it.

Conversely, you might not help others because you think that they will not reciprocate or that it is not worth your time. You may be correct, and you can be discerning about whom you help and how you help them. However, others will be much more willing to help you when you have helped them or people they know. To get help, give it. You can either offer something in exchange or give first to build goodwill. Either way, how much you give often determines how much you receive.

The approach that benefits yourself and society the most is to help others whenever it is appropriate, ask for help when you need it, and reciprocate whenever it is appropriate. Knowing that there will inevitably be a time when you need support, offering assistance to others can build relationships and earn favors for the future. If you need something, making it known to someone who is willing and able to help is important. Otherwise, they may not be aware of your need or may not think that you want help. If someone helps you, reciprocate in socially acceptable ways: show appreciation, purchase a small gift for her, or return the favor in the future. These activities are the crux of cooperation in society.

Support does not always have to be reciprocal. Given how critical support is to human survival, the species evolved so that generous acts, such as donating to charity or volunteering, trigger the brain's reward system.[108] In addition, these altruistic acts have a positive long-term effect on well-being when people are intrinsically motivated to perform them.[109] Helpful acts, therefore, are often their own reward—even without counting the potential social and spiritual benefits of altruism.

To trigger the neurochemical rewards and social praise, you have to provide support without expecting anything in return. This part of altruism evolved so that the group helps its vulnerable members even if they only have gratitude to offer in exchange. Generosity generates trust, loyalty, and goodwill, and it can benefit the giver, the receiver, and the group. Your personal ethics will determine how much you can give to others without receiving any support, but remember that you need to take care of yourself if you wish to continue helping others in the future.

When you are the one in need, asking for help can be one of the hardest things to do if you believe that it is a sign of weakness or failure. Unfortunately, few people can be helped when they do not want to be helped. Instead of letting your beliefs squelch your desire and motivation, remind yourself that you will achieve less if you do not accept help. With this change in your attitude, you can receive support and accelerate your progress.

When looking for support, find people who have the time, means, desire, and trust to help you. The two components you have the most influence over are their desire and trust. When you have social ties with them or have the same goals, common interests, or aligned incentives, they are more likely to help you. Therefore, you need to find people with similar interests and develop social bonds to maximize your probability of success.

Someone's desire to help you is stronger and more organic when he or she shares your passion for a cause or hope for a mutually beneficial outcome. Friends are likely to help you decorate for a party, for example, because they care about the party's success and benefit from their effort. Similarly, you are more likely to receive donations for a charity from people who share your concern for the issue it addresses. By finding shared interests, you can persuade others to work with you toward a common goal.

Trust is critical to receive support as well, which is why familial, social, and professional gatherings are structured to build social bonds in addition to identifying common interests. Small talk, icebreakers, and other introductory activities allow people to learn about each other so that they may develop the rapport necessary to exchange information, resources, and support. Conversation, shared experiences, and cooperative activities solidify the bonds that make you and your peers more willing to help each other.

Depending on how much of a social bond you have developed and how much help you are asking for, you may need to offer to reciprocate. Two popular social models, the in-group/out-group model and the communal/exchange relationship model, provide guidance on the amount of support you can expect and what level of reciprocation is necessary to receive it.

In the in-group/out-group model, individuals readily cooperate with members of their identified group and oppose, shun, or cautiously trade with non-members. Group identification can

depend on the situation and change over time.[110] Group affili-
ations include family, race, gender, age, political party, religion,
shared interests, birthplace, school attended, reputation, social
status, team, gang, club, occupation, gender identity, and sexual
orientation. Using this model, you can maximize the likelihood
that someone will cooperate with you if you can identify a common interest, shared experience, or social tie that makes him or
her consider you both to be members of the same group.

In the communal/exchange relationship model, psychologists find that the type of relationship that one person has with
another will determine whether he or she will help without expectation of immediate reciprocity. In a communal relationship,
people share resources more freely and give help more quickly
without the expectation of receiving something in return. Types
of relationships that typically qualify as communal include family, friends, or comrades. Alternatively, exchange relationships involve two parties that both expect immediate reciprocity. In this
relationship, there is not enough of a social bond to make one party put his or her own needs aside for the other party's benefit.[111]

Using this model, you can expect your communal relationships to be a source of support without you having to reciprocate immediately. If you offer financial compensation in these
interactions, you may unintentionally offend your friends or family members and reduce their motivation to help. Alternatively,
when engaging non-family, non-friend social connections, expect
to offer immediate, fair reciprocation for the value they provide.
While civilized society has developed social norms suggesting
that you should help strangers with small tasks, such as holding
doors open for them, greater support requires a close relationship, altruistic ethics, or reciprocation.

The in-group/out-group and communal/exchange models
are not mutually exclusive; you may have communal relationships with many of your in-groups. Additionally, group affiliation can reduce the amount and timing of reciprocation required,
and communal relationships can make people more likely to help

you. Both models show how social ties can help you when you need support and are unable to return the favor immediately.

When receiving support, do not forget to show gratitude even if it was in exchange for something. Gratitude shows that you have a positive response to another's actions and makes them feel positive emotions from helping or exchanging services. You might feel that there is no need for gratitude if you paid for the service, but remember that you are receiving more value from it than what you are giving in exchange. Otherwise, you would not conduct the transaction. Despite it not being a selfless act, you can still be grateful that someone was willing and able to provide you with what you needed when you needed it.

You may believe that you have to endure great personal sacrifice to help others in a significant way. While helping others will always require effort or resources, you do not have to harm yourself. On the contrary, some of the most generous people work for decades building businesses that provide the world with amazing products in exchange for great wealth that they then spend on philanthropy. They do have to work hard and forego some short-term pleasure for long-term growth, but they do not have to live a life of poverty and misery. By helping themselves, receiving help, and helping others, they impact the lives of billions of people. Similarly, you can be the source of strength for others while simultaneously bettering yourself.

If you believe that the virtue of support is limited to self-sacrifice and charity, expand your definition to include mutually beneficial forms such as volunteering, mentoring, teamwork, and business. When you contribute to a team, everyone works together to achieve the group's desired outcome. When you hire staff for your business, you help others achieve their professional and financial goals while you achieve yours. These investments of your time, effort, and money toward mutual benefit are as important to successful growth as altruism. As with communal relationships, however, be careful when offering financial compensation for altruistic activities such as community service. Turning a charitable act into a paid transaction may decrease the volunteers' intrinsic motivation and reduce the positive feelings they receive from performing a good deed for its own sake.[112]

You may have seen others manipulate or deceive to get others to do what they want, but these tactics are unnecessary. If you have given help in the past, have a worthy, ethical goal, approach the right person, have a clear need, ask properly, and offer reciprocation or gratitude in exchange, you will usually receive help. Conversely, the probability is extremely low that someone will proactively volunteer to help a selfish, ungrateful person who can seemingly solve his own problem easily. Therefore, people who do not meet those criteria might resort to using manipulation and deception to make up the gap at the risk of losing credibility and support in the future. It can garner support in the short term, but it is not an effective strategy to develop healthy, long-term bonds.

Countless classic stories teach others how asking for and giving support can lead to personal growth and happiness. In *It's a Wonderful Life*, for example, George Bailey spends his career helping others achieve their financial goals while he dreams of travel and success. Unfortunately, his uncle loses a routine deposit for their business, the Bailey Bros. Building & Loan Association, and George almost kills himself because he thinks that the situation is hopeless. His extensive support for the community, though, leads his friends and family to rush to save him in his time of need.[113]

They almost never had a chance to support him, though, because he never asks for help from anyone until he prays at the very end. When he learns how much his contribution has benefitted the people around him by seeing a world without him in it, he finally realizes how important his life is. He helped his family, friends, and community grow and thrive, and they delight in the opportunity to show their gratitude.[114]

In another example, *Groundhog Day*, Phil Connors is a selfish weatherman whose off-camera behavior alienates everyone, including his producer, Rita Hanson. After being obnoxious throughout his trip to Punxsutawney, Pennsylvania to cover the Groundhog Day festivities, he gets stuck in a blizzard trying to return to Pittsburgh. He stays in town for another night and awakes to find himself reliving Groundhog Day over and over again. When he realizes that he is stuck in this time loop with no long-term consequences, he indulges in what people often think will make them happy: pleasurable pursuits, selfish, reckless behavior, spending sprees, and unhealthy food. He even tries to win Rita's affections by learning everything he can about her and orchestrating the perfect date. None of it ultimately brings him true meaning or fulfillment.[115]

After thousands of Groundhog Days full of self-serving and self-destructive behavior, he finally decides to ask Rita for help. She becomes his confidant for a day and provides the emotional support that reminds him that life is not all gloomy and meaningless. Almost immediately, he dedicates his indefinite amount of time reliving Groundhog Day to improving himself and the community. Only when he focuses on helping others and achieving personal growth does he finally become a person worthy of Rita's admiration, which ultimately breaks the time loop.[116]

These fictional stories show the transformative impact of support. With your help, their lives are better; with their help, your life is better. In both cases, life becomes more meaningful, valuable, and rewarding.

While the majority of life's meaning has to be found within yourself (even if that meaning is helping others), cooperating with others is critical to making your dreams possible. Support is an essential tool that can protect you from harm, help you break through your individual limitations, and ensure that your group grows to its full potential. Whereas violating others' ethics can create a downward spiral of degrading behavior, showing appreciation and support for others can create a virtuous cycle of improved outcomes for everyone involved.

Support is everywhere, but making sure that you have it when you need it usually requires effort on your part. Look for it, ask for it, accept it, offer it, and give it. These activities will lead you to the help you need. When you work with others to grow and achieve shared goals on your life journey, what you can accomplish is practically unlimited.

QUESTIONS

Questions That Help You Find Guidance and Support

Your answers to these questions will help you find the right support to help you realize your life's purpose. This chapter's content provides guidance on how to think about these questions, but only you can supply the definitive answers for your life.

Receiving Support

1. How do people currently support you in life? Who helps you, and why do they help you?

2. What help will you need to achieve what you want in life?

3. What sources of support are available and accessible to you?

   Examples: Classes, clubs, support groups, teams, associations, community centers, guilds, congregations, organizations, institutes, fraternities, mentors, libraries, books or videos, training programs

4. Which of these sources of support have the resources or knowledge to help you in your specific growth areas?

5. What can you do to secure support from them?

   • For human support, how can you develop social bonds and identify common interests to increase their willingness to support you?

6. What support will you need in the future to achieve long-term goals? What can you do now to have access to that support when you need it?

7. Is it difficult for you to look for and ask for help? If so, what can you do to be more willing to get the help you need?

8. Can you make it easier for others to support you?

9. How can you reciprocate people's support or make the inter-action mutually beneficial?

Providing Support

1. How do you currently help others with their goals in life? Whom do you help, and why do you help them?

2. Do you expect something in return, or do you give freely? Which factors determine when you expect reciprocity?

3. Is it difficult to support others before they help you? If so, what can you do to start a cycle of generosity in your life?

4. When you help people, do they reciprocate or show grati-tude? How does that affect your willingness to help them?

5. How can you find more satisfaction in helping others?

6. Do others have growth areas that you could be supporting? How could you help them achieve their goals?

   • If you are unable to support others directly, can you con-nect them with people who can help?

7. How could you be helping more people with the resources and support that you are able to provide?

8. As you grow, how will you be able to provide more support?

9. Do you sacrifice too much to help others? If so, how can you meet your own needs while still providing support?

10. At what point does helping others feel like enabling others' lazy or self-destructive behaviors? What can you do to make sure that others do not exploit your generosity?

EXERCISES

Activities That Help You Find Guidance and Support

Completing these exercises will result in actionable ideas for securing support to achieve your life goals.

Thought Exercise: If you do not like asking for help, think about what you can offer in exchange. Determine who can help you and how you can develop a mutually beneficial relationship.

This exercise can encourage you to seek help because the interaction will also benefit others. While some support may not require reciprocity, the willingness to give makes it easier to receive.

Brainstorming Exercise: Brainstorm a list of sources of support that you can rely on when you encounter difficulty. Then, consider which types of support are most appropriate for each of your growth areas and match them.

Example:

Available Support: *Friends, family, spouses, pets, support groups, teams, clubs/associations, professional networks, mentors, exercise, meditation, hobbies, favorite restaurants, events, outings, and camping*

Growth Area: *Career*

Best Support for Growth Area: *Mentors, friends, professional networks, hobbies, exercise, meditation*

Next, brainstorm specific hurdles and tasks that will require help. Identify the best source of support for each one and why.

Example:

Growth Area: *Athletic growth*

Hurdle/Task: *Improve my defensive skills*

Support: *A teammate who wants to practice his offensive skills*

Reason/Way It Can Help: *I learn more when I practice against others*

Knowing where to go in advance will make it easier to progress through or recover from challenging tasks and hurdles. For example, if you are trying to be a professional athlete, you need a support structure for when you get injured or lose a competition. If you are trying to overcome an addiction, you need friends or family to talk to during stressful times to avoid relapsing.

Brainstorming several possible sources of support mitigates the risk of one source not being available when you need it. Make sure that your list includes people, resources, or activities, and make sure that you have sources for accelerating progress, overcoming hurdles, recovering from setbacks, and alleviating stress.

Creative Exercise: Look at the collage you have created and enhanced through the creative exercises in the previous four chapters. For each item you have in the Desire column, find pictures that represent the support system that will help you get what you want. You may also refer to your list in the brainstorming exercise of possible support mechanisms, such as people, resources, events, prerequisites, and money, to identify picture ideas. Place the pictures below the Appreciation column of your collage in a section labeled "Support" to symbolize the stable foundation you have for successful growth.

If you already have parts of your support system placed in your Appreciation or Beliefs sections from earlier exercises, you may wish to copy or move them to the Support section so that you can find them more easily when you need help. Make sure that big dreams or long-term goals have enough supporting items so that these goals feel attainable. You may have pictures representing help in overcoming obstacles as well, but you should focus on the support and not the obstacles.

This exercise will remind you that you are not alone on your journey and that the support you need to succeed is available to you.

Example: If you would like to be a lawyer, you can put pictures of scholarships, the school you want to attend, your professors, family, friends, role models, and mentors. You can also add support to overcome specific hurdles, such as loans to meet financial needs and recommendation letters to help you separate yourself from your competition.

Note: You may wish to leave space on or next to your collage for the final creative exercise.

Writing Exercise: Take your list of possible experiences and action items from the writing exercises of the first six chapters as well as the hurdles from the Belief chapter. Review the hurdles to make sure that you have captured potential opposition, setbacks, or large tasks where support may be necessary to accomplish your desired outcome. For each experience or action item, write down who can support you in this area and what resources are available to you. For each hurdle, note how the support you listed will help you to overcome it. If there are steps you need to take to garner the support, update your action items.

Use this writing exercise to record where and how you can get the support you need to prevail through adversity and achieve your goals in life. If it is difficult for you to accept help from people, start with resources such as technology and media. If friends and relatives cannot help, consider public and professional services.

Finally, consider how helping others can help you grow as well. For example, you may develop leadership by coaching a sports team or coordinating a community service event. Your help will be mutually beneficial and will improve your support system.

Example:

Experiences	Action Items	Hurdles	People	Resources	How Support Will Help
Exercise	Go to the gym 3 days per week	Motivation, working late	Gym buddy	Fitness center at the office	I won't let down my friend; I can run before work
Club activities	Make 3 new friends	Social anxiety	Brother, classmate	Book on social anxiety	My brother is social; I can use the book's methods

Note: The above example does not show all of the information you will bring from the previous writing exercises; it is possible that this chapter's teachings may cause you to refine that information.

OUTCOME

After reading this chapter, you should have a clear list of people and resources available to support you in your growth. This support will influence how you approach your growth areas and what you do when you run into difficulties. You should see how support increases your probability of success, and you might reprioritize your growth areas as a result. Finally, you should have an understanding of what support system you need in place for your life journey and how to develop and maintain that system to maximize your likelihood of success.

With your updated list, you should be ready to move forward in your life with meaning and purpose. Now, you must choose what to do next. When you are ready, proceed to the next chapter.

Choice

Your choices create your destiny

"Every man builds his world in his own image. He has the power to choose, but no power to escape the necessity of choice."

— Dr. Hugh Akston in *Atlas Shrugged* by Ayn Rand[117]

"Two roads diverged in a wood, and I—I took the one less traveled by, and that has made all the difference."

— Robert Frost, "The Road Not Taken"[118]

"If then whereas we wish for our end, the means to our end are matters of deliberation and choice, it follows that actions dealing with these means are done by choice."

— Aristotle[119]

PRINCIPLES OF CHOICE

- Choice is the ability of life to determine which actions to take
- A human life's meaning is self-determined
- Your future is largely the result of the choices you make in life
- Without choice, life would be passive, restricted, and boring
- If you do not choose, you let external forces choose for you

CHOICE AND THE MEANING OF LIFE

You control your own destiny. Life forms interact with reality through their actions, and those actions are chosen through their decisions. Choice is the ability to select from multiple options. In a world of infinite possibilities, choice empowers life to determine for itself how to move toward its desired outcome.

Choice is a crucial component of finding your meaning in life because you ultimately decide what is meaningful to you. You cannot live a purposeful life without choice, and your desires, beliefs, emotions, ethics, and support system have no value if you do not use them to make better choices. Choice is your active role in life, and it makes life worth living.

Choice is the ability of life to determine which actions to take

One of the greatest mysteries in the universe is the degree to which life has deliberate control over the world around it. To shed light on this question, philosophers and scientists first ask whether the universe was deliberately created or randomly generated. They then ask whether subsequent events were predetermined by the force that created it or determined by the events before them. Finally, they wonder whether life, which can move and interact with its environment, has agency or is at the mercy of genetics, a creator, external forces, or chance. While these philosophical questions are all interesting, the ultimate goal is usually to understand how much of an organism's fate is self-determined through its decisions or actions.

Research in physics has been able to explain most causal relationships between matter in the universe, and scientists can use that information to conjecture as to how the universe itself formed. In the prevailing model, the Big Bang theory, an explosive reaction of a subatomic particle resulted in an incredibly large universe that continues to expand.[120] From that reaction, the laws of physics can explain the dispersion of matter that became the stars, planets, and other astronomical bodies. Even if a non-physical source caused the initial reaction, all evidence points to the universe unfolding over billions of years in predictable ways that physicists can understand and model.

The emergence of life marked the end of a universe consisting solely of purposeless events. Research in genetics has shown that billions of years were required for spontaneous chemical reactions to lead to complex organic molecules and living organisms. At some point during that time period, the right conditions caused organic molecules to begin to self-organize and self-replicate. This matter could trigger its own chemical reactions instead of having to rely solely on external catalysts. The ability of a molecule to influence itself was the first step toward autonomous life.

From that moment, the universe was no longer purely random. While other molecules could replicate given the perfect combination of materials and conditions, these molecules had more control and required less luck to trigger that process. When they gained the ability to reproduce themselves, they gained control over the continuation of their genetic material. They now had the power to affect their own destiny.

Self-replication is the foundation of growth in all living things. Early self-replication was mostly serendipitous, as molecules still required a near-optimal set of materials and conditions. By the time they evolved into single-celled organisms, however, they had developed greater abilities to influence the conditions and gather the materials necessary to self-replicate. Without the need for an external catalyst, host, or perfect conditions, life could now flourish.

Somewhere along that evolutionary timeline, life made its first choice. After gaining a certain amount of control over itself, a living organism had multiple options for how to proceed but could only take one action. If it gained the ability to move around in its environment, it could move in many directions but had to choose one direction at a time. If it had access to many resources, it had to decide which to use to self-replicate. If some chemicals in the environment were harmful and others were beneficial, it had to move toward and let in the beneficial ones and move away from and keep out the harmful ones.

Despite how rudimentary these choices may seem, they are extremely difficult to make correctly. An incalculable number of organisms have died making the wrong choices about where to move, which resources to consume, and how to defend against environmental threats. The genetic material (i.e., DNA) that contained fatal instructions was destroyed, and the remaining organisms contained DNA that provided the best instructions for survival. While the organisms at this stage may not have had the freedom or ability to choose alternatives to what their innate programming dictated, they were still choosing one of many possible actions that they were physically capable of performing.

Choices from simple organisms can be surprisingly precise. For example, when an amoeba is faced with multiple sources of nutrition, it selects an optimal 2:1 ratio of protein to sugar. If it comes into contact with those nutrients in a different ratio, it will adjust itself to capture its ideal diet.[121] In each of these scenarios, the amoeba makes the best decision to maximize its growth by combining its genetic programming (i.e., "instinct") with the information it gathered about its environment (i.e., "experience").

Despite the surprising level of decision-making ability that these types of life forms demonstrate, their choices are much less advanced and free than the conscious, deliberate decisions of complex life forms. Their DNA provides the instructions for how they should behave, and they execute. However, the freedom to choose any of multiple options did eventually evolve. As life added more abilities and faced environmental changes, its number of options and freedom of choice increased exponentially.

In a relatively static environment, natural selection favors organisms that select the best option for how to behave in those specific conditions. Successful life forms are genetically equipped to execute those specific behaviors effectively and are heavily driven by instinct to perform them. However, in a volatile environment, natural selection favors organisms that have the flexibility to choose the best option for a variety of situations.

Because all environments change over time, life forms evolved the ability to adapt. They experienced random genetic mutations during the replication process, and the genetic variations that improved decision making or enabled new or improved actions were the most likely to increase their fitness. While their DNA still determined their physical properties and behavioral tendencies, they could act in many different ways to improve their survivability. Organisms that did not have the ability or option to adapt to the environmental change either died or migrated to more favorable conditions.

Just as the ability to self-replicate denoted the first instance of matter controlling itself, adaptation is significant because it demonstrates an organism's ability to control itself in response to change. After billions of years of evolution, life forms have an abundance of means through which they interact with and control their environment. Some organisms can change their color or shape, and others can consume many different food sources. The most advanced organisms have the ability to analyze and solve complex problems. Each of these abilities grants more choices to reduce harm and achieve more growth.

There are limits to the number of choices that an organism has at its disposal. First, it cannot choose the DNA that it possesses at birth. Those genes determine much of an organism's physical capabilities and its potential. Single-celled organisms have instructions to gather the resources they need to replicate and then divide into two cells. Plants and animals follow their instructions to grow into their respective forms and reproduce before they die. Their growth continues in the offspring that carry on their genes.

Second, the environment limits the number of options available. For example, an organism living in an environment with a wealth of resources has more choices available to it than life existing in harsh conditions. Additionally, life that is constantly warding off competition and predators cannot safely choose to spend as much time caring for itself and its group. If an organism has more advanced instructions and a more conducive environment, it will have more choices and a higher likelihood of growing to its full potential.

Through natural selection, life has developed ways to overcome or work around these two limitations. Sexual reproduction, for example, allows life forms to overcome the lifespan limitations of an organism's genetics as well as the likelihood that some environmental factor may injure or kill it during its lifetime. It also helps life push the boundaries of its inherited limitations by enabling two organisms to mix their genes to increase their offspring's survivability.

In another example, many animals developed migratory patterns or hibernation cycles to account for seasonal environmental changes. When conditions are intolerable, life can try to change them, adjust for them, or move away from them. By moving to a warmer environment or reducing metabolism during periods of cold weather and food scarcity, these creatures can counteract the effects of the elements. These types of adaptations enable life to protect itself from harm and continue to grow through changing conditions.

The most successful organisms in a changing ecosystem combine sensors to detect change, physical abilities to have a number of ways to respond, and intelligence to choose the best response. A single-celled organism has limited sensors, capabilities, and intelligence, so it relies heavily on its rapid replication and luck to survive. Plants can sense sunlight and adjust their positions to maximize their rate of photosynthesis, but they are unable to uproot and change locations to achieve that goal. Animals can sense light, sound, motion, scent, temperature, and pressure, and they can learn to navigate terrain and manipulate objects. Humans can plan, reason, walk on two legs, and use advanced tools. Life evolved to have more control, freedom, ability, and power, and it has more options to grow and thrive as a result.

These three capabilities often evolve together, as they are all necessary to make better decisions. Greater physical ability enables a greater number of possible actions, and it requires greater intellect to use those actions effectively and improved sensors to monitor the need for and consequences of those actions. Greater sensory capabilities are useless without the intelligence to process the information and the physical ability to respond. Greater intellect benefits from more information about the situation and a greater range of options to achieve the desired outcome. Each organism has slightly different degrees of freedom and adaptability based on these capabilities, so their choices will vary widely.

The most advanced combination of these capabilities includes multiple senses, a sophisticated brain, bipedal movement, and opposable thumbs. Collectively, they allow humans to detect beneficial and harmful aspects of the environment, analyze situations for the best action to take, and move around and manipulate the environment to satisfy their needs. As a result, humans have made decisions that have not only kept the species alive but enabled it to grow into advanced civilizations.

Even with these advances, humans' primary goals are still to seek growth and avoid harm. As such, their choices can seem as simple as performing beneficial actions and refraining from harmful ones. However, they have to know which environmental factors are helpful and harmful, which actions are possible, and how beneficial or harmful each action would be. Unfortunately, no organism has perfect information, so they have to make a choice based on their instinct, knowledge, and predictions.

These components of the decision-making process ultimately define the degree to which humans are free to make their own choices. In effect, freedom of choice (i.e., "free will") is the ability to use sensory inputs, physical abilities, and intellectual capacity to decide the best course of action given instincts, past experience, knowledge of the current situation, and expectations for the future. Humans evolved rational decision-making abilities because instinct cannot provide perfect instructions for every possible situation. By being able to analyze a problem, they can figure out the best decision at any given moment. Rational thought can, therefore, override instinct and cause people to react differently to the current environment than a direct stimulus would trigger. The result is a conscious choice.

Instinct and unconscious processes still exist in advanced organisms and heavily influence their behavior. Because conscious decision making requires attention, concentration, and energy, humans evolved to control only a subset of all biological functions with their conscious minds. Many functions, therefore, follow instructions automatically: eyes blink, hearts beat, and cells divide. A human can influence some automatic activities, such as blinking or swallowing, for a short period of time but cannot stop them completely through conscious thought.

Human biology also includes powerful drives that compel certain behaviors and reward systems that incentivize behaviors. Humans need to eat to live, and the ones that felt the urge to eat and derived pleasure from eating were more likely to survive. Therefore, humans have both a drive and incentive to eat, and the body regularly signals the brain to seek food.

Instinct, therefore, is a strong, sometimes uncontrollable urge to engage in a behavior because that behavior led to the survival of the species. It is a predisposition toward a behavior that was shaped over millions of years, and it drives most behaviors in simple organisms and many behaviors in advanced ones.

Regardless of how strong the drives and incentives are, these behaviors are neither predetermined by a divine force nor purely determined by past, external events. Instincts formed because organisms with advantageous behavioral tendencies were more likely to survive, so they began to exhibit those behaviors in the optimal amounts over millennia of natural selection. While organisms often react directly to internal and external stimuli, advanced decision-making processes require that the organism sense the stimulus, understand the situation, know how to respond, and have the ability to respond effectively. In humans and other intelligent creatures, they can choose where to focus their attention, choose how to evaluate the situation, choose to prioritize certain factors over others, and choose how to respond. They can even decide to change the way they make decisions in the future.

The result of human evolution is an unprecedented combination of genetics, instinct, and rational thought. Genetics give people many options for how to live. Instinct drives them toward options that meet basic needs. Conscious, rational thought gives them the ability to act beyond how genetics, past events, or a divine power would dictate. Humans cannot control everything, and they often follow automatic, predictable patterns to conserve energy and prioritize the use of conscious thought. They suffer from many biases and use their conscious mind to rationalize decisions that they made unconsciously. However, their advanced brain functions are much more effective than instinct at making complex, long-term decisions that involve multiple parties.

These advanced cognitive abilities give them the freedom to choose options that go against what instinct would instruct them to do. Well-behaved children and well-trained animals are examples of how instinctual urges can be overridden by the deliberate choice to behave in ways that are more conducive to group well-being. In extreme cases, that control can even be used to overcome core programming. People committing suicide, protecting strangers in an emergency, or breaking world records for holding their breath are all using their freedom of choice to act in a different way than their DNA would automatically instruct.

Advanced life forms are neither completely free from their genetics and environment nor completely at their mercy, and their degree of freedom can vary greatly. Most people in modern society have the time and potential to make deliberate choices. They can listen to their instincts, follow their logic, or let external forces dictate their behavior. Individuals with genetic defects, brain damage, mental illness, addictions, or less-developed brains may have less conscious control over their behavior. People under stress or duress will be more likely to make choices that they would not have made otherwise. People with less experience may not be as familiar with the options available to them. Everyone will have some limitation or restriction in the choices they make.

Regardless of how limited the ability to make a deliberate, free, conscious decisions may be, there will always be options for how to proceed that will necessitate a choice. Those choices will always have consequences.

Life is constantly making choices regarding how it behaves. Choice is the inevitable result of having multiple options, and organisms gain more options as they develop greater abilities. The only way to limit choice is to inhibit those abilities. When life forms have the power and freedom to perform an act, they have to choose when and how to use it. They may be biased toward a specific option or compelled by genetics, beliefs, or external factors, but they are always making choices. Because humans have the capacity for conscious thought, they can make deliberate choices regarding the meaning and direction of their lives.

A human life's meaning is self-determined

Human life is unique in that it has the intellectual capacity to contemplate its own existence, how it originated, and why. Earlier forms of life without conscious thought and impulse control can neither contemplate nor adjust their instinctual choices. Humans, however, can analyze their internal motivations and the cause-and-effect relationships of their actions so that they can make better decisions in the future. That intellectual power also allows them to determine what they want and what choices and actions will enable them to attain it.

The most important aspect of this ability is that humans can influence both their decisions and their motivations through reason. For example, the smell of nearby food could trigger a person's hunger sensation, but he could then realize that he will be eating dinner with friends soon. He could then make a conscious choice to wait until dinner to eat. In that single moment, the person has an *experience* that triggers a *desire* that conflicts with a *be-*

lief, and he makes a conscious *choice* to ignore that impulse as a result.

The ability to analyze and influence their own motivations is what allows humans to understand what life means to them and to shape what it means to them. They can take the same information and choose to interpret it as good or bad, helpful or harmful, or important or unimportant. They can also decide whether to take action based on that information. Therefore, people are not simply passive recipients of meaning from an external source; they can develop it themselves and adjust it as their lives change.

Because meaning is self-determined, humans can choose to find (greater) meaning in their existence. More accurately, they can choose the (greater) meaning that they give to their existence. People who passively wait for divine inspiration regarding their purpose in life are not actively using their mental and physical capabilities to determine what truly matters to them. Thoughts can be choices. Experiences can be choices. Desires and beliefs can be choices. Ethics can be choices. Happiness can be a choice. Meaning can be a choice.

Having the cognitive abilities to make conscious decisions means that humans control their own destiny. Control over oneself and one's environment is an evolutionary advantage; organisms that can control the world around them can prevent their own deaths. Exercising this control, therefore, is critical to people's success. Psychology research has found self-control to be twice as important as intelligence in predicting academic achievement in children.[122] This advantage is why humans feel a strong need to have personal control or to have a choice.[123]

Choice is not just necessary for a person to succeed; choice is required for a person to have the will to live. Studies have shown that the elderly live longer and are much more satisfied with life when placed in a care facility in which they still have a degree of autonomy over their lives. Even in environments that do not grant them much autonomy, the tenants who exercise control over their lives have lower rates of depression, report a higher level of personal fulfillment, and live longer than their peers who surrender their autonomy.[124]

Psychologists call the attribution of outcomes to one's own actions (i.e., what he or she can influence) instead of environmental factors (i.e., luck) as having an internal locus of control.[125] Individuals with an internal locus of control are also likely to have a sense of purpose in life and an ability to handle life's setbacks.[126,127] These individuals believe that they can influence their own outcomes, so they take responsibility for their own direction and want to have the freedom and power of choice.

Unfortunately, the inherent need to control one's own destiny can cause people to misidentify cause-and-effect relationships and controllable factors, leading to superstitious behaviors. For example, a person may associate wearing a certain pair of socks with performing well in a sport and continue wearing them to maintain a feeling of control over the outcome. While it is irrational to believe that this behavior has a metaphysical influence on a sporting event, the resulting confidence can make them more likely to succeed in what they can control, such as their athletic performance. Despite it sometimes going awry, the feeling of control and choice motivates people to a self-determined path in life.[128]

While humans can heavily influence an outcome, many external factors, such as the weather, the sun, and gravity, are uncontrollable. If people do not accept this reality, they will sometimes go to great lengths to try to gain a sense of control over the uncontrollable. For example, many early humans formed polytheistic religions to explain events with unknown causes and to fulfill their desire for control over factors that significantly affect their lives.

Humans' desire to understand the world around them is an advantage. If they can figure out how a system works, they might be able to predict what will happen and influence the outcome. These early humans had developed the intelligence to understand cause-and-effect relationships[129] but had neither the scientific method nor the technology with which to study advanced concepts such as weather patterns. Since the sun, clouds, wind, and rain significantly influenced their survivability, they were motivated to learn how to predict, influence, or control these elements. As a result, they likely concluded that unseen forces probably caused these events to occur.

Combined with their instinct to see patterns (even in randomness[130]), people likely started associating certain actions with uncontrollable events occurring. Factoring in the belief in non-physical entities, they could conclude that the behavior did not directly cause the event but rather caused a deity to favor them. Over time, rituals and traditions formed to appease these deities so that humans could control the uncontrollable.

For example, when a person cannot directly control when a famine ends or whether there are any complications in childbirth, they instead ask for support from the being that he or she believes does. The desire for control, advanced thinking, creativity, pattern recognition, and confirmation bias combine to lead to superstitious behavior as humans look to find ways to influence outcomes that are largely or completely uncontrollable.

As humans grew intellectually, the scientific method became a superior approach for them to understand, predict, and control the world around them. Science has been able to shift cause-and-effect relationships from deities to natural elements. Their beliefs (i.e., hypotheses) require testing it to see if the opposite of what they believe is untrue (i.e., rejecting the null hypothesis in a scientific study). When they can consistently achieve those results, they have determined the cause of an effect and can now intentionally prevent or ensure that outcome. This greater understanding of how the world works allows humans to control their environment and make better decisions, which lead to better outcomes in their lives.

This analysis has one underlying fundamental question: "Which choices can humans make to live life in the best way possible?" Choices drive the need for research and experimentation to see which option is best. "How much water does my garden need?" "Which foods and chemicals should I avoid consuming to prevent heart disease or cancer?" "What can I do to ensure the financial security of my family?" "Which profession will bring me personal fulfillment as well as an acceptable income?" With so many options, the only way to know which ones are best is to learn which ones provide the desired outcome and why.

The definition of "best" may differ based on what is important to the individual. Someone may prefer the good life, the moral life, the wealthy life, a life of learning, or a life of love. In general, however, most people are looking for one way out of all of the possible ways they can live to be safe, successful, happy, and fulfilled. Religion, science, philosophy, psychology, sociology, academia, and medicine all have the same goal of understanding the world so society can make better decisions and take better actions in life. Everyone wants to make the best choices for his or her growth. These choices are the source of endless debate and soul-searching, but they make life interesting.

The power of choice makes life self-directed and, therefore, meaningful. Humans have a great deal of control over how they live their lives and how they grow. While there are strong genetic and social incentives to behave in one way or another, there is always a choice. Even within the same job, task, or goal, there are many ways to approach a situation.

The abundance of options can be overwhelming. Scientists have found that humans can sometimes encounter the "Paradox of Choice" where they become less likely to make a decision and less satisfied with their choices when they have more options.[131,132] While choice allows people to feel in control, encountering too many options can be frustrating because it is difficult, confusing, and time-consuming to evaluate all of them. It also reduces their confidence that they made the best choice. As a result, people can become discouraged and put off making critical life decisions.

Some scientists have found, though, that it is not the number of options that causes the problem.[133] Instead, many variables factor into the dissatisfaction with the choice, including:

- The amount of information available
- The knowledge the person already has about the options
- The contrast between options
- The clarity of the decision-making criteria
- The certainty of the decision-maker as to what they want

People can experience "paralysis by analysis" when they have too much information without a systematic way to take clear, decisive action based on it. Alternatively, they can "become extinct by instinct" when they make rash decisions without using the information available.[134] The goal, then, is to optimize the process for effective decision making.

People can reduce their anxiety and improve the quality of their decisions by applying the following approach consistently:

- Describe the decision and possible options
- Define the desired outcome
- Uncover and test beliefs that are underlying the decision
- Establish clear decision-making criteria
- Gather information about the criteria for each option
- Prioritize the most important, relevant information
- Eliminate options that are clearly inferior
- Isolate the critical differences between remaining options
- Select the option that best meets the criteria

When facing a difficult choice, people can use this process to clarify and finalize the decision more quickly and confidently.

While having many options ensures that everyone can find what he or she wants, people should quickly eliminate some of them to avoid becoming overwhelmed. One approach is to define requirements and filter out options that do not meet them. For example, someone looking for a mate using a dating service can quickly filter candidates by gender, age range, geographic location, spoken language, income level, education completed, and other factors. This process results in a much more limited number of options that are easier to compare. If she overly restricts her options, she can always loosen those requirements.

In these cases, the clear decision criteria help to define those requirements and narrow the options methodically. The person can give certain criteria, such as geographic location or income level, less importance if they are willing to travel or care more about finding a good emotional fit. She can then choose between the remaining options knowing that her core requirements are met and that she just needs to evaluate attractiveness and personality.

Arguably the most difficult aspect of improving decision making is surfacing the many underlying beliefs, biases, and assumptions influencing the decision. For example, people favor options that look or sound pleasant, are familiar to them, or remind them of themselves or things they like. A peculiar example of this effect is that people with the first letter H are more likely to own a hardware store or how people named Lawrence are more likely to be lawyers than other professions.[135] Knowing that a preference for alliteration can have such a significant influence on a person's choice of vocation, people should be wary of how factors beyond one's conscious awareness are affecting their decisions.

While some of these factors are silly and arbitrary, other biases can be extremely harmful and difficult to overcome. People might prejudge someone based on his or her race, ethnicity, gender, religion, or political affiliation. They may unconsciously think that learning is for nerds, sports are for dumb jocks, domestic work is for women, or men are neanderthals. These biases can influence the careers they pursue, the growth areas they prioritize, the company they keep, or the romantic partner they choose. To surface and address them, people have to search their emotions, beliefs, and ethics, identify the source of those biases, and adjust their decision-making criteria accordingly. Otherwise, those beliefs may cause them to make decisions that could prevent them from achieving their life goals.

Despite the fact that external factors heavily influence people's decisions, they ultimately have freedom of choice. They may have a choice with few, one, or even zero *desirable* options, but the choice still exists. The nature of the options is not as important as the fact that there are options. All humans have the freedom of choice, even in such restrictive conditions where the only choice they have is how to focus their attention and thoughts. In better circumstances, they have the ability and freedom to choose what they wear, with whom they associate, how they make a living, what they do with their time, and how they respond to adversity and setbacks.

Humans can improve their psychological health by remembering that they have the power of choice because their sense of self-efficacy is correlated with their well-being. Humans or animals that experience so many negative effects from uncontrollable external factors may exhibit learned helplessness and give up trying to exercise their autonomy.[136,137] That perceived loss of agency and meaningful choice begins to take away from the pleasure and fulfillment of a person's life journey.

Ultimately, you have more control over your growth than anyone else does. Despite your genes, your environment, and the other uncontrollable factors you face, your life and its meaning to you are still yours to determine. You have the freedom and power to make your life better or worse with every choice you make.

Your future is largely the result of the choices you make in life

Every action you take or do not take has consequences that shape your future. You can choose to pursue desired experiences or choose to do nothing and leave your fate to other people or chance. If you choose to take action toward a goal, you may progress and succeed or might encounter adversity and fail. If you choose to give up, you may shift your focus to another growth area or abandon all hope of getting what you want in life. If you choose to fight, you may win or lose—even live or die. If you choose to follow someone else, you are accepting that person's judgment as to what you should do next.

However you proceed, your path is shaped by your decisions and actions. You have many choices in life: what you want, what you believe, which experiences you pursue, how you respond to your emotions, which approach you take to achieve your goals, and which resources you leverage. Once you make these decisions, you then have to take action.

With enough desire for and belief in a specific path, you will feel like the option that you are favoring has no reasonable alternative. Indeed, desire and belief are all you need to motivate you to select an option and take action. However, if you have them and still do not take action, you are likely having difficulty deciding between multiple competing options that each have their advantages and disadvantages. To get over this indecision, you need to understand how people make decisions and how you can use decision-making techniques to reach better conclusions.

Some choices seem obvious. If you have to choose between a ripe peach and a bruised peach, you pick the ripe peach. In this case, the options are similar enough, the criteria are limited enough, and one option is clearly superior, so the choice is easy. Some may say, "There is no *real* choice here. The ripe peach is clearly the better option." However, it is still a choice, and the circumstances can change which option you select.

For example, if you wanted to retaliate against someone who wronged you in the past, you may choose the bruised peach and give it to that person. If you had only two peaches and you had to eat one and give one to your child, you may choose to eat the bruised one. You may be able to get a third peach and throw the bruised one away. Even with seemingly obvious choices, your perception of the best option will change based on the situation and the evaluation criteria you are using.

Less obvious choices usually involve either similar items where each one has pros and cons or significantly different options that are too difficult to compare. An example of similar options is if you had to choose between a peach that is ripe with a bruise and a peach without a bruise that is less than a day from being fully ripened. Neither is optimal, so you may choose to eat around the bruised area of the ripe fruit now or to choose the other fruit and wait a day or two for it to ripen. Your choice may vary based on how hungry you are now and whether the bruises are substantial enough to make the peach inedible.

In an example of different options, you may win a contest where you then have to choose between a department store gift card, a free hotel stay, or a new microwave. Those three items are completely different and require considering a multitude of factors to determine which is the best option. Because none is clearly better in every situation, you may choose which item has the highest dollar value, which item you like the most, or which item a friend or family member needs. Alternatively, you may use more than one criterion, selecting the option that is worth the most and that is usable within the next month.

Life choices can involve a multitude of different options. For example, you may have to decide which profession you wish to pursue. The options are practically limitless, which can be overwhelming. As a result, many people immediately reduce the number under consideration based on simplistic criteria. Children often only consider well-known, glorified careers or their parents' professions, and adults often only consider a job based on geographic location, salary, or social status. In a world of infinite possibilities, people tend to select from familiar options.

Making major decisions so arbitrarily may seem irrational, but it does avoid the "paralysis by analysis" problem. With so many options and no clear evaluation criteria, people risk procrastinating or doing nothing. As a result, they may prematurely self-limit options to simplify the decision. Instead of researching and gaining experience in a variety of areas to see which options are worth considering, they go with the default option or imitate others. While you can use this approach to make decisions when you are overwhelmed or indifferent, there is a low probability that the decision will be right for you.

The root cause of many existential crises is that people apply these poor decision models to major life decisions. They might select a job without thinking much about it. They might be told that work is miserable or that they would amount to nothing, so they never bother to look for something that they love to do. Years later, they ask themselves why they do not get a sense of meaning and fulfillment from their profession.

Alternatively, they may want to select one option but then change their decision due to pressure from others. For example, a poor, uneducated child in a remote part of China might dream of becoming the leading stand-up comedian in Canada only to be told by his parents that it was impractical. While it might seem improbable, the decision to abandon the dream altogether will prematurely eliminate practical initial options to write a few jokes or research the cost of a flight to Canada.

Even with an appropriate decision model, life decisions are subject to a great degree of uncertainty and change. Few people know what they want to do in life and hold that singular desire throughout their entire lives with no deviation. People are unsure when they are young, indecisive when they have to make major life decisions, and then seemingly trapped after committing to their choices for a few years. With these factors combined, it seems that a single person has a low likelihood of succeeding if they need both a supportive family and certainty early to live a life of meaning.

For example, a person living in a culture where he is expected to graduate, get married, have children, and support the family business may have his life figured out for him before he gets a chance to consider his options. If that person immediately knows that he wants, though, he may take his own path that involves being a single, childless entrepreneur. However, if he is uncertain early on with what he wants in life, he may follow the societal norms because that is what his community expects of him.

In either case, that person has to make a decision at each point: whether to continue education, get married, have children, and pursue a career. Everyone makes these kinds of life decisions, and you have the power of choice to go in any direction at any time. With each choice, you have to balance what you want or need with what others want or need. You might have to choose between doing what you want and having a relationship with your parents. You might have to choose between living in your hometown and living in a place where you can be free of that town's social, vocational, or legal limitations. You might choose to live your life as others wish and be miserable.

You will have varying levels of support from others and certainty of what you want when you face these decisions. You may know what you want, carve your whole path, and achieve everything you want with no restrictions placed on you by your family or society. Alternatively, you may not know what you want, take the wrong path, and then feel restrictions now that you are a parent and a spouse. You might want something that no one will support you in getting and have to choose between your passion and your social ties.

In any case, you have a choice regardless of how impossible change seems under the current circumstances. If you face societal shame, you can choose to move to another city to find people who will accept you. If your career is unfulfilling, you can choose to go back to school or secure a new job in another field. If you are pregnant and realize that you are not ready to raise children, you can choose to help a family looking to adopt. You have so many options in life—at any time and under any circumstances.

Life decisions are complex, difficult, and nuanced. Your best approach to evaluating them should factor in your past experience, desires, beliefs, feelings, ethics, and resources. You also may choose to factor in others' experience, desires, beliefs, feelings, ethics, and resources. However you consider these factors, make sure to create a clear decision-making process so you can make confident, informed choices and avoid getting overwhelmed and procrastinating. By identifying and prioritizing your decision criteria, gathering relevant information on those criteria for all options, and then narrowing down and comparing your options, you can improve your ability to make decisions.

When making any decision, make sure to test your beliefs and assumptions for inaccuracies, as you might be unnecessarily limiting yourself. For example, you may feel restricted in the current moment based on a series of past events, not realizing that conditions have changed. By testing your assumptions, you may find that you have more options than you thought you had. Additionally, you should test the ones behind others' recommendations since there will be biases toward their needs or interests. If you incorporate their advice, you should take into account how they think that you (should) perceive the world.

Belief testing can uncover biases that prevent you from making the best decision. For example, you might believe that you cannot change direction in life because you have already invested so much (i.e., the "sunk cost" fallacy). You might believe that you cannot change or prefer not to change (i.e., the status quo bias). You might always take a risk-averse approach to life (i.e., loss aversion). In the first two biases, your past investments or behaviors may have more of an influence on your future decisions than they should. In the latter bias, losses tend to outweigh equivalent gains, which predisposes you to conservative decision making. These biases can stunt your growth, so you should recognize them and correct your judgment where appropriate.

When the decision is difficult, you may procrastinate because you worry about what will happen after you make it. For example, you may worry that you will somehow be unhappy, worse off, and with no recourse. There are certain decisions, such as ending a marriage or leaving a job without another job lined up, that are worth considering deeply before making because you may be worse off and will probably not be able to undo them. However, many people will fear making the wrong choice so much that they will never make it despite being miserable in their current situation. Alternatively, they may try to keep their options open out of fear of choosing incorrectly and never commit.

Despite what people believe, the science of happiness supports making informed decisions and committing to them. In one psychological study by Dan Gilbert and Jane Ebert, people who were given a choice between several posters of famous paintings and then given the option to change their minds later were less happy than people who were not given that option.[138] Studies such as this one have indicated that your brain will increase your happiness and satisfaction with choices you have made that you cannot change. Choices that you can change do not have this effect. Even research on tragedy and loss from accidents or bad decisions found that people were able to find meaning in these events, learn from them, and be grateful for them.[139]

The results of these analyses are great news if you are faced with a difficult life choice, as you will either be able to change your mind later or will ultimately come to terms with your decision. If you are absolutely sure, you can take the leap and cut out other options to ensure that you go through with it; if you are unsure, you can keep your options open and change your mind later. Your brain is well-equipped to help you make difficult choices with the best of intentions and all factors considered.

As long as you follow an ethical approach, any decision you make under those conditions should be either acceptable or correctable. When faced with overwhelming or difficult decisions, take the time to consider, make, and own your choices. If you make a mistake, learn from it to make better decisions in the future. You will have to make many decisions over the course of your lifetime, so you will benefit from improving your ability to make them. Having choices is a gift, not a curse.

Before preparing to make a choice, however, you must first confirm that there is a choice to be made. As the Serenity Prayer goes, "God, grant me the serenity to accept the things I cannot change, the courage to change the things I can, and the wisdom to know the difference."[140] It requires wisdom to know the difference because there are so many uncontrollable factors in this world that could worry you. You may have to accept them so that you may shift your attention to where your choices matter. Test your assumptions to confirm which factors are controllable and then focus on the decisions and actions that can help you make progress toward your objectives.

When evaluating factors within your control, use both objective and subjective criteria. Objective criteria are factors that make a choice inherently better, such as the calculated benefit or harm of an action or the number of people affected. Subjective criteria are factors that are unique to you, such as the color of a product you are purchasing that may be better for you but not necessarily better for everyone.

For example, you may buy a set of desks for a classroom based on how they objectively fit the children attending and select a certain color because you think it matches the room. The color is a nice-to-have criterion, but it does not necessarily make it an objectively better desk. Together, the objective and subjective criteria help you determine the best option for you to choose.

Additionally, make sure that you have sufficient information regarding the controllable factors to make the right decision. All of the work conducted before the choice—the research, the experience, the thought work, the guidance from peers—culminates in you knowing the best option that works for you. Success in life often results from making informed choices. You want enough information so that you do not act from ignorance, but you also want a clear method of absorbing information so you can effectively factor it all into your decision without becoming overwhelmed. The goal is to make an informed choice to achieve the optimal outcome; not all choices or outcomes can be perfect.

One of the most difficult parts of decision making is not knowing how others will perceive your decision. Humans are a social species, so they inherently care about what other people think about their choices. Specifically, they may fear judgment if others disagree with or misinterpret their decision. Not everyone has the same information or the same perspective, so a single choice is open to multiple interpretations.

For example, one person could see you moving to another country to pursue your passion as following a dream, while parts of your family could see it as abandonment. If you divorce, some people may view you as a failure. If you choose to surprise someone with a gift, that person may suspect that you wronged them in someone way or are about to ask them for a huge favor. Without the same information that you have, others may draw different conclusions about your intentions, perceive your actions and their outcomes differently, and then react in unexpected ways.

If you made the best decision, the only other influence you have over others' opinions of it is your ability to communicate your reasoning effectively. If you do not care what others think, then you do not have to justify your choice to them. You do have to be prepared, though, for the consequences of your actions and others' possible perceptions and reactions. If you are not prepared, then you have to ask yourself whether you want to make a choice that leaves you dissatisfied with how others perceive it. This dilemma exists for every unpopular decision you make: live with regret in choosing an option due to social pressure or live with the regret of the social consequences of your decision.

Others' influence on your decisions can go beyond them judging you. People throughout your lifetime will try to persuade you and sometimes even try to change your entire worldview. Detractors may say that a situation is "the way it is" to convince you to abandon an action that you want to take. They may point to uncontrollable factors, such as demographics, socioeconomic conditions, social norms, and physics, as evidence that you have to accept your circumstances. They may see the other options as too difficult, risky, or impractical. As a result, they may conclude that you should follow the crowd, take the path of least resistance, keep the status quo, or focus your efforts elsewhere.

Not everyone will be honest or accurate when they try to influence you. People who want to exert control or influence over you will try to make you feel like the approach they want you to take is the only option. They will weave compelling, misleading stories to try to get you to their option. In response, you might be susceptible to accepting their argument without questioning it if you believe that you do not have a choice in the matter.

Whether you are faced with detractors or manipulators, you can resist others' influence by not giving up your freedom and ability to choose. You always have a choice, and your choices matter. People who make you think otherwise likely want you to choose the option that benefits them or validates their beliefs.

The factors in your decision making can feel overwhelming: your situation, desires, beliefs, emotions, ethics, resources, past experience, evaluation criteria, consequences, and others' reactions. Adding to the anxiety, the number of decisions you will make in your lifetime is innumerable. To prepare yourself, define a consistent decision-making process and that is as efficient and effective as possible.

By reducing the effort required for commonplace decisions, you can focus your attention on the critical decisions in your life. The most successful people in the world prioritize their time in this way, and the human mind is optimized for this exact approach. Your unconscious mind automates and streamlines regular decision making, leaving the conscious mind to focus its attention on novel situations.

Your life's purpose is a critical decision that influences every other decision you make. Once you decide on your meaning in life and how to go about realizing it, you just need to choose to take the first step, then choose to take the second, and so on until you attain your goal. In every moment, life contains a choice. You can choose to continue, change direction, try a different approach, start over, or give up. Collectively, your choices shape your future. The consequence of those choices is your destiny.

Without choice, life would be passive, restricted, and boring
Imagine life without choice. It would just be a series of events that happened to you with no ability to control any of it or do

anything about it. It would feel like a dull, endless conveyor belt forcing you through a predetermined set of experiences with no input required or allowed on your part.

Imagine being strapped into a chair with your eyes peeled while you stare at images that you cannot control. This situation was depicted in the film, *A Clockwork Orange*. The goal was to expose the main character, an imprisoned gang leader, to experiences that would recondition him to be able to live in normal society. In that situation, he is completely at the mercy of others in how he directs his attention and experience.[141] Most people would consider it torture to restrict a person's freedom of thought, attention, and movement to that extent.

Unfortunately, there are many situations in which choice is removed from people in society. Kidnapping, imprisonment, and slavery are examples of people forcibly restricting the choices of others. Most forms of unnecessarily restricting personal freedom are unlawful or morally reprehensible in free societies. Necessary restrictions to personal liberty, such as imprisonment, are considered to be acceptable and justified if they deter crime, punish and rehabilitate criminals, and protect innocent people. In either case, restricting someone's freedom can have a negative impact on his or her physical and psychological health.

Losing the ability to choose when and what to eat, where and how to live, what to do with your time, what to wear, or with whom to interact can be a significant hurdle to being able to live a fulfilling life. Loss of control, choice, and autonomy can cause you to struggle to keep your spirits, will, and sanity. When you lose your freedom to choose, your meaning in life begins to wane.

Fortunately, humans have some control even in dire situations. Prisoners in developed countries can read, converse, and exercise. They can own and trade possessions. They can choose what they think about in their cells. They can choose how they think about their lives. Even when your circumstances seem dire, you can choose your own thoughts as long as you are conscious.

Under normal circumstances, people will have many more choices. There are always limits to freedom, however, as some uncontrollable factors such as gravity, weather, and lunar activity can be understood, predicted, and worked around but not directly controlled. From those universal restrictions, various segments of the population have additional constraints imposed by authority figures. The degree of freedom and control that these segments have is generally correlated with the responsibility and accountability they assume for the consequences of their actions.

Children and the elderly, for example, may not have the freedom to choose where they live, what they eat, and what they do. However, they also may not be expected to earn an income or pay for the damage they cause. Instead, their caregivers are making those decisions for them and bearing those responsibilities.

People who are responsible for others are constantly making trade-offs between granting their dependents more freedom and restricting their behavior for cost, safety, or health reasons. Too many restrictions can slow the development of dependents and make them feel oppressed and depressed. Too few restrictions can put them in danger. Freedom without responsibility will lead to recklessness. Leaders and caregivers struggle to find the right balance to maximize the benefits and minimize the drawbacks.

Fortunately for parents, restrictions often foster a child's growth rather than hindering it. Young children in developed societies are not allowed to work so that they can go to school and have time to learn. Supervised play allows them to experiment while still having an adult ready to intervene if they attempt an activity that is too dangerous. Chores and rules teach responsibility so they can demonstrate self-discipline in the future.

Limitations on responsible adults are more controversial. Citizens with mandatory military, community, or public service are having their choices restricted for the good of society, but many people would argue that all activity should be voluntary unless absolutely necessary. Even within those restrictions, however, people have a choice to resist, make a half-hearted effort, or try to make the most of their experience.

Constraints may be self-imposed for their benefits as well. For example, the elderly may choose to move to an assisted living facility to offload some life maintenance and gain access to extra care. They willfully reduce several of their options in exchange for convenience and support so that they may focus on other activities in retirement. Students or athletes preparing for a tough test or competition may isolate themselves from other people and activities. In these cases, choosing to eliminate options can reduce the stress of worrying about them and allow people to optimize growth in other areas.

Because everyone faces physical, psychological, and biological constraints, some people will question whether humans have choice or the illusion of choice. They will point to the strong influence of DNA in human behavior as well as physical and intellectual potential. They will point to superstitions for evidence that people believe that they have control over something that they do not. They can even point to research that shows that human brains fire neurons that will lead to actions before the actors consciously perceive them.[142] As a result, many philosophers question the existence of free will and wonder how much of the universe is deterministic.

When defining a choice as a conscious decision made by a person, it is true that many people do not have a choice in certain situations. People with damage to their prefrontal cortex, for example, show impaired cognitive control and decision-making abilities.[143] Mind-altering substances can also inhibit or impair decision-making processes. Some people have addictions, impulse-control issues, or mental illnesses and are so overwhelmed by the chemical drive to perform a certain behavior that their conscious decision-making abilities cannot contain them. These conditions can prevent a conscious choice from occurring.

In these cases, it is important to distinguish the choice from the conscious ability to control which choice is made. People still choose to consume a substance; they just may not have the willpower to choose another option. Knowing this fact, many people can make other choices ahead of time to prevent themselves from making a poor decision later. For example, people who follow strict diets can refrain from bringing home snacks and desserts so that they do not select unhealthy foods to eat when they are hungry. People suffering from addictions can choose to check themselves into a rehabilitation center that will effectively restrict their freedom until their withdrawal subsides and their willpower returns.

While internal and external influencers will always affect your decision making, you still have plenty of choices. You can choose to avoid certain situations or ask someone to make certain choices for you. You can practice new habits so that you make better unconscious decisions in the future, or you can make conscious corrections if your instincts are incorrect. Your preferences and predispositions are powerful drivers of your behavior, but your conscious mind can find ways to override them.

Scientists will continue to become more accurate as to the degree to which you have control over your own behavior. The loss of choice in one area is not a loss of choice in all areas, however, so this information should enable you to update your knowledge of uncontrollable factors so that you can focus on the controllable ones. Self-efficacy is critical to finding meaning and purpose, so overemphasizing the influence of external factors can do more psychological harm than overestimating the degree of control that you have over your circumstances.

Without choice, people's lives quickly enter a dark place. A common reason for suicide is when people experience a series of negative events and begin to feel powerless to change their circumstances. If the will to live is the strongest natural drive, imagine how severe the perception of powerlessness has to be before someone makes that final choice. People who believe that they have control over their lives do not conclude that suicide is a sensible option; it is only a last resort for people who believe that there is nothing they can do to get what they want in life.

Life without options is boring; life without choice is a passive existence. A person usually cannot live for very long without the urge for something new, and he or she usually cannot live for very long under overbearing restrictions without wanting to break through them. Every organism has an instinctual drive to interact with its environment and exert at least some control over its fate. Learned helplessness is just that: learned. The innate need for agency is so strong that people in monotonous or oppressive conditions will begin to exhibit bizarre or even self-destructive behaviors just to exercise control over something in their lives. If you wish to stop feeling like a passive participant in your own life, you should seek choice and exert control over your own destiny.

Alternatively, having too many choices or options can be overwhelming. Small choices, such as what you have for breakfast, and big choices, such as where you work or study, can both cause stress. Too much stress is debilitating, so you can limit your decision making for your own well-being. You may choose the default option or use a consistent, repeatable process to save on mental effort. These approaches can reduce your burden and ensure that you choose wisely when the stakes are high.

In these examples, it is important to note that you are choosing to eliminate options and reduce the number of conscious decisions that you have to make. If someone else were to eliminate choices or options without your consent, it could add to your stress. People's responses to excessive constraints range from disobedience to outright rebellion. Children who hate the rules that their parents place on them will break them out of spite. Citizens living under an oppressive government will risk their lives to regain their lost freedom. While you may appreciate someone making your decisions simpler or easier, you will not appreciate someone taking away your preferred options.

When exercising your freedom of choice, remember that believing in your own self-efficacy is as vital to your well-being as having it. Believing that you do not have a choice is a self-fulfilling prophecy, leading to the same consequences as when you actually do not have a choice. Your belief can empower you to make choices that lead you toward your goals or squelch your desire until you choose to abandon them.

Unfortunately, there will sometimes be circumstances where you do not have a choice. Random events or other people's actions might affect you, or you might have made a choice earlier that you can no longer change. While you may not have control over these situations, you can still make choices regarding how you react to them.

To address the emotional discomfort (known as cognitive dissonance[144] in psychology) resulting from a conflict between competing experiences, desires, and beliefs, your brain has a defense mechanism to change how you interpret the situation. A famous example of this effect is the Aesop fable about sour grapes. In the story, the fox in the fable changed its belief in the desirability of the grapes it was trying to obtain because it could not reach them.[145] Similarly, if your choice is restricted without recourse, you can choose instead to change your beliefs about the situation.

This defense mechanism is common when you make a choice that you cannot undo. When nothing can be done, your brain can change your perception of your decision so that you can accept what happened. For example, people who subject themselves to hazing or pick the wrong major in school will often talk about the value of the experience and express that they would do it again if they could change history. In this example, these people are aligning their desires and beliefs to accept the decision now that they cannot change it.

Amazingly, people are capable of balancing these two seemingly contradictory forces: the strong desire to take control of their own destiny *and* the willingness to accept situations that they cannot control. You can combine these ideas so that you can focus on what you can improve and not worry about what you cannot. This combination is optimal for human beings, as they have an unprecedented level of control over their environment but still cannot understand, predict, and control everything around them.

A world without choice is a world without life. Life gained the ability to control its environment and itself, and now it has many options as to how it grows. Not having or making conscious choices can lead to learned helplessness, depression, and monotony. If you do not exercise your ability to direct your own growth, you will become a passive participant in your life and lose your sense of purpose.

If you do not choose, you let external forces choose for you

Because there is always a choice, not making that choice deliberately is essentially the same as choosing to accept the default option, what other people want, or random chance. You may not like the alternatives to what you consider to be the only option, but they exist.

When people say, "I have no choice," they usually mean, "There's no reasonable alternative." Indeed, there are many times when there is no other viable option. For example, being robbed at gunpoint or being forced into human trafficking under threat of death to yourself and your family are not choices with a reasonable alternative to compliance. While you could risk torture or death by fighting back, the safest decision at the time may be to capitulate until there is a less risky opportunity to escape.

Clearly, "I didn't have a choice," is said for brevity. However, it is also meant to communicate that external forces dictated a course of action. It is commonly accepted that actions performed under duress are the fault of the person applying force, not the person complying. Therefore, the abbreviated phrase implicitly places more responsibility on external circumstances than the longer version, "I had a choice between complying and possibly living or resisting and probably dying."

Remember this distinction so that you can avoid two opposing risks to your psychological health when you are under duress:

- Blaming external factors even when you have control
- Blaming yourself for coerced actions

If you begin to blame external factors for much of your life situation, you may exhibit learned helplessness. To avoid this risk, remind yourself that you are making a conscious choice to comply. This approach will help you maintain your self-efficacy and will help you resist coercion and peer pressure when it is safer to dissent. If you begin to blame yourself for actions taken under duress, you may repeatedly question whether you could have chosen a different approach. To avoid this risk, acknowledge the coercion and the consequences of non-compliance.

Decisions made under duress are difficult, no-win scenarios where you might be choosing between living with guilt or dying with pride. Your cynical side may begin to question the benefit of living when you are eternally miserable or the benefit of pride when you are dead. In life-threatening moments, the best way to empower yourself is to assert that you are making the best choice for yourself and others under the circumstances.

While you will hopefully never face this kind of choice, many others have. Valeen Schnurr, a victim of the Columbine High School massacre, replied, "Yes," when Dylan Klebold asked her if she believed in God after she had been shot nine times.[146] There would have been no shame in lying or saying anything that would have kept her alive, but she chose to affirm her belief to someone with a gun who probably disagreed with her. He could have killed her in response. With her life on the line, Valeen made her own choice rather than let a mass murderer influence it. Miraculously, she survived her wounds.

Other desperate situations can feel comparable to being held at gunpoint. Battered spouses may continue to live with their abusers to protect their children. Straight-A students who are living in poverty may drop out of school to work and earn money for their families. Gang initiates may commit violent acts to become accepted by the group and to avoid its wrath. These situations involve difficult choices between terrible options. These decisions are heavily influenced by circumstances and are not the ones that they would likely make without such pressures.

If you face these types of situations, you should still acknowledge that you have a choice. Otherwise, you may begin to mistake influence for duress or ignore how your past and present actions could change the situation. If you feel forced but actually have reasonable alternatives, authority figures may disagree with your rationale and punish you for your actions. If you begin to exhibit a pattern of not taking responsibility for your actions, you may feel less ownership over your future choices.

Examples of people making these mistakes include students who cheat on tests after not taking the time to study and addicts who lose their jobs and begin stealing food and money to stay alive. While those situations are stressful, objective observers will not accept perceived duress as an excuse when there were other viable options. Also, people who commit those offenses will feel less obliged to follow the rules in the future. They may not even realize that their ethics have compromised until they are caught.

Without understanding that all situations involve choices, you may begin to avoid making decisions and then tell yourself that you had no choice later. Alternatively, you may let other people and outside forces dictate your actions. If you exhibit these behavioral patterns, you may have adopted an external locus of control. This attitude is a self-fulfilling prophecy, causing you to be compelled by external factors in the future because you never change your behavior to change your circumstances. Thus, you will likely give up trying to control your life.

The problem with this attitude is that you will begin to ignore changes and miss new options. Kidnapping victims, for example, often choose to comply under duress and then continue to comply even when the opportunity arises to escape safely. Students might continue to cheat even though they could have begun adjusting their schedule to study more. High school dropouts might believe that resuming their education is impossible even if their reason for quitting was addressed a long time ago. In these kinds of situations, you could become so used to not having a choice that you are unable to see the alternatives.

To avoid being a passive participant in your life, embrace your choices. Acknowledge the fact that your decisions have meaning and impact. You choose to accept the world as it is or choose to try to change it. You choose whether to follow the rules and choose to take responsibility for the consequences. You choose to comply under duress so that you live another day but will choose to retake control of your life as soon as the threat subsides. You choose whether life is a series of events that happen to you or events that you actively shape. To find meaning in your decisions and actions, make them deliberately.

Some people prefer an external locus of control so that they can avoid being blamed for their actions. They may rationalize that they cannot regret actions that they had no control over. However, they will likely regret the actions that they do not take, and they will eventually feel helpless and trapped from letting external factors dictate their lives. Your optimal balance should be to identify and accept what you cannot control and then focus on what you can control. With this approach, you will spend less time worrying, blaming, complaining, and regretting and more time improving your circumstances.

Taking responsibility for yourself is empowering. It drives you to action. Changing your mindset from having no control over outcomes to having control can immediately transform your outlook on life and your actions. In normal situations, it helps you make the right decisions to progress toward your goals. In high-pressure situations, you can decide to let external factors temporarily dictate the situation until you have the opportunity to make a decision that is better aligned with your goals and de-sires. Consciously choose to accept circumstances or consciously choose to change them, and you will feel more control over your life and greater satisfaction with the outcome.

To make the best decisions, you should monitor your options and influencing factors. Choices exist in every moment of your life. You have the choice to live or die. You can fight or flee when threatened. You have the option to harm others or help them. You can follow the law or commit a crime. You can solicit, steal, beg, con, extort, or offer a value-added service to make money. Every action and every decision is at your discretion. You have a multitude of options, and each option has consequences.

You also have the choice to do nothing. Doing nothing has consequences as well. There are some instances when doing nothing is a good option, such as when someone tries to instigate a fight. It may be best to let it go and not risk harm or discipline, or it might be better to hold your ground and prevent the harassment from continuing. Choosing to act prematurely, irrationally, or immorally may be worse than not acting at all. In risky situations, exercising caution is a valid option.

However, avoiding decisions over a long period of time is like gambling in a casino: you choose to leave your fate to luck in a situation where the odds are rigged against you by people who have their own interest—not yours—in mind. You may get lucky once in a while, but long-term probabilities will deliver an outcome that is out of your control and determined by the rules and desires of others.

If and when you do decide to take control of a situation, you still have to factor those external influencers into your decisions. There are plenty of factors to consider, including laws, social norms, others' desires and beliefs, past events, and current conditions. These factors help you determine the best choice to make, and it may narrow down your reasonable options to a few or even one.

The best choice, of course, is the one that leads to the optimal outcome. To identify it, you need to make sure that you have the most relevant information and that you think critically and creatively about your options. If you know that you are going to have to make a quick decision in the future, you should analyze it ahead of time so that you can make it unconsciously. Athletes rehearse plays, and police, firefighters, and medical teams rehearse emergency scenarios. With enough practice, the right decisions become automatic responses in critical situations.

Some of the most difficult decisions involve other people. You can try to understand, predict, and control others to ensure the best outcomes, but remember that exercising influence and authority over others has ethical implications. In general, society accepts that people with more stake in an outcome should have more influence and that people with more responsibility should have more control. Other people have their own thoughts and make their own choices, though, so you will need to factor their thoughts into your decisions and help them make the best choices for themselves and others.

If you do not understand others' decisions, remember that you may not have the same information that they do. They may choose not to help a person because of his or her past misdeeds. They may not reciprocate because they think that your action is repaying them for something that they did for you earlier. Regardless of their reasoning, you can make different choices for yourself. They have to live with the consequences of their actions, and you have to live with yours.

Even with your best efforts, you may never truly be able to understand other people's choices or know what is best for them. At some point, everyone has to accept that people are different and will not agree on everything. People have to live their own lives, and all you can do is hope that their actions are beneficial to themselves and not harmful to you. Governments establish laws to protect you from others' bad decisions, but having freedom always entails the risk of causing harm or being harmed.

While you cannot always control others' actions, you can always control your reaction to them. First, you can control your emotional reaction. If you are angry at someone, for example, you can get away from the situation, take deep breaths, or change what you want or expect from that person. Second, you can control your behavioral response. If you like to help others but become upset with people who do not reciprocate, you can choose not to help them again, ask them for something in return, scold them for not reciprocating, or find someone else to help. Finally, you can control your future decisions and actions. If someone else takes advantage of you, you may decide not to associate with that individual going forward.

It is empowering to acknowledge the influence you have with others as well: you can set expectations, show gratitude, provide incentives, or help them make better decisions. You can also acknowledge that your choices affect their choices. You have the power to perpetuate or stop a downward spiral of spiteful actions. You have the power to start or continue a virtuous cycle of mutual benefit. Your choices have tangible, lasting impact.

Ultimately, you do need to look out for your own best interest as well as others' needs when making decisions. While many people will tout the benefits of helping others and glorify people who help others at great personal sacrifice, every person has to take care of himself to some extent. You can help others more from a position of well-being. If you do not make the right decisions for yourself, few people will. Anyone who tries to make decisions for you can only do what she thinks is in your best interest, and she will eventually give up if her help enables you to engage in careless or self-destructive behavior.

No one can make choices in your best interest better than you can because no one has complete access to your complex set of desires, beliefs, and emotions that inform those decisions. If you do not make your own choices, they will be made for you. If you do not choose your purpose in life, you will be assigned a purpose by someone else.

Unfortunately, some choices can be very difficult, and you may struggle to determine the best option given the many factors involved. To make the best choice, decisive people develop a set of decision-making techniques to help them better understand their options. These approaches reduce uncertainty so that you can get past forks in the road and continue on your journey.

Below is a list of difficult situations with associated techniques that can lead to better outcomes. Adopt these approaches to become a more active participant in your own destiny:

Scenarios for Using Special Decision-Making Techniques

- *Too Few Options* – If there are only two sub-optimal options, test your situation for a false dichotomy. You may be able to find alternatives, do both, do neither, see a compromise, or make a temporary decision that you revisit when circumstances change.

  Example: If you have to choose between going to college and working to help your family, you could do one or the other, take night courses so you can do both, delay going to school for a year, work while you are at school, or find a job that will pay you while they train you.

- *Too Many Options* – Turn unlimited options into the few best options for you by asking a series of simple filtering questions. Each answer eliminates suboptimal options, making it easier to make a final decision from a shorter list.

  Example: If you cannot decide where to live, use simple filters to narrow the options: Do you prefer warm weather or cold weather? Do you care whether you already speak the language? Do you have to be close to your family? Do you like urban or rural areas?

- *Options Are Too Similar or Too Different* – Some options are too difficult to compare if they are too similar or too different. Each one may have its pros and cons, and a head-to-head comparison may not lead to a clear conclusion. In this case, ask yourself why you would choose each option. This approach changes your analysis from which option is objectively better to which one is subjectively better for you and your needs.

  Examples: When comparing two similar meals, you may enjoy both of them equally and cannot choose from their objective merits. To break through this indecision, identify what you want in a meal right now. How hungry are you? Do you need certain nutrients?

When did you last have each meal? Do you prefer different types of meals for breakfast, lunch, or dinner? Then, choose which satisfies those needs rather than which one meets objective criteria.

When comparing very different careers, you may get caught up in the details of the skill sets you will develop, potential career paths, salary potential, benefits, and work-life balance. Before you decide, remind yourself what you want in a career. One may not seem to be objectively superior, but you may notice that your most important factors are prestige and quality of peers. You can then emphasize those more in your evaluation and finalize your decision.

- *Analysis Still Leaves You Uncertain* – If you are still stuck after thorough analysis, pick one at random or let someone else choose for you. Then, pretend that you have to choose that option and assess how you feel. By having the choice be taken away from you, your true feelings (e.g., disappointment, regret, satisfaction) will surface about which option is right for you. You can then make your final decision with greater confidence.

  Example: If you are having difficulty deciding on a movie to watch, ask a friend to decide what you should watch. Notice how quickly you realize that you have a preference for a certain type of movie when the suggestion makes you feel excited or dreadful. If it was not the right movie, you will begin to think about movies you would rather watch and get closer to a satisfying choice.

- *Too Tempted by the Instant Gratification Option* – If you have to choose between experiencing pleasure now or being better off later, picture yourself with the end result of each option. Imagine yourself feeling bad in the future after choosing the gratification option and feeling good after selecting the better option. This approach counteracts the temptation of immediate rewards by introducing the threat of regret before you decide.

  Example: If you have to choose between going to sleep on time or staying up late watching television, make yourself feel the regret of waking up tired in the morning. The negative emotions will begin to offset and overtake your desire to procrastinate by watching the next program.

- **Each Option Detracts from the Other** – If you have to choose between investing time in multiple competing growth areas, identify how much investment is required to make progress in each area. Then, see if you can allocate enough time to work on both areas. If you cannot, you may then prioritize which is more important to you in the long-term and assess how much of one is sacrificed when you spend more time focusing on the other.

  Examples: If you are focused on both academics and athletics, determine how much time you need for each and if they can both fit into your schedule. If they cannot, determine which is more important: incrementally better athletic performance or incrementally higher grades. Then, based on how much you are willing to sacrifice for the other, determine the amount of time you will dedicate to each.

  If you are balancing work and personal commitments, assess the sacrifice to the latter if you need to spend more time working on an important project. Determine if you can accept the trade-off or make it up later. If you cannot, see if you need to move deadlines, get additional support, or consider other job opportunities. Monitor the situation over time for changing conditions so that your temporary sacrifice does not turn into a permanent one that costs you your spouse or your family.

You will face a multitude of decisions in your lifetime, so optimizing your decision-making processes will help you succeed. As you make better choices in life, your life will improve.

Your family, friends, classmates, coworkers, and employers will also face difficult decisions in their lifetimes. If they have more knowledge or experience, then you might defer to their superior judgment. However, if they have less knowledge or experience, you can give them your opinion or teach them the appropriate decision-making processes or decision criteria. As you help them make better choices, both of your lives could improve.

Finally, you will often be one of many options in other people's decisions. The most fundamental way to persuade them to select you over alternatives is to *be the better option*. If you are the best option or pose the best idea or solution, you make their decision easy. To do so, learn their needs, their decision-making processes, and their decision criteria. Use them to position yourself effectively and make the most persuasive argument. Through this approach, you can help them see that you are the right choice.

Choice may be considered the ultimate human ability because it enables you to grow in your own way. You determine your own path forward. This knowledge may empower you or overwhelm you, but it ultimately will allow you to find your meaning. When you realize that meaning is a choice from within and not a mandate from without, you are now in control of your own destiny.

To make the most of your ability to choose, use your experiences, desires, beliefs, emotions, ethics, and support structure as guides. They are not perfect, however, so you should frequently test and calibrate each of them. Continuously improving your decision-making processes will help you make the best life choices and help you live with meaning and purpose.

The decisions you make will shape your future. Your past, your current situation, your external factors, and your genetics all influence what your choices are and what your potential is in the near term. However, they do not define you. You define yourself. You have as much control over your long-term fate as you are willing to take. Own your choices, own your future, and own your destiny. Choose to pursue and foster growth, and you will choose to have meaning.

QUESTIONS

Questions That Help You Make Life Choices

Your answers to these questions will help you to understand the degree to which you can make decisions or take action in your current circum-

stances to realize your life's purpose. This chapter's content provides guidance on how to think about these questions, but only you can supply the definitive answers for your life.

1. Regarding your identified growth areas, what choices do you have to make to move toward your goals?

2. In which areas do you feel that you do not currently have a choice in the matter? Why?

   - For these areas, are there options that you immediately discount? How would your feeling of choice change if you remembered that you have these options?
   - In areas where one option is the only reasonable one right now, what could you do going forward to give you more or better options in the future?
   - If you cannot control an external factor, can you choose how you view the situation or how you react to the situation? Can you use the restriction to your advantage?

3. Based on what is in and out of your control, what will you choose to do in each of your growth areas? How will you choose to spend your time and focus your efforts?

4. What will happen to your growth or development if you choose to do nothing?

   - If you choose to do nothing for now, are you procrastinating or waiting for circumstances to change?

5. Has analyzing your experiences, desires, beliefs, emotions, ethics, and support changed your plans going forward?

6. What do you choose to do, be, or have? What is your first step, and when do you get started?

EXERCISES

Activities That Help You Make Life Choices

Completing these exercises will help you break through indecision and make difficult, critical life choices.

Thought Exercise: If you have a difficult time making a choice, ask another person to make it for you or randomly select an option. For a moment, assume that this option is the final decision. Assess how you feel about it now that the choice is made and is out of your control. Then, imagine what happens next as a consequence of that decision.

This exercise will trigger a reaction within you about how you truly feel about a choice. You may notice two reactions that will guide your decision making:

1. A desire to have control over your choice again
2. An emotion that will indicate which option you prefer

This exercise also simulates hindsight. Many people who regret decisions mention how hindsight gave them a better perspective. While you cannot know for sure what the consequences of a decision will be, you can try to estimate them as accurately as possible by imagining yourself looking back on the decision in the future.

Brainstorming Exercise: If you are unsure of what choices you have, brainstorm the various options that might be available to you. First, list these options regardless of their practicality. Then, assess each option's desirability (i.e., your preference for it) and feasibility (i.e., its likelihood). Finally, determine how many options you will possibly be able to choose based on time or resource limitations.

This exercise is meant to free you from the constraints of your past thinking to find new options you may not have thought of before. Given enough thought and consideration, there is practically no limit to the number of ways that you can grow in an area. It also allows you to have alternatives ready if you run into limitations in the future. Through this process, you should have a robust list of options for the decision you are trying to make.

Sample Use Cases:

If you want to get an academic degree, you may think that you do not have that choice because it costs too much money. However, there are loans, grants, scholarships, in-state tuition rates, online courses, or part-time programs that are all options for getting a degree given your financial means. You may also start with a lesser degree and then get a job that pays well enough to be able to save for the next degree. Through this process, you may discover that you want multiple degrees and have to choose two fields out of the five or six that you are considering.

If you have always wanted to join the military or a sports team, you may have a physical limitation that prevents you from participating as a soldier or player. If so, there are plenty of roles in those fields that allow you to contribute, such as being an analyst in the military or a manager, coach, or scout for a sports team. Getting a sense of what your options are, how you feel about them, and how many you can choose will make you faster and more confident in your future decisions.

Creative Exercise: Look at the collage that you have created and enhanced through the creative exercises in the previous five chapters. By completing those exercises, you should have a visual understanding of your desired future state, the beliefs and support that make your desires attainable, and the feelings and ethics associated with your approach.

Now, it is time to choose a course of action. Start by writing numbers (e.g., 1, 2, 3) and symbols (e.g., star, circle, square) on small pieces of paper to place against your Desire pictures. Each number represents a priority, and each symbol represents a category. You determine how to classify each picture; useful classifications include:

- *Major versus minor objectives* – e.g., stars for major objectives, circles for minor objectives
- *Short-term goals versus long-term goals* – e.g., stars for long-term goals, circles for short-term goals
- *Type of growth area* – e.g., circles for family, stars for social, hearts for relationships
- *Readiness to work toward* – e.g., gold stars indicating that you have strong desire and belief, silver stars indicating that you

have desire but need to improve your beliefs or support, bronze stars indicating that you need to do more research

- *Big bets versus incremental improvements* – e.g., currency symbols for significant monetary investments, clocks for significant time investments, scales for trade-offs, stars for "quick wins"

Note: You can change the sizes and colors of the symbols to add classifications without increasing clutter (e.g., large symbols denote large investments, green symbols denote that you are ready to get started)

Start by categorizing your pictures. Then, use the numbers to rank-order your pictures in order of priority. You may prioritize all of your items on one ordered list or prioritize within each category. Either approach works, but many people find that it is easier to compare items within categories before (or instead of) comparing items across categories. Finally, you can add dates, time commitment, money required, or other details to begin to visualize your journey toward your objectives.

The goal of this exercise is to prepare yourself to choose and act on those choices. You can determine where you will start, which areas you will focus on first, and how you will organize and manage your goals collectively. Visualize your choices and actions, and you will be more confident and effective in making and taking them when you are ready to proceed.

Writing Exercise: Take your list of growth areas, goals, possible experiences, and action items from the writing exercises of the previous seven chapters. It is finally time to create a detailed action plan. To begin, select your top three priorities and review the goals and action items that you have for them. For each priority, decide on the relevant details, such as the timeline for completion, the effort required, the investment required, your schedule, your main contacts for support, the order of activities, your motivation plan, and ideas for revisiting decisions as conditions change.

Be as specific and detailed as you possibly can. Make sure that you incorporate both short-term and long-term goals into your plan so that you have believable, achievable milestones with accurate estimates along with bigger objectives with fewer details. Commit to your choices by assigning time on your calendar, allocating the funds, conducting the research, and gathering the resources necessary to act. Finally, decide to act on the first action item, decide to act on the second item, and continue deciding to spend your time progressing toward your goals.

If at any time you feel limited in your ability to attain a goal, refer back to the brainstorming exercise in this chapter and write down your list of possible opportunities. You can then choose which ones to include in your action plan. If you are unsure of your next step along the way, you can make the next step in the action plan to research options before you make a final decision. If your conditions change, you may reprioritize your growth areas, adjust your goals, or change your decisions accordingly.

At the end of this exercise, you should have a concrete plan to grow and develop in the areas of life that you care about the most. This document is a written articulation of your life's purpose that you created. You have just found your meaning in life and have just chosen to take control of your future. You now just have to execute and make your destiny a reality.

Example:

Priority	Growth Area	Action Items	Detailed Plan
1	Physical growth	Go to the gym 3 days per week	Timeline: 1 month Effort: 3 hours per week Schedule: M-W-F Cost: $50/month Gym Buddy: Kaitlyn (412-555-5741)
2	Social growth	Make 3 new friends	Schedule time to attend the next club meeting. Introduce myself to everyone. Have one good conversation with someone in the first meeting I attend. Volunteer to host the next meeting.

Note: The above example does not show all of the information you will bring from the previous writing exercises; it is possible that this chapter's teachings may cause you to refine that information.

OUTCOME

After reading this chapter, you should understand how you can make the right life choices for you based on a thorough understanding of how your desires, beliefs, emotions, ethics, resources, and experiences help you grow. You should commit to your choice, take action, and look for feedback or changes that will indicate that you need to adjust your course or approach.

Action is a chosen outcome; inaction is a chosen outcome. Consequently, success is an outcome achieved by continuously choosing to take actions that lead you toward your goal. Success in life, therefore, is determined by the many choices you make throughout your lifetime, not the few memorable ones. You can be successful in life regardless of whether you choose to pursue one career or another, to marry or remain single, to have children or not, or to attain an advanced degree or not. It is the choice to grow in life that is the most important choice you will ever make. Make the choices that will be the best for your growth and the growth of those around you, and success is inevitable.

When you have your final action plan, you should already be moving forward in your life with meaning and purpose. Living a life of meaning is a choice, and you have just given yourself the very meaning in life that you have been seeking.

Conclusion

How do you find your life's meaning?

"Three things are necessary to man for salvation, that is to say: 1. a knowledge of what he must believe; 2. a knowledge of what he must desire; 3. a knowledge of what he must do."

— St. Thomas Aquinas[147]

"Well, life for none of us has been a crystal stair, but we must keep moving. We must keep going. And so, if you can't fly, run. If you can't run, walk. If you can't walk, crawl, but, by all means, keep moving."

— Martin Luther King, Jr.[148]

PRINCIPLES FOR FINDING YOUR MEANING

- Identify your desired growth areas and define success in each
- Trace your goals to their requisite experiences
- Build desire for and belief in those goals and experiences
- Check your emotions to confirm your direction
- Follow ethics to grow in the best way for yourself and others
- Find people and resources that can support you
- Make the choices and take the actions required to progress
- Monitor your emotions and adjust your path as necessary

GUIDANCE ON FINDING YOUR MEANING

"Your life is what you make of it." These words are either em-powering or daunting. You may see them as either an inspiration or a trite platitude. Your view depends on whether you have the autonomy and the ability necessary to make something of it. It also depends on your *perception* of your autonomy and ability to make something of your life.

You may feel or be limited by your current conditions. Note, however, that the goal is *not* to make *everything* of it—just to make *something* out of it because you can make *anything* out of it. That "something" is for you to determine; you can build, nurture, or develop anything within your control. While people or circum-stances may restrict your freedom or hinder your progress, they can neither dictate your purpose nor take away your ability to find meaning in however you choose to live.

Meaning is within your ability to determine for yourself. Many people look for external guidance, which is necessary to explore options but also involves the risk of being led down the wrong path. Other people, books, or philosophies may provide recommendations that are not aligned with your desires, beliefs, and abilities. The best decisions and actions come when you are willing to listen to both external advice and your own reasoning.

Equipped with the knowledge from this book, you should now know how to use experience to gain more information and then use your internal mechanisms—desire, belief, emotions, and ethics—to determine what growth is best for you. You can then make the conscious choice to secure the support you need in your endeavors and move forward. These tools are all that you need to find meaning in your life, regardless of which path in life you decide to pursue.

To find meaning with these tools, you must use them effec-tively both individually and as a complementary set. However, you may have been misinformed about how these tools work, usually by caregivers, instructors, leaders, or authority figures who wanted you to do what they asked of you. You may have been taught that what you want does not matter, that you have to believe what they believe, that you should ignore your emotions, or that you should follow the rules without questioning them. In many cases, using these concepts effectively will require you to reprogram yourself so that you are able to understand and view them differently.

For example, if you were abused as a child, you may now believe that the people you care about most will hurt you, that people are inherently untrustworthy, and that no one could possibly care about you. You might also believe that you cannot amount to anything, that your emotions need to be suppressed, and that you cannot have what you want. This combination of beliefs is what abusers want so that their victims become stuck in abusive relationships without being able to escape. If an abuser can make the victim think there is no way out, then there is no way out. Life becomes nothing more than survival, doing whatever it takes to appease the abuser and minimize the abuse.

Recovering from this troubling past is very difficult but not impossible. You have to learn that it is okay to want things and have your own opinion again. You have to believe in other people again. You have to let your emotional scars heal. You have to exercise your freedom of choice again. This process may be long and arduous, but you can use the very system that is in a state of disrepair to recover from the most tragic life events. You must repair or even reset these mechanisms to get back on the path toward having a meaningful life.

Fortunately, you have the power to turn your worldview around when you feel pessimistic and seem to lack desire. If you are distressed and feel defeated, you want to be happy. You want to believe in the world. You want to help yourself and others. These desires are just suppressed by your experience and beliefs. If you can rekindle that desire for just a moment, you can muster the will to improve your beliefs and ethics, to understand and manage your emotions, and to make choices that get your life moving in the right direction.

When you control your desires, beliefs, emotions, ethics, and choices, you have the power to change your life circumstances. Through it all, you can always find and secure support to help you. You may also find that by helping others, you help yourself.

No matter how good or bad your life situation is, you can find meaning in your life if you accept the power and responsibility that comes with your ability and freedom to shape your own destiny. You are the only one with the most, best information on what matters to you in life. You have to make the choices and take the actions that lead to personal fulfillment; no one can find fulfillment for you.

You have the power to contribute to your own growth and happiness. The world does not have to be different for you to start today. You can wait for people or conditions to change, but it takes much longer and is less under your control than changing yourself. If you make your happiness dependent on everyone in the world behaving in ways that you deem appropriate, then you will never be happy. Others may neither want to change nor believe that they can change. You can change yourself, however, starting immediately.

If you wish to make it your life purpose to try to influence others to your way of thinking, then you can decide to do that. If giving other people more freedom, support, or protection is your purpose, then you can decide to do that. If you have many goals, then you can either spread your time evenly or prioritize your primary objective and support secondary objectives financially. If you wish to escape others' control, then you can work incessantly toward your own independence.

You choose how to spend your time in this world to contribute to your own and others' growth. You owe the world nothing, and the world owes you nothing. Other people will judge you no matter what you do. Just as it is easier to change yourself than to change others, it is easier to be yourself than it is to live to meet others' expectations and influences. As long as everyone follows the necessary laws that prevent harm to others, you should live life on your terms and let others live on their terms.

The point of understanding how life works is to get as much from your limited time in this universe as you can. You can do that when you know how to control your own destiny and then take ownership of it. However, understanding how it works is not about good and bad, winning and losing, or blame and regret. What is good or bad is dependent on the person and the situation. There is no special way to live that will make you better than everyone else. Others do not necessarily have to lose for you to win in life. When mistakes occur, it is not about blame, shame, and righteous indignation. Life is about making progress, solving problems, and continuously improving.

Through that lens, "good" becomes more about avoiding harmful outcomes and achieving beneficial outcomes than about conforming to group norms. Competition becomes a means to improve the ability of all involved, not to make some people better off at the expense of others. Correcting mistakes becomes more about improving future outcomes, not satisfying the instinct for revenge.

What this means for you is that having missed an opportunity, made a mistake, lost, failed, or fallen victim of another's bad choice does not mean that you need to let that experience consume you. Wherever you are now, that is your starting point on your journey going forward, and you can do your best to make better choices for yourself and others. All you can meaningfully do at any point in life is work to be a better person in the future—in other words, to grow.

People will probably debate for the rest of human existence whether there is any meaning to life at all. Many will say that there is no meaning in life, while others will point to God's will. Both arguments assume that it must come from an external source, but meaning comes from within. Without life's ability to assign meaning to things, there is no meaning. With this ability, there are infinite possibilities for meaning and purpose in life. It is for you to discover for yourself what makes your life meaningful.

The concept of infinite possibilities can be overwhelming, and it may seem that having a purpose bestowed upon you would be easier. Imagine someone forcing you to do the worst thing that you can think of doing, though, and you will quickly realize that you would not want someone dictating your life from above or behind the scenes. You may even incidentally begin to see what you do want in life by thinking about what you do not want. After imagining a predetermined existence, the first thing that you will want is control over your life. Take it.

Once you are in an autonomous mindset, your blueprint for finding meaning in your life consists of just eight principles that help you grow in the way that is best for you, the people you care about, and society as a whole:

- Determine which growth areas are of most interest to you
- Identify related experiences
- Build desire and appreciation for them
- Believe that you can attain them
- Monitor your emotions for feedback
- Establish ethics to guide your approach
- Garner support to help you succeed
- Make choices and take actions that lead you to your goals

These principles are all that you need to find your meaning. Experiences and beliefs shape your perception. Desire, ethics, and choice shape your direction. Emotions provide feedback on your progress, and support helps you through challenges. Growth is life's objective. Continue to internalize and operationalize these concepts, and you will have the ability to control your own destiny and derive your own meaning from events. Collectively, they will help you determine what you want to do with the limited time you have in this universe.

"Why am I here?" can ask either the cause of your existence or the purpose of it. The former is an interesting question for humanity to answer; the latter is a necessary question for you to answer. Where you came from before your life began and where you are going after your life ends are two fascinating thought exercises. However, they have no practical bearing on your meaning while you are here. Your creator does not dictate your purpose. You will not be assessed in the afterlife and given an "ethical life score" that determines your eternal reward or punishment. You are an autonomous being applying subjective, situational ethics that evolve over your lifetime. Your indicators of meaning in this physical reality are your emotions; you do not need to understand anything beyond the physical universe to use them properly.

Self-determination is unique to life. Purpose is not intrinsic to non-living things because they do not have the ability to control themselves and interact with the environment. A rock cannot think or act in the physical world, so it cannot have its own purpose. Any purpose it has is given to it by a living thing that can use it. Life can have an intrinsic purpose because it exists as a form of self-controlled growth. With that ability, there is no need for an external force to decide its purpose for it.

All eight concepts are involved when a life form demonstrates self-determination. An organism that can control itself and interact with its environment can have experiences. It has to decide how to use its abilities in that environment, so it has biological drives, beliefs about how the world works, rules for how to act in the given the situation, and feedback mechanisms to monitor the results of its behavior. Environmental factors are either supporting or hindering its ability to perform those actions. The primary purpose of any organism's activities is growth.

These concepts are interconnected. Depressed people have little desire, do not believe in themselves, treat themselves poorly, avoid experiences, retreat from their support network, and make very few choices in their lives. Consequently, they make less progress in life. Happy people have a lot to live for, want to experience life, believe that life is valuable and meaningful, live with a set of guiding principles, seek and provide support, and appreciate the choices they have in life. As a result, they thrive.

Together, these concepts can create either a virtuous cycle or a downward spiral. In a virtuous cycle, support increases belief, belief strengthens desire, appreciation reinforces support, and support fosters appreciation. In a downward spiral, negative beliefs can defile ethics and desires, diminished desire can change beliefs, and a loss of autonomy can break a person's will.

Now that you understand how these concepts work together, you can use them to keep striving toward your goals. To build momentum, strengthen one of them and then use it to bolster the others. To reverse a trend of negativity, you can develop techniques to address each component, such as meditating to calm negative emotions or exploring options to clarify your desire. If one component is too difficult to improve, you can always try focusing on another one to start the virtuous cycle.

If you are in an extreme negative state, a turnaround may seem impossible. People who are recovering from the sudden death of a loved one or years of unlawful imprisonment may need to start with small shifts and improve gradually. In these types of situations, their emotions, desires, beliefs, and ethics are often severely affected by their past experience. They can start with one minor change, such as finding the desire to take a walk outside on a sunny day. As they progress, they can make more significant changes such as regaining their positive outlook on their future or beginning to trust other people again. No matter where you start, you can always find your way to a meaningful life by improving in these eight areas.

Whatever the situation, do your best not to let your current circumstances dictate your direction. Your circumstances will never be absolutely perfect. Many people use setbacks as the driving force to propel them to succeed. Successful investors make some of their most important investments during market downturns. The first person to invent, discover, or achieve something had to overcome the reality that no one had done it before.

Do not succumb to peer pressure or current conditions if it means suppressing a strong, positive desire. There will always be nay-sayers and obstacles, and your life will be at the mercy of them if you always surrender to them. Set your direction based on where you want to be before you adjust it to account for where you are.

Similarly, do not overemphasize immediate results. Many people will quit if they do not see initial success, but natural talent is not necessarily an accurate predictor of long-term achievement. Some people may give up trying to find their purpose if they do not figure it out right away, but many successful people only found their true purpose in life after years of focusing on the wrong goals. Growth by definition is an evolution. You will not automatically do everything perfectly. You will not immediately understand everything and know exactly what to do. You can improve anything over time, so you should let your desire drive you instead of allowing limiting beliefs to creep in too quickly.

If you are starting from a place of uncertainty, you may look to others for advice on the meaning of life. Given the limitations of a short conversation, people will simplify the meaning of life as they understand it. The meaning of life is to serve others. It is to love. It is to learn. It is to get better every day. They are all right, as these are all ways to grow or foster growth in others. Each person's meaning is much more nuanced, however, so it is important that you incorporate any advice that you find valuable into what you already know about yourself. Your path will be unique. Some of the advice that helps someone become an expert painter may help you grow into a successful businessperson, and some of it may not. What worked for your parents or friends may or may not work for you. You need to balance learning from others' wisdom with listening to your inner guidance.

If you choose a different path than others, they may look down on you because they think that their way of life is best. Conversely, you may feel that another person is squandering their talent by focusing on something that you deem unimportant. Everyone has a right to their opinion, and there is not much that you can or need to do in either case. There is room in life for everyone to pursue their own paths while cooperating with others to achieve societal objectives. If someone's wish for you is not in line with what you want (or vice versa), then it is important to live and let live. Everyone has his or her own meaning and needs to follow his or her own path.

You will find yourself in situations where you are severely restricted by external forces and cannot grow in the way that you want. For example, you may have to take care of a suddenly ailing loved one or have a significant amount of debt. These situations require considerable time and effort in areas that may not be your preferred option. Regardless of the circumstances, there is one powerful ability that you can always exercise: you can find meaning in what you are doing. If you cannot do what you love, love what you do.

Because meaning is up to you, you can decide today to find meaning in the work you are doing, the support you are providing, the food you eat, and the choices you make. If you could escape your current life at any time through a variety of means, then you must have a purpose in choosing to face the current situation. If you are cleaning a floor, it is to make it safe and pleasant for others. If you are supporting a dying loved one, it is to help him or her leave this world as comfortable and loved as possible.

Everything you do is a means to an end, and you can find meaning in both the activity and the outcome. Every decision and action has a purpose, and you can assign significance to anything you do. You can give meaning to everything in your life: everything you think, everything you do, everything you have, everything you want, everything you are.

Finding meaning when you have restrictions is crucial because you will always have short-term limitations. You have limited time, attention, funds, and resources. Therefore, you may have to prioritize your desires and identify short-term goals that can make long-term goals possible. However, you can accomplish virtually any long-term goal with growth. Humans instinctually test limits because growth requires them to expand the boundaries of what existed before. Keep your belief and meaning when encountering those boundaries; if you lose them, you will stop pursuing that path regardless of your probability of success.

One way that people find more meaning in their daily activities is to be mindful and deliberate in performing them. It is easy to automate operations so that they do not require conscious thought, and that is a valuable function of the brain to allow you to focus on the most important things in life. However, many parts of this process can go wrong: you may deprioritize important decisions, miss when conditions change, and solely focus on stressful future and past events.

Automating when you should be acting deliberately will leave you automatically making the wrong decisions, so check your routines and assumptions frequently. If you solely focus on problems in life, you will eventually tire of the constant stress and pain. Automating too much of the present while thinking about the past or future can reduce the meaning and importance of the moment. When you are mindful and deliberate, you make more meaningful decisions and make decisions more meaningful. When you make meaningful choices throughout your lifetime, you will logically conclude that your life was meaningful. Make it your deliberate intention to grow, and you have the potential to become or achieve whatever you want.

While you can choose any meaning that you wish, be careful when making decisions in the interest of pleasure instead of fulfillment. Hedonism, the idea that life's primary goals are to seek pleasure and avoid pain, is slightly mistaken; pleasure and pain are life's primary *incentives*, not its ultimate *goals*. The goal is to grow, and organisms generally receive neurochemical rewards for performing growth-enabling activities and alarm signals for experiencing growth-inhibiting events. This distinction is important because pleasure is an imperfect indicator that people have learned to manipulate. As such, you can stimulate your reward system in ways that are detrimental to your long-term growth.

The correlation between dissatisfaction with life and plea-sure-seeking addictions such as drugs, alcohol, sex, or gambling shows that manipulating your neurochemicals for short-term pleasure is a losing strategy for long-term fulfillment.[149,150,151] The boredom, emptiness, or pain that these temporary pleasures are masking can only be truly alleviated with growth-enabling ac-tivities. Having meaning can be everything to a person. It is the difference between being a contributing member of society and a detractor. It is the difference between happiness and despair, self-actualization and disappointment, and even life and death.

You must be careful in your search for meaning because all as-pects of the process can be gamed. You can game your emotions and desires by abusing pleasure-inducing chemicals or activities. Someone can manipulate your beliefs and ethics to achieve their own goals. Someone may pretend to be supporting you but ac-tually be undermining you. Someone may rig your experiences to lead you to the wrong conclusion. Someone may provide you with the illusion of choice or make you think that you have no choice. Because of this potential for abuse, you need to be wary of attempts by anyone—including yourself—to derail your quest for a fulfilling life.

If any of these components are manipulated or inaccurate, your understanding of your meaning could be wrong. Given that your meaning is also frequently changing and evolving, you should check your current state periodically to ensure that you are on the right path. This analysis will be unique to you, so oth-ers can provide guidance but will not have all the answers.

The subjectivity of meaning is why general recommendations from authoritative sources may seem incomplete or inaccurate. These recommendations usually either assume a purpose, such as making money, being healthy, or starting a family, or instruct you to pick a specific goal or aspiration before following them. These types of guidance require you to know what you want in life or how to figure it out before they can help. Other guides as-sume that a successful life generally consists of a common set of goals, such as health, wealth, happiness, and love. They aim for broad applicability, but they usually focus on what to do and why rather than helping you understand how it all works so that you can set your own direction.

You may listen to that type of advice to see if you are interested in those goals, but make sure that you have a clear direction before you follow it. Only then will you maximize its value because you will see its applicability and take action. Hopefully, you now understand how you can set your direction and derive your meaning in life. Using the eight fundamental concepts in finding meaning, you can control your own destiny.

As for the idea of there being a greater meaning in life, many debaters will create a false dichotomy between a divine purpose for everyone and no purpose for anyone or anything in the universe. The growth-centric view of meaning provides another possibility: the meaning of life is to grow, and humans have the ability to assign meaning to their lives and anything in them.

The ability to assign meaning is just one of humans' many advanced capabilities that give them an unparalleled level of influence over their own reality. While the word "reality" often refers to scientific absolutes that are unchanging, undeniable, and eternal, it can also refer to artificial systems and structures that people can change. Absolute reality includes physics, chemistry, and mathematics; malleable reality includes laws, social norms, and technology. Humans cannot alter absolute reality; they can only work within or around its boundaries. Humans can influence malleable reality, however. They can agree to new rules and norms, and they can invent new technologies. These aspects of reality only exist because people created them.

Therefore, what you know as your current "reality" is part absolute and part malleable. While the elements used to construct buildings, cars, and computers existed before humans did, the inventions themselves are a result of human imagination and action. Reality is constantly changing as laws change, human potential increases, science evolves, and new ideas are explored.

People created much of the reality that you experience every day. Therefore, you can create your own reality—not in a metaphysical sense, but in a tangible sense. You can change where you live. You can get an education. You can find a mate. You can pursue a career. You can change your life and make your wishes come true.

Unfortunately, the difference between absolute and malleable reality is not always clear. In addition, reality is a complex combination of factors that cannot be analyzed or changed all at once. As a result, there are plenty of disagreements and conflicts over what is real, what is controllable, what conclusions can be drawn from the facts, and what to do as a result. There will never be a time where everyone agrees on everything because everyone perceives the world differently.

This fact is why there is yet another definition of the word "reality" in common use: the world as understood by the person perceiving it. In that definition, perception *is* reality. Humans have their own perception, so they live in their own reality. People decide, act, react, and vote based on how they perceive the world, even if that perception is not in line with scientific absolutes or objective truths. Humans then create their systems, rules, customs, services, and products based on that perception, which is a self-fulfilling prophecy that alters malleable reality to match their worldview. What reality they create, then, is based on their experiences, desires, beliefs, emotions, ethics, support, and choices—the same concepts that determine meaning. In that regard, reality itself is heavily determined by human thoughts and perception.

People will conflate these three definitions of "reality" because human laws can seem as immutable as the law of gravity. Human perception feels real. The past is unchangeable, and most of the current state cannot change instantaneously. Conflating these three definitions, your detractors will tell you to face reality because that is how it is...but that may be neither how it is nor how it has to be. It is your ability to change your current circumstances—your current reality—into the reality you want that is the greatest power that you have as a human being.

Humans are truly free when they realize that they can shape the terms of their existence. Being poor, having a disability, experiencing trauma, or living in an oppressive situation does not have to define you. For every problem that humanity has ever had, people have either found or are looking for a solution. Advances in society, including medicine, nutrition, technology, law, politics, and economics, have vastly improved human well-being and quality of life. People have even proactively pushed the boundaries of what is physically possible when they escaped the Earth's gravitational pull or created chemical elements that never before existed in nature. Humans break boundaries every day, and you can, too, by growing beyond your previous limits and limitations.

You can shape your reality, and you can determine your meaning. The only thing that meaning requires is a life form that is able to assign a purpose and significance to something. You give something significance and meaning by caring. Care about your family, your friends, your job, your home, your health, and your education, and they will have meaning to you. When you find something you care about or decide to care about it, you will have just found meaning in it.

Meaning cannot exist without you. With you, it can be anything you want it to be. You just have to find what you care about. You have to find what you want. You have to find what you believe in. You have to find what makes you happy. Then, make those things your reality. Do not just find your meaning; make your life meaningful.

While humans have an unprecedented ability to perceive and shape the world around them, all life has a fundamental commonality: growth. All living things grow, and growth is the primary objective of all life. If you live a life full of meaningful growth, then you will have found the meaning of life.

Post-Book Assessment

Track growth in your ability to derive meaning in life

Rate the degree to which you agree or disagree with the following statements using this scale:

1	2	3	4	5	6	7
Strongly Disagree	Disagree	Somewhat Disagree	Neither / Uncertain	Somewhat Agree	Agree	Strongly Agree

Statement	Score
1. I understand the ways in which I can grow as a person.	_____
2. I understand how I define success in my life.	_____
3. I know what I can do to make progress in my life.	_____
4. I appreciate what I have in life.	_____
5. I desire activities, abilities, or things that I currently do not have.	_____
6. I believe that I can do, be, or have what I want in life.	_____
7. I understand what my emotions are communicating to me.	_____
8. I follow rules in life that protect and benefit myself and others.	_____
9. I know how to use the resources I have to support my goals in life.	_____
10. I feel like I have a choice in what I do or accomplish in life.	_____
11. I live my life with a sense of purpose.	_____
12. I am pleased with how my life is progressing.	_____
13. My life will be better in the future than it is today.	_____

Total: _____

Results

13-39: Struggling to find meaning in life; dedicate time to life exploration and analysis

40-65: Experiencing some issues or uncertainty in life direction; focus on clarifying specific areas

66-91: Living life with purpose; monitor for changes and opportunities for improvement

Upon completing the assessment, compare these answers to your pre-book assessment and see if your scores have increased. If you scored low in a particular statement and wish to focus on improving it, refer to the following mapping of the assessment's statements to the relevant parts of the book:

Section to Reference When Scoring Low in a Statement

Statements 1–2: Growth
Statement 3: Experience
Statements 4–5: Desire
Statement 6: Belief
Statement 7: Emotions
Statement 8: Ethics
Statement 9: Support
Statement 10: Choice
Statements 11–13: Each Chapter's Questions and Exercises

Glossary

Terms defined within the context of the meaning of life

Appeal to Improbability – A logical fallacy in which something is assumed to be impossible because it is improbable; in life, it is very easy for people to deter others from their desired path through an appeal to improbability

Appreciation – Desire for what you already have in life; gratitude and positive feelings toward things that you can be, do, or have in life or that you have been, done, or had

Attention – The object or focus of a person's consciousness or senses; attention is required to experience something and influences your desires and beliefs based on how you feel about the focus of your attention

Belief – Life's sustaining force; the assumption that something is true; your experiences are influenced, shaped, and framed by your beliefs; your beliefs may strengthen or weaken your desires and lead you to continue on a path, change direction, or give up

Caring – The act of attaching meaning or importance to something; feeling concern about something or taking an interest in it; for humans, caring is how they give something meaning and is an indicator that something has meaning or significance to them

Choice – A decision between multiple options; in life, choice is the ability to set your own path, to pursue what you want, and to take action toward your goals instead of conceding to circumstances or other people

Conditional Probability – The probability of an event occurring given that another event has occurred; people who try to discourage others from going into their chosen path in life often cite misleading statistics that are true as a percentage of the total population but do not factor in conditional probability

Confirmation Bias – The tendency for people to notice and look for evidence that confirms their beliefs and dismiss evidence that contradicts it; should be eliminated in scientific research but can be used in life to help you grow if you focus on things that support your desired outcome while discounting the detractors

Contrast – The difference between what you want and what you do not want; contrast must exist in the world for growth to be possible, as it would be impossible for something to be better tomorrow if it were not worse today; it is the contrast between where you are now and where you would prefer to be that creates desire that leads to action that leads to growth

Desire – Life's driving force; the drive to be, do, or have something; you choose your experiences based on your desires; desire motivates humans to strive to be better in life and is the first step toward growth, accomplishment, and success

The "Don't Look Down" Principle – The idea that if you tell someone, "Don't look down," they almost immediately look down; explains two concepts: 1. if you talk in terms of what a person should not do, all the person receiving the message can think about is doing what you said they should not do; 2. if you focus on the undesired outcome, you are distracted from both the desired outcome and the path to getting there (including obstacles)

Double-Blind Experiment – A method of experimentation where neither the experimenter nor the subjects know which participants are in the control or test group to avoid the expectations of either group affecting the study; an example of expectations significantly altering outcomes that is critical to avoid in research but can be used by people to expect and be more likely to attain better outcomes in life

Emotions – Life's feedback mechanism; emotions indicate whether you are growing in the way that you want to grow and believe you can grow; they provide guidance for you to continue doing things that lead to desired outcomes and to discontinue or avoid things that lead to undesired outcomes

Ethics – Moral principles that life follows to allow for safe, mutually assured growth with other life; rules that prevent you from hurting others or hindering their ability to grow; principles for how you can grow in the best way possible

Expectations – Predictions about the future that are determined by your beliefs; these predictions influence your desire to do something, the effort you will exert, your approach, and the results that you are able to achieve

Experience – Observation of or engagement with a thing, event, activity, or idea; to experience something includes observing it with the senses, learning about it, or participating in it; experiences can result in added knowledge, changed beliefs, progress toward your desired goals, and new desires; experience is the medium through which growth occurs

Failure – The inability to attain your desired outcome; in life, failure is always an occurrence (e.g., "he failed to achieve his goal on that attempt") and never a state of existence of a human being (e.g., "he is a failure"); failure is a learning opportunity to either improve your ability or change your desired outcome

God – According to monotheists, a non-physical entity that exists either separately from this universe or within all living things, that created the universe, and that may or may not exercise the ability to influence the physical world; in the life of believers, God acts as a catalyst for spiritual growth and experience, a receiver of their gratitude, desires, and beliefs, a symbol of the emotions of love and compassion, a provider of universal ethics, a source of support during difficult times, and a spiritual guide for life choices; for humans, God can be a source of meaning or a guide toward meaning but is not required for everyone to have meaning; the existence of God is untestable by science (i.e., the study of the physical universe cannot test for the existence of a non-physical being) and can only be a belief that people hold; the origins of the belief in God may include the human capacity to feel interconnected with other people and life forms, the sensation that life has a non-physical, spiritual component, and the desire to explain the unexplainable and control the uncontrollable in the physical realm; for those who believe in the being's omniscience, omnipotence, or omnipresence, God is the most logical source of answers regarding meaning; God is an effective means for people lacking belief in themselves to believe that positive outcomes are still possible

Growth – Growth is the ability of a living organism to make more of itself; the meaning of life is to grow, as growth defines life, is the reason why it exists, and is the ultimate goal of life

Growth Area – An improvement that a person has identified that he or she would like to make in life with a directionally correct understanding as to how much he or she wants to improve

Hedonic Treadmill – Also known as hedonic adaptation, it is a concept of human resiliency that states that people tend to return to a relatively stable level of happiness regardless of positive or negative events that occur throughout life; strongly suggests that increasing and maximizing happiness is not the ultimate goal of life; happiness is temporary feedback indicating growth and prosperity; overall satisfaction with life, while influenced by genetics, comes from your ability to find long-term meaning and not from quick fixes or short-term gratification

Life – Refers to either all life on Earth or your existence and time lived on Earth as a human being; the critical attributes of life for the purposes of finding meaning include growth and the ability to sense and interact with the environment

Meaning – The significance and purpose of life, which is to grow and become better or more in the future than you were in the past; meaning can be found in many forms of growth, including physical, intellectual, social, spiritual, and financial growth; the term is often used to describe the definition, intent, or goal of life

Negative – The absence or lack of something; when referring to emotions, negative emotions signal an absence of or a threat to growth; when referring to thoughts, negative thoughts are the focus on the absence or lack of the desired outcome (or presence of or potential for an undesired outcome); negative people, things, or events are ones that detract from your growth or desired outcomes; negative is not necessarily synonymous with bad, but your perception of something as negative is a sign that you do not want it or believe that it is undesirable

Non-Life – Refers to everything on Earth that does not qualify as life, such as inorganic compounds; non-life is not able to grow, intend, or sense and interact with the environment, all of which are key to deriving meaning; non-life only has the meaning or purpose that is assigned to it by living things that are capable of these activities

Optimism Bias – An effect where humans are likely to overestimate the likelihood of positive future events and underestimate the likelihood of negative future events compared to what probability and statistics would suggest; the optimism bias comes as a consequence of the inherent belief that a person's circumstances in the future will be better than they are today because growth is the point of living

Outcome – The result or consequence of thoughts, actions, or events; growth begins with the desire and belief in an outcome and ends with the attainment of that outcome (before beginning anew with a different or better outcome); desired outcomes may change with experience

Personal Growth – Refers to the many different ways that a human being can grow in life, such as physical, intellectual, spiritual, social, and emotional growth

Placebo Effect – An effect found in scientific studies where patients achieve a desired health outcome (or experience the expected effects) solely by believing that they will attain it; the "treatment" provided has no ability to cause the desired outcome by itself because it has no active ingredient; in life, belief alone can have a powerful effect on how your brain and body respond to situations; it is important to believe in an outcome so that you maximize the likelihood that you will strive to attain it

Positive – The existence or presence of something; when referring to emotions, positive emotions signal the existence of or progress toward growth; when referring to thoughts, positive thoughts are the focus on the existence or attainment of the desired outcome; positive people, things, or events are ones that contribute to your growth or desired outcomes; positive is not necessarily synonymous with good, but your perception of something as positive is a sign that you want it or believe that it is desirable

Priming – An effect where focusing on or paying attention to one thought or experience unconsciously influences how you perceive a future experience; priming shows that your prior thoughts set the foundation for how you perceive a future situation and should be used to prepare you to see opportunities to grow that you may otherwise miss

Reproduction – Life's fundamental form of growth where an organism creates a copy or new version of itself to continue its existence

Self-Fulfilling Prophecy – An expectation or belief that, through the believer's resulting actions and behaviors, lead to consequences that confirm that expectation; believing that you can do something will lead you to try harder, and your success will validate that initial expectation; believing that you cannot do something will lead you to give a half-hearted effort, and your failure will validate that initial expectation

Success – The accomplishment of an aim or purpose; having grown into the desired state; having achieved the desired outcome

Successful – Accomplishing important life goals or making consistent, visible progress toward them

Support – The ability of life to cooperate with other life to grow more safely and effectively; social behaviors that have been critical to humanity's survival and success; support is necessary for humans to reach their full potential; supporting others increases one's own sense of purpose; while support from people can have the most meaning, resources can also be part of a support system

Afterword

The following sources are examples of the wealth of materials that were researched in the writing of this book and have either provided motivation for its creation or influenced the concepts described, conventional wisdom challenged, examples used, or the nature and structure of key points and arguments:

Evolutionary Biology

The meaning of life is often conflated with the origin of life because people are looking for the intent of the creator. Therefore, an understanding of biology, the origins of life, and basic evolution is necessary to discuss the connection between life and the physical universe.

Studies of the origins of life show that life grows, interacts with the environment, and uses energy. Scientists have possible explanations for how life began, and so it helps eliminate the need for a deity as an explanation. Humans' emotions, social nature, development of ethics, and greater capacity for growth can all be explained through biological study. Evolution explains how life has become more sophisticated over time, which explains the many additional options for humans to live and grow compared to other forms of life.

Examples of media studied:

- *On the Origin of Species* by Charles Darwin
- *Origins of Life* by Robert M. Hazen
- *The Selfish Gene* by Richard Dawkins

Religion

Religions were studied to analyze historical recommendations for how to live life. This analysis led to the finding that these teachings combine how life began, how it works, and how a person should live. Religions make the argument for a God-created universe, suggest universal ethics bestowed upon humanity by its creator, and provide story-based explanations of the best way to live life. Famous scientists and religious skeptics, such as Stephen Hawking and Richard Dawkins, have argued how religion made sense before science as a way to explain things but is no longer necessary now that the universe can be explained scientifically.

While religion as a means for explaining the origins of life and the nature of physical reality has been largely replaced by science, people still look to religion for ethical guidance and for a spiritual purpose. These texts provide insight into early ways of explaining life, giving humanity a higher purpose, and establishing rule sets across different cultures.

Examples of media studied:

- Christianity: *The Bible*
- Judaism: *The Torah*
- Islam: *The Quran*
- Hinduism: *The Bhagavad Gita*
- Buddhism: *Dhammacakkappavattana Sutta*
- Spirituality: *A Course in Miracles*
- Atheism: *The God Delusion* by Richard Dawkins

Psychology

The study of the human mind and how it works is one of the most critical components to understanding how human beings derive meaning from their existence. Hundreds of psychological studies and psychology books were reviewed to investigate how the mind processes and interprets information about its environment and experiences. The findings from these studies provided the scientific basis for how a person can live purposefully.

Specific examples of insights from this material include how a growth mindset influences the probability of success in life, how beliefs influence behavior, what motivates people, why humans have emotions, and how human variation allows for different meanings for different people.

Examples of media studied:

- *The Blank Slate* by Steven Pinker
- *Drive* by Daniel H. Pink
- *Flow* by Mihaly Csikszentmihalyi
- *The Great Ideas of Psychology* by Daniel N. Robinson
- *Mindset* by Carol S. Dweck, Ph.D.
- *Predictably Irrational* by Dan Ariely
- *The Optimism Bias* by Tali Sharot

Philosophy

Countless books have been written on the nature and meaning of human existence. These books have provided insight into which forms of meaning humans derive from their existence, how ethics work, what rights every person should have, and how people should live.

Studying philosophical works led to the conclusion that they are often focused on a specific concept, are too abstract, or make too many assumptions to provide practical guidance for people looking to figure their lives out for themselves. Recommendations around meaning and fulfillment include hard work, service to others, learning, and finding love and happiness, but explanations focus more on how they improve life outcomes than how someone can identify meaningful activities.

Specific ideas from this material include the nature of reality and existence, the degree to which humans have free will, ways in which society balances the rights of the individual with the safety and well-being of the group, and concepts such as virtue, choice, and good versus evil.

Examples of media studied:

- *Critique of Hegel's Philosophy of Right* by Karl Marx
- *Critique of Pure Reason* by Immanuel Kant
- *Elements of the Philosophy of Right* by Georg Wilhelm Friedrich

Hegel
- *Fear and Trembling* by Søren Kierkegaard
- The Four Noble Truths by Siddhartha Gautama
- *The Great Ideas of Philosophy* by Daniel N. Robinson
- *Great Philosophical Debates: Free Will and Determinism* by Shaun Nichols
- *Meditations on First Philosophy* by René Descartes
- *Metaphysics* by Aristotle
- *Philosophy as a Guide to Living* by Stephen A. Erickson
- *Tao Te Ching* by Laozi
- *The Republic* by Plato
- *The Sayings of Confucius* by Confucius
- *A Treatise of Human Nature* by David Hume
- *Two Treatises of Government* by John Locke
- *Vindication of the Rights of Men* by Mary Wollstonecraft
- *Vindication of the Rights of Woman* by Mary Wollstonecraft

Economics and Business

Success in business requires people to work together to achieve an outcome. Behavioral economics studies how people make economic decisions based on various factors and incentives. These fields provide a wealth of research on why people engage in certain behaviors, how they successfully cooperate, and how they plan and execute a strategy.

A few ideas were triggered through studying these materials: most business and self-help books tell you to start with a goal but do not tell you how to identify a goal; any creation of a plan for success works back from the outcome to what you need to do to achieve it; and you will be more successful if you help other people to achieve their goals. Finally, most business books follow underlying business ethics such as providing value to others and treating your associates well. These ethics show the importance of fairness and reciprocity in business dealings.

Examples of media studied:

- *The 7 Habits of Highly Effective People* by Stephen Covey
- *Behavioral Economics* by Scott Huettel
- *Bringing Out the Best in People* by Alan Loy McGinnis
- CEB Research by CEB Inc. (acquired by Gartner, Inc.)
- *Freakonomics* by Steven D. Levitt and Stephen J. Dubner
- *How to Win Friends and Influence People* by Dale Carnegie
- *An Inquiry into the Nature and Causes of the Wealth of Nations* by Adam Smith
- *Manifesto of the Communist Party* by Karl Marx
- *Start with Why* by Simon Sinek

The Meaning of Life

Within philosophy are specific texts focused directly on meaning. Some are trying to answer the "What does it all mean?" question, while others are explaining how to find meaning without religion. Insights from these materials include how to define meaning, how philosophers have tried to figure out why they exist, why people live the way that they do, why they pursue certain goals, how they identify meaningful activities, and how and why they find meaning in them.

Examples of media studied:

- *Quest for Meaning* by Robert H. Kane
- *The Meaning of Life: Perspectives from the World's Great Intellectual Traditions* by Jay L. Garfield
- *No Excuses: Existentialism and the Meaning of Life* by Robert C. Solomon
- *How Will You Measure Your Life?* by Clayton M. Christensen, James Allworth, and Karen Dillon
- *Life Driven Purpose* by Dan Barker
- *Why We Do What We Do* by Tony Robbins

Happiness

Happiness is a popular answer for what the meaning of life is. Therefore, there has been a wealth of research on what makes people happy. The research has found that happiness through material goods is short-lived and that things that people think should make them happy, such as choice and positive thinking, can actually become sources of stress.

The findings seem to contradict what people think will make them happy. However, happiness is a term that can refer to the emotional state, to pleasure, or to life fulfillment. While they use the same term, the pleasure received from food and material goods is very different from the fulfillment received from donating to a cause. The conflation of meanings leads to confusion around what actually makes someone happy. The insights from these materials point out and clarify these issues, and the research on mindfulness notes that your perception and state of mind can influence your happiness, appreciation, contentment, and fulfillment as much as your external conditions can.

The insight that most of these materials miss is that happiness is really an indicator of growth and prosperity and not the ultimate goal of life. While many of them explain how addictions are artificial manipulations of the brain's reward system, they do not always make or explain the connection between growth-enabling activities and fulfillment.

Examples of media studied:

- *10% Happier* by Dan Harris
- *The Antidote* by Oliver Burkeman
- *The Happiness Hypothesis* by Jonathan Haidt
- *The Paradox of Choice* by Barry Schwartz
- *The Psychology of Happiness* by Arlene Matthews Uhl
- *The Science of Mindfulness* by Ronald Siegel
- *Stumbling on Happiness* by Daniel Gilbert

Ethics

Because there have been many ethics and ethical systems that humans have established over the course of history, there are countless documents on the way that people should live. Sources include religious texts, philosophy texts, academic texts, business books, self-help books, biographies, governing documents, and codes of conduct.

Insights from these materials include why humans have ethics, how ethics evolved, how ethics are set and enforced in society, and how people make ethical decisions. This information is critical to understanding how to establish the best ethics for your life.

A deliberate attempt was made to study less common ethics. Examples include media that pushed for ethical principles to expand to non-humans, media that questioned the ethics of free-market corporations that legally sell products that harm the consumer, people who were willing to listen to multiple perspectives with compassion on controversial topics, and philosophies that recommended entirely new or different governmental, social, or economic systems. While this book does not recommend a specific set of ethics, the best way to determine the right set of ethics for you is to evaluate them and see if they lead to better outcomes.

Examples of media studied:
- *Accidental Courtesy* by Matthew Ornstein
- *Beyond Good and Evil* by Friedrich Nietzsche
- *Beyond Religion: Ethics for a Whole New World* by The Dalai Lama
- *Common Sense* by Thomas Paine
- *The Ethics of Ambiguity* by Simone de Beauvoir
- *Live and Let Live* by Marc Pierschel
- *The Moral Animal* by Robert Wright
- *Moral Decision Making* by Clancy Martin
- *Nicomachean Ethics* by Aristotle
- *The Red Pill* by Cassie Jaye
- *The Theory of Moral Sentiments* by Adam Smith

The New Thought Movement
The New Thought Movement was studied for its claims of how a human being can influence the world around it starting with

his or her thoughts. The ideas go beyond provable science by suggesting that the universe responds to a person's thoughts in non-physical ways, lining up experiences that match those thoughts so that they occur in his or her reality. Other than that faith-based claim, however, its explanations of why people exist and how they can achieve their goals align well with the advice that most successful people would provide:

- You exist in this universe to grow through life experience
- You know where to focus your attention based on your desires
- Your belief in your ability to attain an outcome helps you to attain it
- Your emotions tells you if your desires and beliefs are in alignment

While this book keeps all explanations within the realm of what could be reasoned or scientifically tested, it must be acknowledged that several of these resources articulate the importance of desire, appreciation, belief, and emotions in living a meaningful life more effectively than most philosophy and psychology books.

Examples of media studied:

- *Ask and It Is Given* by Esther and Jerry Hicks
- *The Biology of Belief* by Bruce H. Lipton
- *The Secret* by Rhonda Byrne
- *Think and Grow Rich* by Napoleon Hill

Bibliography

1   Frankl, Viktor E. *Man's Search for Meaning: an Introduction to Logo-therapy*. Part One translated by Ilse Lasch, Preface by Gordon W. Allport, Beacon Press, 1992.

2   Jhaveri, Vithalbhai, director. *Mahatma: Life of Gandhi, 1869-1948*. Gandhi National Memorial Fund, 1968.

3   O'Toole, Garson. "Life Is a Journey, Not a Destination." *Quote Investigator*, 31 Aug. 2012, quoteinvestigator.com/2012/08/31/life-journey/. Accessed 4 July 2017.
    (Note: This quotation is often attributed to Ralph Waldo Emerson but is of unknown origin)

4   Morihei, Ueshiba, and John Stevens. *The Art of Peace*. Boston, Shambhala, 2010.

5   Miller, S. L. "A Production of Amino Acids Under Possible Primitive Earth Conditions." *Science*, vol. 117, no. 3046, 1953, pp. 528–529.

6   Patel, Bhavesh H., et al. "Common Origins of RNA, Protein and Lipid Precursors in a Cyanosulfidic Protometabolism." *Nature Chemistry*, vol. 7, no. 4, 2015, pp. 301–307.

7   Herschy, Barry, et al. "An Origin-of-Life Reactor to Simulate Alkaline Hydrothermal Vents." *Journal of Molecular Evolution*, vol. 79, no. 5-6, 2014, pp. 213–227.

8   McMaster, Joe. "How Did Life Begin?" *PBS*, Public Broadcasting Service, 1 July 2004, www.pbs.org/wgbh/nova/evolution/how-did-life-begin.html.

9   "The Meaning of Life." Huntley, Matthew, director. *Stephen Hawking's Grand Design*, Discovery Channel, 24 June 2012.

10 Lipton, Bruce H. *The Biology of Belief*. Carlsbad, CA, Hay House, Inc., 2008.

11 Lipton, Bruce H., et al. "Microvessel Endothelial Cell Transdifferentiation: Phenotypic Characterization." *Differentiation*, vol. 46, no. 2, 1991, pp. 117–133.

12 Freud, Sigmund. *Project for a Scientific Psychology*. 1895.

13 Maslow, A. H. "A Theory of Human Motivation." *Psychological Review*, vol. 50, no. 4, 1943, pp. 370–396.

14 Roosevelt, Eleanor. "My Day, August 2, 1941." *The Eleanor Roo-

sevelt Papers Digital Edition, 2017, www2.gwu.edu/~erpapers/myday/displaydoc.cfm?_y=1941&_f=md055954. Accessed 4 July 2017.

15 Kant, Immanuel, et al. *The Critique of Pure Reason*. Cambridge, Cambridge University Press, 2009.

16 Einstein, Albert, and Sonja Bargmann. *Ideas and Opinions*. New York, Dell Publ. Co., 1978.

17 Csikszentmihalyi, Mihaly. *Flow: The Psychology of Optimal Experience*. HarperCollins e-books, 2009.

18 Csikszentmihalyi, Mihaly. *Flow: The Psychology of Optimal Experience*. HarperCollins e-books, 2009.

19 Metcalf, T. "Listening to Your Clients." *Life Association News*, vol. 92, no. 7, 1997, pp. 16–18.

20 Dweck, Carol S. *Mindset*. New York, Random House LLC, 2006.

21 Kumar, Amit, et al. "Waiting for Merlot." *Psychological Science*, vol. 25, no. 10, 2014, pp. 1924–1931.

22 Gibran, Kahlil. *Sand and Foam*. New York, Alfred A. Knopf, 1926.

23 "Quotes by Ella Fitzgerald." *Ella Fitzgerald*, Universal Music Enterprises, 30 Mar. 2017, www.ellafitzgerald.com/about/quotes. Accessed 4 July 2017.

24 Nathan, R., et al. "A Movement Ecology Paradigm for Unifying Organismal Movement Research." *Proceedings of the National Academy of Sciences*, vol. 105, no. 49, 5 Dec. 2008, pp. 19052–19059.

25 Grant, Adam M., and Francesca Gino. "A Little Thanks Goes a Long Way: Explaining Why Gratitude Expressions Motivate Prosocial Behavior." *Journal of Personality and Social Psychology*, vol. 98, no. 6, June 2010, pp. 946–955.

26 Post, Stephen G. "Altruism, Happiness, and Health: It's Good to Be Good." *International Journal of Behavioral Medicine*, vol. 12, no. 2, June 2005, pp. 66–77.

27 Twain, Mark. *The Adventures of Tom Sawyer, Part 1*. Project Gutenberg, 2015.

28 Twain, Mark. *The Adventures of Tom Sawyer, Part 1*. Project Gutenberg, 2015.

29 Pink, Daniel H. *Drive: The Surprising Truth about What Motivates Us*. New York, Riverhead Books, 2011.

30 Pink, Daniel H. *Drive: The Surprising Truth about What Motivates Us*. New York, Riverhead Books, 2011.

31 Shakespeare, William. *Hamlet*. Amazon Classics, 2017.

32 Brickman, P., and D. T. Campbell. "Hedonic Relativism and Planning the Good Society." *Adaptation-Level Theory: a Symposium*, New York, Academic Press, 1971, pp. 287–302.

33 Emmons, Robert A., and Michael E. McCullough. "Counting Blessings versus Burdens: An Experimental Investigation of Gratitude and Subjective Well-Being in Daily Life." *Journal of Personality & Social Psychology*, vol. 84, no. 2, 2003, pp. 377–389.

34 King, Laura A. "The Health Benefits of Writing about Life Goals." *Personality and Social Psychology Bulletin*, vol. 27, no. 7, 2001, pp. 798–807.

35 Loewenstein, George. "Anticipation and the Valuation of Delayed Consumption." *The Economic Journal*, vol. 97, no. 387, Sept. 1987, pp. 666–684.

36 Wallace, DeWitt, and Lila Acheson Wallace, editors. *The Reader's Digest*. Sept. 1947, p. 64.

37 Dychtwald, Ken. "Powers of Mind: A New Age Interview with Arnold Schwarzenegger." *New Age*, Jan. 1978, pp. 38–52.

38 James, William. *The Will to Believe: and Other Essays in Popular Philosophy*. Urbana, IL, Project Gutenberg, 2009.

39 Sharot, Tali. *The Optimism Bias: a Tour of the Irrationally Positive Brain*. New York, Vintage Books, 2012.

40 Sharot, Tali. *The Optimism Bias: a Tour of the Irrationally Positive Brain*. New York, Vintage Books, 2012.

41 "The Roger Bannister Effect: The Myth of the Psychological Breakthrough." *Science of Running*, 16 May 2017, www.scienceofrunning.com/2017/05/the-roger-bannister-effect-the-myth-of-the-psychological-breakthrough.html.

42 Chan, Melissa. "10 Crazy Things More Likely to Happen to You Than Winning the Powerball Jackpot." *Time*, Time, 23 Aug. 2017, 11:54, time.com/4171474/powerball-lottery-more-likely-win/.

43 Dweck, Carol S. *Mindset*. New York, Random House LLC, 2006.

44 Dweck, Carol S. *Mindset*. New York, Random House LLC, 2006.

45 Merton, Robert K. "The Self-Fulfilling Prophecy." *The Antioch Review*, vol. 8, no. 2, 1948, p. 193.

46 Weinstein, Rhona S., et al. "Pygmalion and the Student: Age and Classroom Differences in Children's Awareness of Teacher Expectations." *Child Development*, vol. 58, no. 4, 1987, p. 1079.

47 Buks, E., et al. "Dephasing in Electron Interference by a 'Which-

Path' Detector." *Nature*, vol. 391, no. 6670, 1998, pp. 871–874.

48   Rovelli, Carlo. "Relational Quantum Mechanics." *International Journal of Theoretical Physics*, vol. 35, no. 8, Aug. 1996, pp. 1637–1678.

49   Clarke, Arthur C. *Profiles of the Future; an Inquiry Into the Limits of the Possible, by Arthur C. Clarke*. Harper & Row, 1973.

50   Turner-McGrievy, Gabrielle M, and Deborah F Tate. "Weight Loss Social Support in 140 Characters or Less: Use of an Online Social Network in a Remotely Delivered Weight Loss Intervention." *Translational Behavioral Medicine*, vol. 3, no. 3, 2013, pp. 287–294.

51   Gollwitzer, Peter M., et al. "When Intentions Go Public." *Psychological Science*, vol. 20, no. 5, 2009, pp. 612–618.

52   Littlefield, Bill. "Hollywood Scores A 'Miracle' With Locker Room Speech." *wbur.org*, 90.9 WBUR-FM, 6 June 2015, www.wbur.org/onlyagame/2015/06/06/us-miracle-olympics-herb-brooks.

53   Laozi. *The Tâo Teh King (Tao Te Ching)*. Translated by James Legge, Wisehouse Classics, 2016.
(Note: literally translated as, "A journey of a thousand li starts beneath one's feet," while commonly translated as, "The journey of a thousand li commenced with a single step.")

54   Martin, Douglas. "Roger Ebert Dies at 70; a Critic for the Common Man." *The New York Times*, 4 Apr. 2013, www.nytimes.com/2013/04/05/movies/roger-ebert-film-critic-dies.html. Accessed 4 July 2017.

55   Roosevelt, Eleanor. *You Learn by Living: Eleven Keys for a More Fulfilling Life*. New York, NY, Olive Editions, 2016.

56   Yeats, John Butler., et al. *Letters to His Son W.B. Yeats and Others: 1869-1922*. London, Faber and Faber, 1999.
(Note: This quotation is commonly attributed to W.B. Yeats but originates from his father)

57   Gros, C. "Emotions, Diffusive Emotional Control and the Motivational Problem for Autonomous Cognitive Systems." *Machine Learning: Concepts, Methodologies, Tools and Applications*, 2012, pp. 1784–1797.

58   Olds, James. "Pleasure Centers in the Brain." *Scientific American*, vol. 195, no. 4, 1956, pp. 105–117.

59   Witters, Weldon L., and Patricia Jones-Witters. *Human Sexuality, a Biological Perspective*. New York, Van Nostrand, 1980.

60   Moan, Charles E., and Robert G. Heath. "Septal Stimulation for the Initiation of Heterosexual Behavior in a Homosexual Male." *Journal of Behavior Therapy and Experimental Psychiatry*, vol. 3, no. 1, 1972,

pp. 23–30.

[61] Bellows, Alan. "Technology and the Pursuit of Happiness." *Damn Interesting*, Article #36, 26 December 2005.

[62] Seligman, Martin E. P. *Authentic Happiness: Using the New Positive Psychology to Realize Your Potential for Lasting Fulfillment*. New York, Free Press, 2013.

[63] Brickman, P., and D. T. Campbell. "Hedonic Relativism and Planning the Good Society." *Adaptation-Level Theory: a Symposium*, New York, Academic Press, 1971, pp. 287–302.

[64] Lyubomirsky, Sonja, et al. "Pursuing Happiness: The Architecture of Sustainable Change." *Review of General Psychology*, vol. 9, no. 2, 2005, pp. 111–131.

[65] Sheldon, Kennon M., and Sonja Lyubomirsky. "Achieving Sustainable Gains in Happiness: Change Your Actions, Not Your Circumstances." *Journal of Happiness Studies*, vol. 7, no. 1, 2006, pp. 55–86.

[66] The idea of emotions being an indicator of how you are progressing in life is influenced by the Emotional Guidance System created by Jerry and Esther Hicks. However, the emotions used in this list are different, growth-focused, and devoid of unprovable non-physical elements (e.g., "connection to source energy").

[67] Csikszentmihalyi, Mihaly. *Flow: The Psychology of Optimal Experience*. HarperCollins e-books, 2009.

[68] Chandola, Tarani, et al. "Chronic Stress at Work and the Metabolic Syndrome: Prospective Study." *BMJ*, vol. 332, no. 7540, 2006, pp. 521–525.

[69] Moore, Zella E. "Mindfulness, Emotion Regulation, and Performance." *Mindfulness and Performance*, edited by Amy L. Baltzell, Cambridge, Cambridge University Press, 2016, pp. 29–52.

[70] Teper, Rimma, et al. "Inside the Mindful Mind: How Mindfulness Enhances Emotion Regulation Through Improvements in Executive Control." *Current Directions in Psychological Science*, vol. 22, no. 6, 2013, pp. 449–454.

[71] Streeter, Chris C., et al. "Effects of Yoga Versus Walking on Mood, Anxiety, and Brain GABA Levels: A Randomized Controlled MRS Study." *The Journal of Alternative and Complementary Medicine*, vol. 16, no. 11, 2010, pp. 1145–1152.

[72] Heim, Christine, and Charles B Nemeroff. "The Role of Childhood Trauma in the Neurobiology of Mood and Anxiety Disorders: Preclinical and Clinical Studies." *Biological Psychiatry*, vol. 49, no. 12, 2001, pp. 1023–1039.

73 Wegner, Daniel M., et al. "Paradoxical Effects of Thought Suppression." *Journal of Personality and Social Psychology*, vol. 53, no. 1, 1987, pp. 5–13.

74 Pavlov, Ivan Petrovich, and G. V. Anrep. *Conditioned Reflexes: an Investigation of the Physiological Activity of the Cerebral Cortex.* Mansfield Centre, CT, Martino Publishing, 2015.

75 Finkenauer, Catrin, et al. "Flashbulb Memories and the Underlying Mechanisms of Their Formation: Toward an Emotional-Integrative Model." *Memory & Cognition*, vol. 26, no. 3, 1998, pp. 516–531.

76 Godden, D. R., and A. D. Baddeley. "Context-Dependent Memory In Two Natural Environments: On Land And Underwater." *British Journal of Psychology*, vol. 66, no. 3, 1975, pp. 325–331.

77 Dumas, Alexandre. *The Count of Monte Cristo.* Penguin, 2003.

78 Gensler, Harry J. *Ethics and the Golden Rule.* New York, Routledge, Taylor & Francis Group, 2013.
(Note: The Golden Rule comes in many forms; this source lists many versions of it used throughout history and quotes this version as the most common form in use in 2013)

79 Seaver, George, and Albert Schweitzer. *Albert Schweitzer: The Man and His Mind.* London, Adam & Charles Black, 1947.

80 Brown, William D., and Katherine L. Barry. "Sexual Cannibalism Increases Male Material Investment in Offspring: Quantifying Terminal Reproductive Effort in a Praying Mantis." *Proceedings of the Royal Society B: Biological Sciences*, vol. 283, no. 1833, 2016.

81 Packer, Craig, and Anne E. Pusey. "Adaptations of Female Lions to Infanticide by Incoming Males." *The American Naturalist*, vol. 121, no. 5, 1983, pp. 716–728.

82 Masuda, Naoki, and Feng Fu. "Evolutionary Models of In-Group Favoritism." *F1000Prime Reports*, vol. 7, Mar. 2015.

83 Alan, Sanfey. "Fairness, Trust & Reciprocity in Social Decision-Making." *Frontiers in Neuroscience*, vol. 4, 2010.

84 Fehr, Ernst, and Klaus M. Schmidt. "Theories of Fairness and Reciprocity: Evidence and Economic Applications." *Advances in Economics and Econometrics*, pp. 208–257, 2003.

85 Rosas, Alejandro. "Beyond the Sociobiological Dilemma: Social Emotions and the Evolution of Morality." *Zygon®*, vol. 42, no. 3, 2007, pp. 685–700.

86 The model behind the Prisoner's Dilemma was originally designed by Merrill Flood and Melvin Dresher in 1950, while the exact name and scenario was formalized by Albert W. Tucker.

87   Hardin, Garrett. "The Tragedy of the Commons." *Science,* vol. 162, no. 3859, 1968, pp. 1243–1248.
(Note: The name comes from a story told in *Two Lectures on the Checks to the Population* by William Forster Lloyd)

88   Kinnier, Richard T., and Arlene T. Metha. "Regrets and Priorities at Three Stages of Life." *Counseling and Values,* vol. 33, no. 3, 1989, pp. 182–193.

89   Milgram, Stanley. "Behavioral Study of Obedience." *The Journal of Abnormal and Social Psychology,* vol. 67, no. 4, 1963, pp. 371–378.

90   Haney, Craig, et al. "Interpersonal Dynamics in a Simulated Prison." *International Journal of Criminology and Penology,* vol. 1, 1973, pp. 69–97.

91   Darwin, Charles. *On the Origin of Species by Means of Natural Selection, or the Preservation of Favoured Races in the Struggle for Life.* London, 1859.

92   MacIntyre, Alasdair C. *After Virtue: a Study in Moral Theory.* University of Notre Dame Press, 1981.

93   Glass, Jennifer, et al. "Parenthood and Happiness: Effects of Work-Family Reconciliation Policies in 22 OECD Countries." *American Journal of Sociology,* vol. 122, no. 3, 2016, pp. 886–929.

94   *The King James Bible.* Project Gutenberg, 2011.

95   Ariely, Dan. *The (Honest) Truth about Dishonesty: How We Lie to Everyone—Especially Ourselves.* Harper Perennial, 2013.

96   Lash, Joseph P. *Helen and Teacher: the Story of Helen Keller and Anne Sullivan Macy.* New York, Delacorte Press, 1980.

97   Newton, Isaac. "Letter from Sir Isaac Newton to Robert Hooke." Received by Robert Hooke, 5 Feb. 1675.

98   Donne, John. *Devotions upon Emergent Occasions and Severall Steps in My Sicknes: Digested into, 1. Meditations upon Our Human Conditions, 2. Expostulations, and Debatement with God, 3. Prayers, upon the Severall Occasions, to Him.* Printed for Thomas Jones, 1624.

99   West, Stuart A., et al. "Social Evolution Theory for Microorganisms." *Nature Reviews Microbiology,* vol. 4, no. 8, 2006, pp. 597–607.

100   Dawkins, Richard. *The Selfish Gene.* Oxford, Oxford University Press, 2016.

101   Plunkett, Jevon, et al. "An Evolutionary Genomic Approach to Identify Genes Involved in Human Birth Timing." *PLOS Genetics,* Public Library of Science, 14 Apr. 2011, journals.plos.org/plosgenetics/article?id=10.1371%2Fjournal.pgen.1001365.

102 Dunswortha, Holly M., et al. "Metabolic Hypothesis for Human Altriciality." *Proceedings of the National Academy of Sciences*, National Academy of Sciences, 16 Apr. 2012, www.pnas.org/content/109/38/15212.full.

103 Tennov, Dorothy. *Love and Limerence: the Experience of Being in Love.* Scarborough House, 1999.

104 Liebowitz, Michael R. *The Chemistry of Love.* Little, Brown, 1983.

105 Swain, James E., et al. "Parenting and Beyond: Common Neurocircuits Underlying Parental and Altruistic Caregiving." *Parenting*, vol. 12, no. 2-3, 2012, pp. 115–123.

106 Holt-Lunstad, Julianne, et al. "Influence of a 'Warm Touch' Support Enhancement Intervention Among Married Couples on Ambulatory Blood Pressure, Oxytocin, Alpha Amylase, and Cortisol." *Psychosomatic Medicine*, vol. 70, no. 9, 2008, pp. 976–985.

107 Algoe, Sara B., et al. "The Social Functions of the Emotion of Gratitude via Expression." *Emotion*, vol. 13, no. 4, 2013, pp. 605–609.

108 Moll, J., et al. "Human Fronto-Mesolimbic Networks Guide Decisions about Charitable Donation." *Proceedings of the National Academy of Sciences*, vol. 103, no. 42, Sept. 2006, pp. 15623–15628.

109 Wilson, John, and Marc Musick. "The Effects of Volunteering on the Volunteer." *Law and Contemporary Problems*, vol. 62, no. 4, 1999, pp. 141–168., doi:10.2307/1192270.

110 Masuda, Naoki, and Feng Fu. "Evolutionary Models of In-Group Favoritism." *F1000Prime Reports*, vol. 7, Mar. 2015.

111 Clark, Margaret S., and Judson R. Mills. "A Theory of Communal (and Exchange) Relationships." *Handbook of Theories of Social Psychology: Volume 2*, Paul A. Van Lange, Arie W. Kruglanski, and E. T. Higgins, vol. 2, London, SAGE Publications, Ltd., 2012, pp. 232–250.

112 Frey, Bruno S., and Lorenz Goette. *Does Pay Motivate Volunteers?* Institute for Empirical Research in Economics, University of Zurich, 1999.

113 Capra, Frank, director. *It's a Wonderful Life.* Liberty Films, 1946.

114 Capra, Frank, director. *It's a Wonderful Life.* Liberty Films, 1946.

115 Ramis, Harold, director. *Groundhog Day.* Columbia Pictures, 1993.

116 Ramis, Harold, director. *Groundhog Day.* Columbia Pictures, 1993.

117 Rand, Ayn. *Atlas Shrugged.* New York, New American Library, 1957.

118 Frost, Robert. "The Road Not Taken." *Mountain Interval*, New

York, Holt, 1921.

119 Aristotle, et al. *The Nicomachean Ethics*. Hertfordshire, Wordsworth Editions Limited, 1996.

120 Lemaître, G. "The Beginning of the World from the Point of View of Quantum Theory." *Nature*, vol. 127, no. 3210, 1931, p. 706.

121 Dussutour, A., et al. "Amoeboid Organism Solves Complex Nutritional Challenges." *Proceedings of the National Academy of Sciences*, vol. 107, no. 10, Aug. 2010, pp. 4607–4611.

122 Duckworth, A. L., and M. E. P. Seligman. "Self-Discipline Outdoes IQ in Predicting Academic Performance of Adolescents." *Psychological Science*, vol. 16, no. 12, Jan. 2005, pp. 939–944.

123 Inesi, M. Ena, et al. "Power and Choice." *Psychological Science*, vol. 22, no. 8, 2011, pp. 1042–1048.

124 Langer, Ellen J., and Judith Rodin. "The Effects of Choice and Enhanced Personal Responsibility for the Aged: A Field Experiment in an Institutional Setting." *Journal of Personality and Social Psychology*, vol. 34, no. 2, 1976, pp. 191–198.

125 Rotter, Julian B. "Generalized Expectancies for Internal Versus External Control of Reinforcement." *Psychological Monographs: General and Applied*, vol. 80, no. 1, 1966, pp. 1–28.

126 Ryff, Carol D. "Happiness Is Everything, or Is It? Explorations on the Meaning of Psychological Well-Being." *Journal of Personality and Social Psychology*, vol. 57, no. 6, 1989, pp. 1069–1081.

127 Jackson, Laurence E., and Robert D. Coursey. "The Relationship of God Control and Internal Locus of Control to Intrinsic Religious Motivation, Coping and Purpose in Life." *Journal for the Scientific Study of Religion*, vol. 27, no. 3, 1988, pp. 399–410.

128 Schwarzer, Ralf. *Self-Efficacy: Thought Control of Action*. Hemisphere Publishing Corporation, 1992.

129 Wolpert, Lewis. *Six Impossible Things before Breakfast: the Evolutionary Origins of Belief*. W.W. Norton & Company, 2008.

130 Taleb, Nassim Nicholas. *Fooled by Randomness: The Hidden Role of Chance in Life and in the Markets*. New York, Random House, 2016.

131 Schwartz, Barry. *The Paradox of Choice – Why More Is Less*. Ecco, 2016.

132 Schwartz, Barry, et al. "Maximizing Versus Satisficing: Happiness Is a Matter of Choice." *Journal of Personality and Social Psychology*, vol. 83, no. 5, 2002, pp. 1178–1197.

133 Scheibehenne, Benjamin, et al. "Can There Ever Be Too Many

Options? A Meta-Analytic Review of Choice Overload." *Journal of Consumer Research*, vol. 37, no. 3, 1 Oct. 2010, pp. 409–425.

[134] Schwartz, Charles R. "The Return-on-Investment Concept as a Tool for Decision Making." *General Management Series*, New York, American Management Association, no. 183, 1956, pp. 42–61.

[135] Pelham, Brett W., et al. "Why Susie Sells Seashells by the Seashore: Implicit Egotism and Major Life Decisions." *Journal of Personality and Social Psychology*, vol. 82, no. 4, 2002, pp. 469–487.

[136] Seligman, M. E. P. "Learned Helplessness." *Annual Review of Medicine*, vol. 23, no. 1, 1972, pp. 407–412.

[137] Seligman, Martin E. P. *Helplessness: on Depression, Development, and Death: with a New Introduction by the Author*. Freeman, 2000.

[138] Gilbert, Daniel T., and Jane E. J. Ebert. "Decisions and Revisions: The Affective Forecasting of Changeable Outcomes." *Journal of Personality and Social Psychology*, vol. 82, no. 4, 2002, pp. 503–514.

[139] Altmaier, Elizabeth M. *Reconstructing Meaning after Trauma: Theory, Research, and Practice*. Academic Press, 2017.

[140] Shapiro, Fred R. "Who Wrote the Serenity Prayer?" *The Chronicle Review*, 28 Apr. 2014, www.chronicle.com/article/Who-Wrote-the-Serenity-Prayer-/146159/.

[141] Kubrick, Stanley, director. *A Clockwork Orange*. Warner Bros., 1972.

[142] Soon, Chun Siong, et al. "Unconscious determinants of free decisions in the human brain." *Nature Neuroscience*, vol. 11, no. 5, 2008, pp. 543–545.

[143] Glascher, J., et al. "Lesion Mapping of Cognitive Control and Value-Based Decision Making in the Prefrontal Cortex." *Proceedings of the National Academy of Sciences*, vol. 109, no. 36, 2012, pp. 14681–14684.

[144] Festinger, Leon. *A Theory of Cognitive Dissonance*. Stanford University Press, 1957.

[145] Aesop. *Aesop's Fables; a New Translation*. Translated by V.S. Vernon Jones, 1912.

[146] Cullen, David. *Columbine*. Twelve, 2016.

[147] Thomas, and H. A. Rawes. *St. Thomas Aquinas on the Two Commandments of Charity: and the Ten Commandments of the Law. Translated, with Prayers Added, by Father Rawes, D.D.* London, Burns and Oates, 1879.

[148] King, Martin Luther. "Martin Luther King Jr.'s Glenville High School Speech." 26 Apr. 1967, Cleveland, Glenville High School.

[149] Zullig, Keith J, et al. "Relationship between Perceived Life Satisfaction and Adolescents' Substance Abuse." *Journal of Adolescent Health*, vol. 29, no. 4, 2001, pp. 279–288.

[150] Grant, Jon E., and Suck Won Kim. "Quality of Life in Kleptomania and Pathological Gambling." *Comprehensive Psychiatry*, vol. 46, no. 1, 2005, pp. 34–37.

[151] Zapf, James L., et al. "Attachment Styles and Male Sex Addiction." *Sexual Addiction & Compulsivity*, vol. 15, no. 2, 2008, pp. 158–175.